Playing and Exploring

Playing and Exploring

Education through the discovery of order

R. A. Hodgkin

METHUEN

London and New York

First published in 1985 by
Methuen & Co. Ltd
11 New Fetter Lane, London EC4P 4EE

Published in the USA by
Methuen & Co.
in association with Methuen, Inc.
29 West 35th Street, New York NY10001

© 1985 R. A. Hodgkin

Photoset by Rowland Phototypesetting Ltd
Bury St Edmunds, Suffolk
Printed in Great Britain by
Richard Clay (The Chaucer Press) Ltd
Bungay, Suffolk

British Library Cataloguing in
Publication Data

Hodgkin, R. A.
Playing and exploring: education
through the discovery of order.
1. Education
I. Title
370   LB17

ISBN 0-416-40180-5
ISBN 0-416-40300-X Pbk

Library of Congress Cataloging in
Publication Data

Hodgkin, R. A. (Robin A.)
Playing and exploring.
Bibliography: p.
Includes index.
1. Learning by discovery.
2. Cognition in children.
3. Play
4. Teacher–student relationships.
5. Socialization.   I. Title
LB1067.H62   1985   370.15'23   85-4883

ISBN 0-416-40180-5
ISBN 0-416-40300-X (pbk.)

For E. M. H.

Contents

Figures

Acknowledgements

Many people have helped in the preparation of this book. Some have read through large tracts of text at various stages and have offered encouragement, suggestions and, occasionally, sharp criticism. Others – colleagues and students at Oxford, at Abbotsholme and in the Sudan – have unwittingly assisted by their questioning, by forcing our discussions down to deep, unexpected problems and principles. I owe them all a debt. I am grateful, too, for the generosity of the Joseph Rowntree Charitable Trust: on two occasions the Trust helped with David Warr's research on visual aids and it has made a grant towards the cost of publishing this book.

Thanks are due to the following authors and publishers for some of the longer quotations which I have used and for other borrowings: to the BBC for the passage by Professor Norman Geschwind; to Professor J. S. Bruner for his letter on roles; to Mr Tony Buzan and The Learning Methods Group for 'pattern notes'; to Mr Peter Cropper and South Western Arts for the passage on rehearsing and performing; to Dr Paulo Freire and his publishers (Messrs Sheed and Ward) for the picture and related 'generative words'; to Professors Gazzaniga and LeDoux for their diagrams, which I have borrowed (and modified) from *The Integrated Mind*; to Professor Seymour Papert for two quotations; to Mrs Magda Polanyi for several quotations from her late husband's works; to Routledge and Kegan Paul Ltd. for the quotation from C. G. Jung; to Professor Charles Taylor; to William Collins Sons and Co. Ltd for the passage from T. H. White and to several other authors for shorter passages.

The epigraph on page 5 is from *Collected Poems* by Conrad Aiken, © 1953, 1970 by Conrad Aiken; renewed 1981 by Mary Aiken. Reprinted by permission of Oxford University Press Inc.

The author also wishes to acknowledge that the quotation from C. G. Jung appears in *The Collected Works of C. G. Jung,* revised trans. R. F. C. Hull, trans by J. G. Baynes, Bollingen Series 20. Vol. 6: *Psychological Types.* Copyright © 1971 by Princeton University Press.

Introduction

Believing is where learning starts. We know first, act on such knowledge and then get to know more. We may acquire sharp knowledge, built around reasons, causes and calculations, or vaguer knowledge, in which hopes, enigmas and alluring problems form the thread. The two ways often go together, for the activity of getting to know is compounded of feelings as well as of intellectual curiosity, of hunches as well as of facts.

The purpose of this book is to open up a way of thinking about education which is marked throughout by the concept of an exploring, hopeful, fallible and potentially responsible person. The main themes which run through it are as follows:

  (i) the importance of psychological 'space', of the play and the exploring which happen in it;
 (ii) the nature of skill, tools and competence;
(iii) the frontiers where we perceive problems and possibilities limiting our competence;
 (iv) orderliness arising from disorderliness, sometimes through our own creative efforts;
  (v) the teacher–learner relationship, exemplified by apprenticeship;
 (vi) the watershed of adolescence;
(vii) the various levels of interlocking human culture in which we exercise our competences, serve our apprenticeships and do most of our exploring, from childhood to old age.

There is one particular cultural boundary zone on which I shall focus – where pictures mediate between bodily action and language. Two chapters are devoted to exploring this new ground.

Education needs to be seen in a new light, not so much as the opening up of an already known world but as the continuous discovery and celebration of form in nature, in art and, not least, in the processes of human community. A profound change in thinking is already going on around us which impinges on many disciplines. Many teachers are aware of this, mainly through the work they do; but the assumptions which still prevail in popular discussion and even, sometimes, in universities and colleges make it difficult for teachers to fit their hunches about the good practice which they experience, into a coherent and trustworthy framework of knowledge. Though I say very little about religious belief, and though a reader might agree with much of the book without verbally 'believing in God', the possibility of such belief is implicit throughout. Good education and certainly an adequate theory of it must always be open towards the experience of the numinous. Taking such experiences seriously will often lead to religious words and to religious practice.

If you have taught for ten years or have enjoyed working with, and learning from, your own children as they grow towards maturity, you have a rich store of empirical knowledge of education. You may indeed be better equipped to think about it than many so-called experts. The research of educational and social psychologists can undoubtedly be of great importance and their extensive terminology merits critical attention. However, to understand it we need to be interested in the everyday experiences of children and also in many 'primitive' forms of education, outside the schooling system and in simpler societies than ours.

Where do the ideas of this book come from? A partial answer lies in the bibliography and footnotes, for even those ideas which may display some originality have been formed by bringing together two or three insights from other people. I cannot properly acknowledge the many debts I owe to those who, somehow, happened to be *there*, crucially, near a turning point in my own journey and who knew more than I did. Sometimes they were there after some catastrophe or failure, or they seemed to point the way out of one task and into another. Michael Polanyi and Marjorie Grene (who made me read Polanyi) were in this category. Just as important and even harder to list were all those people I learnt *with*: to many friends in the Sudan and at Abbotsholme School I owe especial debts – the debt of an apprentice as well as that of a tolerated authority.

One of the problems about this book has been how to end it –

how to deal with all the practical implications which it points to. There are, for example, interesting questions about openness and closedness in the curriculum, about adventure and risk and learning from failure. There is much more to be said about the nature of authority and about the law-making process in schools. And there is a range of ideas to be explored which bear on the educational needs of young adults – what have we to learn from anthropology about *rites de passage* and the rituals and symbols of initiation? The agenda is certainly extensive and so I decided to include, as a tailpiece, a broadcast – 'Education 2000' – which I made two years before starting work on the main book. It does touch, in a glancing manner, on many of these problems, and it illustrates some of the controversial ideas around which the rest of the book came to be constructed.

1 New ground

You went to the verge, you say, and came back safely?
Some have not been so fortunate – some have fallen.
Children go lightly there, from crag to crag,
And coign to coign, – where even the goat is wary, –
And make a sport of it . . .
        Water and fire were there,
And air and earth; there too was emptiness;
All, and nothing, and something too, and love.
                      (Conrad Aiken, 'Memnon')

Human infants hold powerful inarticulate beliefs. They believe, or soon learn to, that parents come back, that time has a pattern, that space and things are both interesting and, up to a point, explorable. By the child's second year one particular wordless belief must move to the forefront of consciousness – *that language is, and can be, spoken.* In ways which are only partly understood, this belief is supported by many innate endowments which are in the brain and body of every child. The capacity to believe and to hope must grow around each child's exploratory journeys and around all its active experiments with speech.

One can learn something about this rather mysterious, early triumph of informal education by watching infants make the marvellous creative blunders which characterize their exploration of the threshold of language. But there is more to it than trial and error. As Margaret Donaldson has stressed, the basic problem in education 'is to understand how something that began so well can often end so badly' for the majority of children (1978, 14). It is a problem with wide practical and philosophical ramifications.

I do not know a better word than 'belief' for that initial, energized attitude of commitment and curiosity in children. The creative bundle of communicative skills which they so rapidly acquire has properly been called linguistic 'competence'. A child's attitude, during this prolonged endeavour to master language, is only a naive version of any competent and confident adult explorer's attitude of believing-what-might-be. This kind of commitment or belief precedes and accompanies all purposive action. It guides such action and is often guided by what it finds. Once an act of learning has been achieved a person may look back on it and theorize about it and, as likely as not, will falsify it: 'it was easy, really,' he or she will say: 'I only did it for the money'. The passage of time also dims the memory of all the emotions – hopes, desires, fears – which accompany the early stages of getting to know. My own, most vivid memory of this is the combined feeling of commitment, caution and zest which run together when one is attempting, perhaps for the first time, a difficult mountain climb. In the heat (or chill) of such early ventures the explorer knows much more, and also feels much more, than he or she can tell.

All education starts when someone else tries to enrich a learner's inarticulate system of skills and feelings. It was Michael Polanyi (1958, 1966) who coined the term 'tacit knowledge' to describe the underlying mass of experience, attitudes and information patterns, out of which emerges that other, more explicit and articulate kind of knowledge which dominates our books and our conversations. Educationists quite rightly value 'learning by doing' whether it is an infant or an adult who is being active; and one reason for this is clear, that it is then, in action, that the tacit foundations of knowledge are enriched. Part of the essential asymmetry of education lies in the fact that the teacher has already travelled further than the learner, and therefore much that is obvious and discussable by him is only tacitly and inarticulately known by the learner.

Young teachers are often needlessly anxious about whether they will have enough to say in their lessons. What should concern them, however, is the need for appropriate and varied forms of *action* by their pupils. It is the learner's own doing that counts because he or she is in the process of taking patterned information in, much of it without words. Such a pattern might, for example, be the apprehension of a causal explanation in science or of a trend in history or a harmony in music. The activity of learning may be that of hand or eye, or it may be activity shared with others, or it may be hidden, 'in the mind', where words and pictures work together. It may be fun and involve play, or it may involve sustained effort and practice. J. S. Bruner (1968) has stressed how varied all these transforming, internalizing actions are.[1] The learner shifts from bodily movements to picture-making, to story telling and questioning and back again. So it is not easy for an apprentice teacher to know just what educational activity is likely to be appropriate at any particular moment and this is why practical experience is so important. Still, the key problem remains – not, can a teacher produce a date or a formula – but what can Jean or Peter *do* as they enter, what is to them, new ground?

Skilled acts are rooted in tacit knowledge

One of the central problems of education concerns a child's desire for freedom and how this can be reconciled with a teacher's or a parent's knowledge that the road is long and stony and that, as well as happiness, there are bound to be testing times ahead. Education involves freedom and happiness; but it is also about less comfortable things. One of the paradoxes generated by libertarian educational reformers, such as A. S. Neill of Summerhill, has been that their theoretical prescriptions in favour of freedom and of short term satisfactions have been at variance with their unspoken, tacit messages – their personal dedication, their authority and their broad humanity. It was these qualities which carried their schools along and influenced their pupils, much more than the wisdom of their theories.

It is strange that, in the thirty years since Polanyi wrote *Personal Knowledge*, his philosophy has had so little impact on education. All his main themes – the process of discovery, personal responsibility and commitment, the dangers of totalitarianism, the nature of skill and technology, the importance both of tradition and of open enquiry – could have been used to illuminate much of the doubt and confusion which has spread over teachers and schools in the materialistic, technologically advanced countries of the world. Polanyi invites us to be less obsessed with certain and testable knowledge, to make a *volte face*, and to focus on hazardous but skilled acts of making and of getting to know. His claim about belief is that we are committed to truth, not when we have proved it, but from the moment we start searching for it.[2]

Anyone who wants a preliminary understanding of Polanyi's thought, and of the way in which he develops it around skilled acts of making and discovering and judging, would do well to read chapter 4, on skills, in *Personal Knowledge*. Here he develops his central idea that all skilled acts are rooted in the soil of a person's tacit knowledge – millions of grains of information which have been uniquely patterned by heredity and by experience. When we do anything original or creative we are actively drawing on this material. Then we integrate it, generally not knowing clearly what it is, *towards a focus of intent* which lies ahead of us in the near or distant future. Observe, for example, the various skills which enable you to drive a car, and reflect on where the material basis of those skills is now, and where their focus will be when you put them into action.

Polanyi's theory of tacit knowing is just as relevant to intellectual and abstract skills as it is to manual and physical ones. This is one reason why it is important for education: it helps us to understand the various levels at which a child and an adult interact. Polanyi refers, several times, to the similarity between a beginner learning to use a hammer and an experienced judge working out a novel decision in the law courts (1958, 54–5, 117, 308–10). Both of these are pioneers trying to bring various skills to bear on what is, to them, a difficult problem. All the sensory or motor skills and the rules and values which make up such a person's tacit knowledge have a history of development in early childhood. It has been said that a child learns more physics in the first five years of life than Einstein learnt in the rest of his. How is it that we learn to mobilize all this mental and bodily material whenever we face new ground? It cannot only be a matter of trial and error. The infant explorer of language does not 'correct his errors'; he *uses* them till something better is discovered. There is no easy way by which to describe this process, but Polanyi makes an important point when he writes about apprenticeship:

> The apprentice unconsciously picks up the rules of the art, including those which are not explicitly known to the master himself. These hidden rules can be assimilated only by a person who surrenders himself to that extent uncritically to the imitation of another. A society which wants to preserve a fund of personal knowledge must submit to tradition. (1958, 53)

Polanyi was not popular with some scientists and philosophers for writing so deferentially about tradition. But is it not clear that children and adult explorers do need a blend of humility and courage if they are to throw themselves, unselfconsciously, into what seems a difficult task? Polanyi makes it abundantly clear that he is not talking about slavish following of tradition. He is referring to many levels of learning and to an irregular oscillation between times of boldness and times of cautious reflection.

The distinction between the routine performances of habitual skilled acts and doing things which are new and difficult is important. Every skilled act, many of which may now seem easy and automatic, started as an achievement in face of difficulty and danger. I shall be using the term 'frontier' to describe that unique zone of individual experience where new skills and new concepts are born. Polanyi does not use this term but in much of his writing he is very conscious of the growing edge of human knowledge as part of the advancing life system of the world. He turns, for example, from animal learning to the subtle discriminations of a connoisseur, and back again to his own childhood memories of learning how to swim or to play the piano, or to that seemingly elementary skill of hitting nails squarely on the head.

> When we use a hammer to drive in a nail, we attend to both nail and hammer, *but in a different way*. We watch the effect of our strokes on the nail and try to wield the hammer so as to hit the nail effectively. When we bring down the hammer we do not feel that the handle has struck our palm but that the head has struck the nail. Yet in a sense we are certainly alert to the feelings in our palm . . . [These feelings] are not watched in themselves; we watch something else while keeping intensely aware of them. I have a *subsidiary awareness* of the feeling in the palm of my hand which is merged into my *focal awareness* of my driving in the nail. (1958, 55)

Polanyi then goes on to discuss the interesting fact that subsidiary awareness and focal awareness are mutually exclusive. 'If a pianist shifts his attention from the piece he is playing to the observation of what he is doing with his fingers while he is playing it, he gets confused and has to stop' (1958, 56).

Later in *Personal Knowledge*, and with the examples of hammering and judging in mind, Polanyi stresses that we explore the meaning and scope both of a word and of a tool by using them and so making them, in a sense, a part of ourselves. Words such as 'truth' or 'justice', he writes, 'accumulate through the centuries an unfathomable fund of subsidiarily known connotations which we can bring partly into focus by reflecting on [their] use' (1958, 115). This similarity between a word and a tool, between the meaning and scope of each, running backward and forward in time, is an idea which Polanyi does not follow far. Nevertheless, as we shall see the parallel is highly significant because the emergence of the finest tool-using skills and the emergence of language may have been two aspects of one evolutionary process.

Apprenticeship and the field of discovery

Educational philosophers have neglected apprenticeship as a central model of education. All human relationships are open to abuse, and examples of insensitive instructors, of oppressive workshops and of exclusive guilds show how apprenticeship can easily be exploited for selfish ends. Nevertheless the authentic experience of apprenticeship is good and it is still not uncommon. In highly developed countries – certainly in Britain – formal apprenticeship has been seriously eroded. Any adult who recalls the vivid, inspiring and disastrous moments of his or her education is almost certain to have memories of a teacher who represented excellence in some way and who helped, sometimes almost by accident, to open windows of hope to a good world.[3] Apprenticeship can be seen in any small teaching group – the Hindu *guru* and his *chela*, Tortelier and his master class, the bushman hunting party, the athletics coach and his pupil and, in its most familiar form, the mother with her dependent but exploring infant. In all these there is asymmetry, not merely at the cognitive level (one knowing more, one less) but at the level of feelings, including respect – by the learner for achievement and by the teacher for a learner's potential. Bruner (1968, 70) refers to the fundamental relationship as 'the unique . . . dyad of teacher and pupil which lies at the heart [of all education]'. Some of Bruner's most important research, on the early patterns of skill and language, was concerned with the most basic apprenticeship of all – the mother and infant as they explore together the nature of time and of sequential behaviour – the idea, for example, of 'your turn, my turn' in games such as peep-bo (1983).

None of this reciprocal activity takes place in isolation; the context is all important. The context can be regarded as a time-space *field* which, as we shall see in the next chapter, may be more or less constrained. At the end of *Personal Knowledge* Michael Polanyi starts to discuss the same idea. He calls it 'a heuristic field' by which he means a field in which discoveries can be made. Any inquisitive animal may be thought of as working in such a heuristic field, and wherever a more experienced animal (or person) helps a less experienced learner we are justified in calling the process educational. Some birds and mammals certainly educate their young in this sense.

Why complicate matters by introducing this idea of *field* from physics and biology? The reason is that we need such a concept in order to escape from the crude mechanical explanations which dominate so much educational thinking. We need to understand the subtlety of a process in which causes from present time, causes from near and distant past and causes from a hypothetical future can all operate together. This is what biology and information theory offer.

The idea of a formative or morphogenetic field is now a commonplace. It refers to a situation in which messages or causal pressures operate from many different levels of complexity on a single entity. Such an entity might be a living cell or an individual learner in a school or a citizen wondering which way to vote. Leaving aside problems of free will, the fact is that all such entities do contain a wide variety of 'programs' which give them the power to respond in many different ways. The embryo of a plant or animal contains, in almost every cell, its own genetic program and this information interacts with physical causes, with external causes such as physical pressure, with micro-electrical gradients, and with chemical causes (enzymes, for example, which trigger or inhibit growth), as well as with diffuse ecological and environmental influences such as plenty or scarcity of nourishment. These affect not only the speed of the cell's growth but also the eventual form which it takes. Cells which start by being identical can thus grow into perfect bone cells or into liver cells or into neurons. They are guided in this both by their 'programs' and by the context or formative field in which they develop.[4]

The value of understanding growth in this way is that it assumes causal complexity without invoking magical or metaphysical entities. Causes which operate predominantly 'from the past', such as the information from DNA, are termed 'diachronic', while those which operate from the environment are 'synchronic'. The growth of a seed illustrates this. The genetic determinants were originally shaped during hundreds of millions of years of evolution, though plant breeders may have altered them more recently. These genes contain diachronic causal elements (in the DNA) – all affecting what is termed the genotype of an individual or species. Soil and climate and competition and many other synchronic factors, often grouped together under the general term of 'environment', affect what actually appears – the particular manifestation or phenotype of the species.[5]

There is a third level of influence which is, strictly speaking, not causal. It eludes measurement and prediction and yet its effect can be critical. It operates when a teacher and a learner, or any trusting human group, engage in some joint action. They then influence each other by a process of constantly interweaving initiatives, of responses and mutual learning. They do not *cause* each other; their currency, rather, is reason and reasons. They share intentions, hopes and problems and so the future, in a sense, is with them. Education cannot always be at that level; but it sometimes can.

We may think of the curriculum, therefore, as a special kind of environment or shared collection of learning fields. It is certainly complex, but compared with the natural and cultural worlds from which it is abstracted, it is relatively simple, as it is open to change and to being steered. It is created mainly by teachers for learners to act on, to react to and to grow in. Past, present and future causal factors have to be ordered and allowed for. Yet we must remember that the teacher is not controlling such a curriculum instrumentally, from outside. Teacher and learner are in the field – acting, interpreting, questioning, and themselves growing. Three special features characterize the two-way activities which go on in an educational field.

(i) The teacher (mother, schoolmistress, *guru*) deals with explicit knowledge which she intends for the learner; at the same time she will also, unconsciously, make available some aspects of tacit knowledge by her mood and by negative and positive signals in regard to long-term intentions, hopes and values.

(ii) The learner (infant, pupil, *chela*) responds actively and thereby assimilates new information. Here too the focus will usually be some intended activity. Other tacit elements will also be assimilated from outside the shared area of intentional activity. Consider, for example, how a young child not only learns to speak but speaks with intonations and mannerisms which the mother may be quite unaware of in her own speech.

(iii) There is feedback from teacher to learner – affirmation, evaluation, criticism; and also from learner to teacher.

Our basic concept of education, therefore, is certainly not of a mental pot to be filled, nor is it even the idea of an individual being sent on some 'fulfilling' trip. It centres on activity and on two-way feedback, on a teacher and learner practising a skill and sharing, with different degrees of clarity, the lessons of failure, the lessons of success and a vision of what might be. Because these interactive, personal processes are at the heart of education we should not be surprised that, if *people* are removed from the teaching side of the process and are replaced by measuring systems called IQ tests or Objective Examinations, something vital is lost. The same is generally true of television 'education', for here too there is no joint action and no feedback (see chapter 9).

So much for the heart of the educational process; what of the periphery? The educational influences of a lively teacher–learner interaction run out far beyond the space and time of a classroom and of a face-to-face encounter. Though this is not our immediate concern, a teacher does have an important responsibility for the outer boundaries of a learning field: for questions that can, reasonably, be asked and for those that cannot – yet; for risks that should be run when learners are being supervised and for those times – which can be profoundly formative – when a learner is alone.

On the beach: the solitary explorer

You can only be said to possess what will not be lost in a shipwreck. (Idries Shah 1966)

Solitariness, at first sight, seems to be a denial of education and yet perhaps the occasional experience of solitariness may be a condition for its full effect, as appetite is for the enjoyment of a feast. Kurt Hahn, founder of Gordonstoun and of the Outward Bound schools and a man of many good hunches, believed this and he used to suggest chosen loneliness as a restorative and therapy, though never as a punishment. The solitary student, working alone in a library and following, perhaps for the first time, a sustained thread of interest, the boy or girl walking (or running) decisively away from school towards some chosen wilderness, or the prophet in the desert – they all choose the lonely road. In literature, both sacred and profane, such archetypal characters have an almost mythical ring. I propose to use Robinson Crusoe as an adult example of loneliness with which to contrast my more sociable and juvenile model of the solitary explorer. Both models, the castaway and the exploring child, are 'existential', or at least they have an existential dimension. How? At the heart of each is a unique person, the very essence of whose being is to know, to choose and to get to know. They do so both in solitariness and in community, and the explorings of both imply existential space and an existential frontier.

The emphasis of these early chapters is on the frontier of exploration which limits a learner's field of knowledge. The reason for this 'focus on frontiers' (Goodman 1968, 259) is that teachers need to develop a special sensitivity to the reality and importance of the 'high tide' aspect of every learner, even though it only appears twice a month. One difficulty about the frontier emphasis and the whole desert island picture is that it can deflect our attention away from the essentially social and cultural nature of education. John Shotter, who has pioneered a new way of thinking about the humanizing work of the mother and infant interaction, expresses clearly the existential quality of the infant explorer and also the sharedness of his 'ecology' or little world of learning:

> The strength of a thoroughgoing ecological approach is . . . that it emphasizes the interfittedness of things and directs attention away from the child as a wholly isolated entity (and away from the hidden 'inner' processes presumed to be going on inside her somewhere). It directs us instead towards what is out there *in her world* at each moment in her development for her to grasp or 'pick up'. . . . The child and her world exist only

in reciprocal relation to one another and they are mutually constitutive and mutually defining. Then, what we might call the child's practical environment-for-action . . . becomes a very special environment existing just for her. It becomes 'her' world, a world into which she is dovetailed, feels at home in and knows how to operate because it is a world made (with the help of others) by her. (Shotter 1984, 80)

I was brought up on a number of desert island tales. The things which stayed in my memory about Robinson Crusoe were the way he built himself a house, his parrot and the marvellous moment when Crusoe saw another, 'native' footprint on the shore – a symbol of all that our solitary model leaves out. Recently, on rereading the book, several things which I had forgotten struck me: that Defoe seemed, at first sight, to be cheating by allowing an improbably rich store of material to be available in the wreck; and secondly, that the story is, among other things, a religious tract which tells of Robinson Crusoe's rediscovery of the faith and the values of his childhood – from scratch, as it were.

The Crusoe metaphor reminds us, in the first place, that someone who survives a shipwreck, who is 'forced' to explore new ground, is not to be seen as a *victim*, as being moulded, nor is he a superman, moulding everything. He or she is a complex, self-motivated individual, interacting with an extremely problematic world. Too many discussions of education omit this and swing away from the interactive middle ground towards those false antitheses of victim versus exploiter or putty in the hands of a paragon.

The Crusoe metaphor is also useful in helping us to think about the ways in which chance and orderliness interact. And when we survive any kind of shipwreck we tend to appreciate some of the many gifts and fundamental perceptions which we share with all other human beings. Obviously there is, common to all men, a wide range of innate capacities. If you or I were thrown onto a desert island with a total stranger, the exercise of these would enable us to join forces and to rediscover and share solutions to many of the basic problems of culture. That piece of driftwood? Yes, it was once a tree; but as we consider its kind and nature – using what language we can – we discuss its possibilities. It is then that common meanings are established. The wood might burn or make a roof beam. We can readily share newly minted meanings, when old meanings would divide us. That is why a crisis at school or on a holiday expedition, a crisis shared and coped with, either by equals or by a teacher and a learner, can be a source of much unspoken common understanding. The Crusoe metaphor also stresses that the survivors are working at a common boundary. It is the classic version of what is now termed 'marginality'. On this side is chaos and watery destruction; on the other are the palm trees and new possible systems of order, such as a hut or a friendship. This aspect of the metaphor is of use not only when we have to think about intercultural (so called 'racial') problems, it is relevant to the predicament of young adults. They certainly need occasional solitariness and they also need first hand experience of crises – of understanding, managing and surviving them.

Who can doubt that our way ahead, into the twenty-first century, is going to be intensely problematic? Resilience, ingenuity and staying power will all be at a premium. As we clamber, rather uncertainly, towards this new ground we find it hard to guess just how much violence these technical, intellectual and ecological revolutions will generate when the wave breaks. Our remote ancestors coped with catastrophic transitions in their time – encroaching ice, encroaching desert, 'barbarians' and the sea. We often vaguely remember this when we return for a while, in what we call 'recreation', in order to struggle amiably with the sea or with the mountains. We too easily forget about the need for challenge and frontier experience in our discussions of education's future. It is astonishing how much contemporary cant there is about leisure. Round the corner, so we are told, is an age of chips and free time; but remarkably little thought is given to what leisure *is*; or to what work is, for that matter. Can such soft scenarios be anything other than delusion? The world will almost certainly be physically hard for most of our children and grandchildren; it will be intellectually and spiritually hard for all of them. This has always been so – more or less – but it has been especially so at times of profound change. So resilience (which can be defined as adaptability combined with integrity) – physical, intellectual and spiritual resilience – should be an underlying aim of all education. This is why the myth of Robinson Crusoe, or the richer Prospero version, is so apt. One man or a group of puzzled friends and a clown or two make a new world out of driftwood *and* discover old wisdom.

Some might argue that we should educate people to be resilient in order that they might stand some chance of coping with life after a nuclear catastrophe. Despite the example of Noah and the flood, that line seems much too defeatist. The case for resilience as a basic aim in education is that adaptability and integrity are qualities that will make people less fearful, less neurotically prone to put their heads in the sand, less grasping of material reward, less deferential to big brother (or big sister) and more ready to innovate and to trust other human beings who at first sight may look like strangers.

Think, if you can, of these three images in the same breath: Robinson Crusoe making sense of his island, a teenager exploring his or her chosen wilderness and a one year old infant being helped to make sense of some intriguing new play space. The desire of each to survive, to grow and to find more truth, is part of their very essence as they interact with that bit of the universe which faces them. And it is first and foremost a peopled universe. The isolation of these desert islands is a conceit, reminding us that humans are not, in essence, victims but responsible *agents* within a society, within a culture; and this means that they are, above all, co-operative doers and makers, and lovers.

Notes

1 Bruner's position as a popularizer of cognitive science may rate higher than his reputation as a researcher. Teachers, however, owe him a great debt. His books in the 1960s and his curriculum innovations must have caused many of us to think more deeply and to experiment more confidently.
2 Polanyi's expression of this idea that commitment and believing precede effective action and especially acts of exploring, runs through much of *Personal Knowledge*. Perhaps the most striking and candid example is on p. 299: 'Logically the whole of my argument is but an elaboration of this circle; it is a systematic course in teaching myself to hold my own beliefs.' This ironic confession is not so well known as his aphorism that 'we can know more than we can tell', paraphrased on p. 6 above. The latter comes from p. 4 in *The Tacit Dimension*. Polanyi does not make clear the distinction between belief

'in' and belief 'that', between holding and explaining a belief. He would, perhaps, have agreed that such terms refer 'to the same thing in different stages of our awareness' (Coulson 1981, 42, 167).

3 For a statement of how traditional learning worked see Coomaraswamy (1956, 38–40) or Pallis (1939, 334–40). Even these strong advocates do not underrate the importance of individual style and its development – *within the tradition*. See also Gardner (1984, 338–45).

4 Controversy has been aroused by Rupert Sheldrake's very drastic extension of the concept of *morphogenetic field*. In his *A New Science of Life* (1983) he suggests that such fields, as they are commonly understood in discussions of embryonic and regenerative processes, have influence far beyond the living systems in which they can be identified. I find his arguments unconvincing. The more modest ideas of Waddington (1968, 1969) and Weiss (1975) are quite complex enough to serve as useful models for education. If Sheldrake were right, teachers would be able to perform a good many more miracles than they do.

5 In the 1980s there has been a burst of research interest in the subtle triggering mechanisms within cells. These speed up or slow down the development of special cell characteristics and sensitivities. The research has focused on the regeneration of nerve cell axons in both mammalian and insect brains, after damage. The swing of interest, therefore, has been away from contextual influences, such as chreods, and towards particular mechanisms. This does not reduce the usefulness of field-like models when they are applied appropriately. There has always been in science, and, perhaps, always will be, an oscillation between more and less holistic interpretations of phenomena.

The concept of frontier

The educational importance of the concept was sketched in my *Reconnaissance on an Educational Frontier* (1970, 7): 'when anyone faces an area of doubt and reacts to it positively . . . he enlarges his own field of consciousness and thereby prepares the ground for creative action. . . . Whenever his imagination is engaged in trying to project a pattern onto chaotic or conflicting experience, he is at the frontier; his own particular sector of a much greater frontier, which runs through time and space.' Subsequently in *Born Curious* (1976, 11–13), the need for a distinction between an individual's developmental frontier ('f') and that of his whole culture ('F') was emphasized.

Anthropologists and sociologists have shown interest in these and related ideas, especially in regard to their relevance to young adults

(Turner 1974, 1982; Martin 1982). Philosophers, too, have discussed frontiers in their bearing on the arts and on creativity in general. Jaspers in his writings on higher education stresses the importance of *Grenzen-situationen* (= my 'Frontiers') and these include 'boundary situations, points of potential growth, clarity, vision and human achievement'. 'The scholar exists (i.e. attains his true being) at a boundary, but to have arrived there is an achievement.' This is from J. F. Wyatt's (1982) 'Karl Jaspers' *The Idea of a University:* an existential argument for an institution concerned with freedom', *Studies in Higher Education* 7 (1), 21–34.

2 Education – making space for instruction

> If I could tell you what it meant there would have been no point in dancing it.
>
> (Isadora Duncan, quoted by Bateson 1973, 110)

> No art without play! No games without rules.
>
> (Eigen and Winkler 1982, 221)

Play and the playful practice of skills is where education starts but unless these competence-enriching activities open onto an attractive, yet ultimately daunting frontier zone, education stays swaddled. The whole business, as Dickens reminds us after his attack on 'facts' in *Hard Times*, is to do with quality, with keeping open and lively 'those subtle elements of humanity which will elude the utmost cunning of algebra until the last trumpet ever to be sounded shall blow even algebra to wrack'.

How are we to hold all these elements in the educational process together in a coherent conceptual bundle – learner, teacher, play, skill, feeling, doubting and believing, instructing and discovering? The time-honoured blank slate to be written on, the half empty jug to be filled, are discredited; though they still loom large in many conversations about education. Even that richer metaphor of carefully tended plants in a garden will not serve. It too easily implies an all-knowing Mr McGregor, pliant plants and a vegetable utopia just around the corner. The great advantage of approaching cultural change, and especially education, via the 'Crusoe model' is that it confronts us with unexpected space and time. It points up the beach, towards higher levels of human achievement and value and it emphasizes what a risky business human culture always is. Further, it denies the possibility of an objective human planner who can be appealed to for answers to difficult questions and it emphasizes, on the contrary, that there must be an essentially personal element, an interplay of freedom and discipline, responsibility and courage, at the heart of all lively culture.

Knowing what is and what might be

Nothing is 'nothing but . . .'. When a child first smiles or starts its explorations, wise parents will not be too quick and matter-of-fact in their interpretations of what is going on. D. W. Winnicott, in an oracular phrase, warns us that when a child discovers a plaything we must never challenge it by asking, 'did you create that [object] or did you find it?' (1971, 12, 89). Winnicott cannot have supposed it likely that one would often ask a child so strange a question. He is warning us all – parents, teachers, therapists – about certain deadening and belittling attitudes to which we are prone. He is emphasizing that the infinite possibilities of both the knower and the thing known must always be left open. Nothing that a child makes his own is 'nothing but . . .' or 'merely . . . lying around'. When we adults are derelict, washed up on some strange shore, then more than at any other time, the things we find lying around may be full of meaning and hope. Interpreting them becomes even more important than explaining. For meaning means, not only what is there, but what there might be: all those future possibilities which we may have a hand in making real – a hut among the palm trees, a friendship or a peaceful nation.

It is sad that so much of education, so much of social science and of mass culture, has the effect of shutting meanings down to the 'mere' and to the matter-of-fact. What seems to count is whatever it is that enables someone to shine in a radio quiz or to fail in an 'objective examination' – a neatly wrapped fact or the lack of it. In too many conventional educational encounters there is no house to build, no fire to kindle, no achievement, not even an argument. 'I'm afraid that's wrong,' says the quiz master, 'that's not the answer which I have on the card.' And that's the end of it. But all culture, including education, should be about beginnings and makings and about moving towards shadowy, problematic frontiers.

Our basic model, whether it takes the form of an exploring infant or an adolescent facing the wilderness or a castaway making a new start, contains the same cluster of ideas – a person with energy and limited but growing competence, encounters some space or freedom in which he is ready to explore and press back the frontier which limits that field. This is the model which is generalized on p. 25. When we think of early childhood, the juvenile version is preferable – an infant exploring its more or less protected play space. At this stage what is explored is, very largely, an interactive social world. When, however, we turn towards adolescence and to a young adult's struggle towards maturity, the Crusoe version is often appropriate. It emphasizes the human need to escape, temporarily, from crowds and from security; the need for young adults to be alone or with their peers for a while, in order that various types of growing competence may be stretched to their shifting and sometimes dangerous limits. Even in Defoe's story the importance of tradition and history, though it had been attenuated by the storm, is not eliminated. Old skills and values are remembered and the eventual return to community – the community in this case of a wise 'native' – is implicit. There is however a further important meaning suggested by the Crusoe model of youthful human nature.

In the last fifty years the idea of man as 'thrown' into a dangerous world, as an explorer of frontiers, has been taken seriously by existentialists and by some Marxists, though it is not fashionable among English-speaking philosophers. The central concept of man groping, enlarging a sector of clarity in a strange and yet fundamentally orderly world obviously applies to small children, but it is also extremely important when one thinks about young adults. It helps to hold a tension, recognized in many theories of knowledge, between that which we expect to know clearly and the penumbra of problems, ambiguities and intentions where conflicts may be kept in balance but are unlikely to be resolved. In science we work on the assumption that some day the shadows will be illuminated; in 'the arts' we accept that they may not, and we often positively seek out and exploit ambiguity. The distinction is close to that which Wilhelm Dilthey[1] drew between knowledge of nature (coherent science or *Naturwissenschaft*) and knowledge of those subtle elements of mind and spirit which he termed *Geistwissenschaft* – words which, in English, have no satisfactory equivalents.

There are always some problems which we have a good chance of solving and explaining and we tend to construe these as 'scientific'; but there are many others looming in our minds – directions, fears, hopes and loves – which we may never either explain or clearly express. They claim our acknowledgement and because we are living beings and, even more, because we are human beings, we are committed to values from the beginning. To live is to live on a slope. The slope may be perceived in many ways, as being about surviving and dying, or about creating more order or less, about truth or falsehood or – focusing on our own sense of personal being – about honour or shame. So commitment to values is not some optional extra for those who are civilized. It is part of our very being-in-the-world. Existentialist philosophers have argued in this way but among writers in the English tradition Polanyi is one of the most persuasive. He possesses the particular advantage, in the present climate of opinion, of approaching all these problems of knowledge primarily, but not solely, as a scientist.

Polanyi often refers to the shared values, concepts, problems and procedures which unify a similar-minded group of explorers – scientific researchers for example. This is approximately what Kuhn (1962, 1974) meant by a shared *paradigm*. Such a unifying network of ideas certainly can refer to a group of teachers or to a group of learners. It will now be clear that to understand education we need a concept of the defining relationship between teacher and learner which is asymmetrical, in which feelings, problems and concepts are shared, but not equally shared, by both members of the dyad. Progressive writers on education are far too ready to ignore this essential asymmetry. It is at this point that Winnicott's ideas become particularly apt, for not only does he start with asymmetry in a heuristic field but he also considers the nature of the objects which children encounter there.

Room to be and to become

A baby sucking is constructing a world of suckable things and not merely finding things in the world that she (or he) sucks.[2]
(Boden 1979)

Donald Winnicott, writing in the early 1970s, seemed to be asking his readers to accept a concept of a heuristic field somewhat similar to Polanyi's. He used the term 'potential space' to denote this and he emphasized three attributes which made the idea particularly relevant to education: (i) that such a heuristic field or space was the creation of two interactive, but very different, people, such as a mother and infant; (ii) that the things which are used or played with in such space change their perceived nature. At one moment, for example, an infant will see some things as 'me', at another as 'not me'; (iii) that here we approach the genesis of all cultural 'things'. Though Winnicott did not state categorically that this potential space is essentially a four-dimensional space–time concept, his emphasis on the *process* nature of all that happens in it makes this meaning clear. By combining Polanyi's and Winnicott's ideas, it seems to me, we can make an interesting ground plan for fundamental thinking about education.

A brief definition of potential space is: *room to be and to become.* One of a teacher's or parent's central tasks in dealing with children is to create a sense of such space surrounding them both, as members of the teacher–learner dyad. In one sense this potential space is always a joint creation. But in its origins it is essentially *for* children and so generally the teacher takes the initiative. He or she creates a space where learners can fail, but not disastrously; space where they can venture up to and know their own local frontier of discovery, explore it and then return to the security of more familiar play or practice. These ideas can all be summarized in the competence-play-frontier model (Figure 1), which is fundamental to the argument of this book. It represents the existential dimension of an exploring learner which runs from competence and security, through play, to danger. This dimension becomes one axis of a more comprehensive cultural model which I shall develop in subsequent chapters. It can also be seen as a diagrammatic version of Crusoe 'making it' from the sea to the unknown palm trees. Its primary reference, however, is to a child exploring a small world *and being helped by someone else.*

When we speak of space for education there must be some mature person in the offing – parent, teacher or master craftsman – to sustain it and enrich it. Even a distant radio pundit can, in these terms, be seen as an educator *provided that he is subject to feedback from the learners*, but not, I would claim, otherwise. So into the Winnicott concept of potential space we begin to introduce the Bruner–Piaget concept of 'in-struction' – of how a learner's experience becomes progressively structured by the help of someone outside who makes available appropriate 'representations' of the world and whose appropriateness is constantly

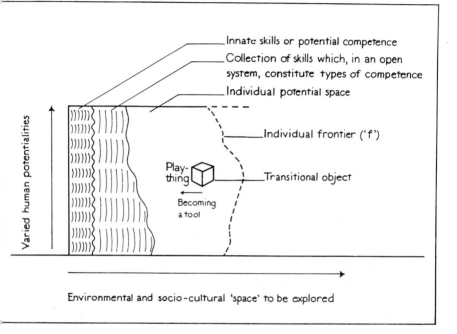

Figure 1   A basic model: the exploring learner

The diagram sums up the relationship between competence – the system of innate and acquired skills relevant to a task – and freedom. The horizontal boundaries represent social and environmental constraints, within which competence is exercised. The frontier is the existential limit to this space, at which a person explores and copes with problems and ambiguities. The transitional object (Winnicott) is proto-typical of all play-things and tools (skill things) as well as of those things, such as probes, hypotheses and symbols, with which we explore. A person's competences develop at different rates. His or her achievements also vary and do not necessarily match competence and, as is suggested here, the possession of a tool (or symbol) may greatly enhance achievement.

monitored. The cube in Figure 1 stands for any toy or piece of apparatus which carries some intrinsic structure – in this case rectangularity and cubeness – and of corresponding problems and possibilities. Here then are what I believe to be the two essential and complementary aspects of education – its freedom ('space') and its inner discipline (structure). *The teacher is responsible both for making and protecting the child's space and for introducing into it appropriate structural elements which derive from the surrounding culture.* Many philosophically-minded biologists regard a constructive balance between an organism's openness *to* environment and its internalizing of rule-governed patterns *from* the environment as a fundamental dialectic of living processes (Boden 1979, 116–25). We should not be surprised, therefore, to find a similar balance at the centre of a broadly based account of education. In Figure 1 the teacher's and society's protective, space-creating function is indicated by the horizontal side walls, while their instructional function is suggested by the cube. This refers, not only to toys and to all the apparatus and suitably selected pictures and words which a teacher uses, but also to all those books and other structural things which furnish a curriculum. Whenever a teacher has abstracted some pattern from the world and embedded it in an attractive context or posed it as an intriguing problem or thrown it down as a moderate challenge, he or she is shaping the curriculum with an eye to making it interesting. All this is diagrammatically signified by that simple rectangular building block or cube.

One further point should be emphasized about the balance which must be maintained between the space-creating functions of a teacher and his or her function as an introducer of appropriate representations of structure. Up to approximately the age of puberty the protective aspect of education should predominate over the challenging, problem-posing aspect. During adolescence, at least for the great majority of young people, the balance should be gradually reversed. Young adults must sometimes sense freedom and danger. Yet our exam-orientated, dais-dominated secondary systems are singularly ill-adapted to meet this deep need for personal experiment, for questing and challenge and for real responsibility, all of which are characteristic requirements of human beings in their transition to adulthood. Our central and immediate concern, however, will be the nature of play and toys and tools. It is amongst these that all culture and all technology take root.

Games and play

An obvious but significant thing about the play and games of adults is that they happen mainly in special fields and at special times. For ball games and athletics there are carefully defined territories and seasons. These are not only marked by physical boundaries but also by special vocabulary, by rituals, and, above all, by rule systems, which themselves are controlled by little parliaments – national associations for this and that sport. We take all this for granted, but when called on to explain a rule or a custom in a game which we know, we tend to do so in terms of the little universe of that particular game. On the other hand if we stand outside these universes and ask what is really going on, why so much dedication and fuss, then we come to other interpretations: that these mini-worlds of golf or football exist partly to create an alternative pattern for those who enter, and they offer much-needed psychological space whose boundaries hold back the greater pressures of the world outside. Once inside we can play different roles, we can subject ourselves to different tensions and explore different potentialities. This is recreation, the adult version of playing. In many forms of play, and especially in those such as mountaineering and ocean sailing, whose space is the world's wilderness, the boundaries may be far out but there are still rules and conventions. There is another important aspect here – access to natural frontiers, to the experience of wild nature and of the elements. Every mountaineer and ocean yachtsman knows the powerful allure of such apparently unbounded playgrounds.

There is a still more general and abstract way of understanding play which can be seen to encompass all the meanings of the word. In all play, whether it be weekend golf, the ritual aggression of the football stands (Harré 1979, 320–2) a practical joke, a zen *koan* or the play or tolerance in a machine (where space fractionally distances a bearing from the axle within) there is something in common. This 'something' is an absence. It suggests a novel definition of play as intentional absence of pressure and the response or activity which characterizes such a condition. Openness is incorporated within a larger system so that the whole system may function without breakdown under the probable range of stresses to which it may be subject.[3]

Consider a common example from cybernetics. In complex mechanical systems, as for instance those space heaters in which feedback information alters the behaviour of the machine according to changing circumstance, such adaptability is part of the design. The concept of adaptability, whether in sophisticated machines or in living organisms, cannot be understood only in terms of parts moving in space, for the future is always being anticipated by some plan or plans built into the system. So play often involves an organism or an organized system acting directionally but leaving some outcomes open. Here the games model can be misleading for it implies fixed goals and targets and unchangeable rule systems. With living creatures, and especially with sentient living creatures, their openness to new kinds of information and their resilience always need understanding in terms of a time–space field – a field which is open to the future. This means being adaptable not only to the vicissitudes of the game but also to emergent patterns and rule systems which had not previously been encountered (Eigen and Winkler 1982, 320–30).

The ethologist, Robert Fagen, is one of a small group of writers on this subject who take the future-directed aspect of play seriously. Fagen suggests that play 'means behavioural performances that emphasize skills for interacting with physical and social environments and that occur in circumstances *under which the function of the exercised skill cannot be achieved*' (Smith 1984, 160, my italics). If we were to rephrase this in the kind of terms we have been using we would say that play happens most characteristically *away* from those frontiers where serious problems might be encountered; that is, it happens in potential space. This does not mean that play is purposeless or inefficient. The player will often strive for mastery, but within a relatively small framework. An observer of that play, or that same player thirty years later, may see it in a wider setting. Fagen gives illuminating examples of how the appropriate forms of play are often not those which would appear, with hindsight, to be the most relevant. He suggests, for example, that the best way for a human to gain competence as a future mountaineer may not be by climbing rocks but by wrestling; and others have suggested dancing. Why? Because when we play with people we have to keep seeing ourselves and the world from a variety of shifting viewpoints. Our antagonist is a kind of mirror. Thus we maximize the amount and diversity of feedback coming in from the context of our acts. J. S. Bruner makes similar suggestions in his paper 'Nature and the uses of immaturity' (Bruner *et al.* 1973). Common to all these accounts of play is the idea that its proper explanation is not to be sought in the here and now, but in some larger, superordinate system whose functioning transcends the immediate scene – the whole life cycle of a mammal for example.

Winnicott's term 'potential space' and the concept of frontier which relates to it can now be understood as overlapping ethology, cybernetic engineering and cognitive science. It means taking the pressure off the immediate situation for a purpose which will need to be understood in terms of some larger system, spanning a longer time. Yet into this space may enter structured novelty – toys, say, or nursery rhymes – which will, from time to time, be introduced by a teacher. Winnicott's own studies and those of other child psychologists have focused on the way in which parents and infants interact with each other from the moment of birth. In the loving interplay of their first few years together they are constantly creating shared 'space' and, within it, they lay down a patterned texture of behaviour which has enduring influence. One of the reasons why psychologists, and others who write on the subject, have had so much difficulty in saying what play *is* derives, I believe, from the necessity of defining play both in terms of absence of pressure ('space') and, at the same time, in terms of presence of observable rhythmic and often rule-governed activity. Yet if one watches a sensitive parent and infant interacting, these two aspects are clear to see. Stimulus is given; space is given – the space of a pause, the space of a raised eyebrow. It is from such ground that all subsequent social, emotional, cognitive and linguistic developments stem.[4]

Throughout this book education will always be taken as implying some variation on this shared theme:

Parent/teacher creating . . .
Learner enjoying, playing in,
   and exploring . . .   } SPACE

Teacher introducing appropriate . . .
Learner actively internalizing new . . .   } STRUCTURE

In *Born Curious* (1976, 54) I suggested that this dual definition of education is useful in sorting out some well-known issues regarding the distinctions between educating, instructing, training, indoctrinating and brain washing. Briefly, the more a teacher reduces a learner's sense of openness, of personal responsibility for choice in learning, the more he or she will move the interaction down the scale – away from an I–you relationship of education and towards an I–it encounter. Indoctrination means a critical reduction of 'play' and freedom while the instructional aspect remains the same. The happy mother–infant dyad usually shows both aspects in balance and yet, no matter how old the learner, both 'space' (in our sense) and structure should be present if the relationship is to be regarded as educational.

There have been many filmed and videotaped studies of mothers and infants interacting. John Shotter has drawn attention to the great qualitative differences which can be observed between those mothers who are responsive and positive towards their infants and those who are not (Shotter 1984, 86–9). Another relationship which is coming to be better understood is the rich interactive effect of siblings on each other. This often leads to differences, rather than to similarities, in development (Dunn and Kendrick 1982) and undoubtedly it causes some of the wide, subsequent variations in intellectual competence and temperament which are common among members of the same family. Even so, such examples should not be taken to imply that inherited factors are unimportant; but they are very difficult to disentangle.

I propose to describe a film of Janet Adler's therapeutic work with severely retarded children. Here the therapist is trying to do what a mother had failed to do for one inturned and solitary infant. Because such a child's need is acute and because the teacher in the film is outstandingly gifted one is able to see an everyday process highlighted as an exceptional achievement. It illustrates all those elements which it is so hard to hold together – play, the making of space, skill, interaction, feeling, the transmission of structure, the frontier, and the innate and acquired competence of the learner. The term 'frontier', it will be recalled, means the existential limit of the child's own exploration, while 'boundary' – in this model – will refer to the normative limits made by the teacher or by some other external agency – a fire-guard, for example, or bedtime.

The dancers

Janet Adler's film is entitled 'Looking for Me'. It demonstrates vividly the nature of 'potential space' and other elements of instruction in the form of dance episodes. The child, at first reluctantly, takes something and the adult gives; but the dance is, in the end, a joint creation. Here we can see, in heightened form, what a mother, interacting effectively with her infant, also demonstrates: that the first need of any child who is learning is a sense of secure, existential space in which it can be and act. In the early sessions of dancing the therapist constantly backs away from the child, engaging with it in both movement and music, but rarely encroaching, always leaving room for some infinitesimal advance. She weaves patterns in the room, on the walls and floor. Sometimes these are focused on the child, who may withdraw, but the dance goes on. A flicker of interest shows on the child's face. A coloured rope is introduced and emphasizes circles of movement, loops and figures of eight. It can be used to signify a bond or a boundary or it can be thrown away. Gradually the cord, then the hands and arms, become links held by each dancer; not controls or threats. In the last sequence, after days of work, there is trust, reciprocity of movement and a loving embrace. All the positive moves of the therapist – her pauses, interrogative glances, slight approaches – are done with the utmost gentleness and are barely perceptible when compared with her negative, space-creating movements of withdrawal and invitation. But the space that is being made is increasingly framed and defined by both participants. The whole is a work of art. The outcome is not only the dance, the enhanced experience of an impoverished child; it is also the establishment of a *we*, that incipient, asymmetrical learning community of two, the dyad on which all education is built.

It is important to note that the therapist used no language, drew no pictures – apart from the mobile picture of the dance. By avoiding words, which may well be an aspect of the world which the child fears, Janet Adler makes it easier for positive feelings, especially for love, to thaw. She uses the two most basic forms of human interaction: first the fundamental interpersonal mode which is so much concerned with the patterning of time. In it there is a kind of unspoken syntax – sequence, pause, interroga-

tion and hopeful waiting. Such interpersonal exchanges foreshadow the emergence of speech. It is as though the two are in
wordless communication – 'my turn', 'your turn?', 'perhaps',
etc.[5] And secondly the dancer is using what Bruner (1967) calls
'the enactive mode' – communicating, demonstrating, experiencing, exploring *by bodily action*, long before the learner is ready to
use other more sophisticated methods such as pictures or speech
for questioning or telling stories.

Structure and instruction

Even though language may still be over the learner's horizon the
teacher (or therapist or parent) is often *in-structing*; she is introducing structure to the learner in a variety of ways. First, she is
cultivating the early groundwork of sequential communication,
in her movements and responses, in her expressions, pauses and
gestures. Here we have the basic interpersonal mode of instruction. Secondly, the dancer is using her bodily movement to
explore space. We see her repeatedly acknowledging and responding to the child's own tentative efforts. It is a kind of mirror
activity, a sensitive feedback which invites the child to strengthen
its own sensorimotor learning and its own sense of being.
Thirdly, Janet Adler used the coloured rope – a toy – to play with,
which can be used to emphasize many of the interpersonal and
enactive exchanges just mentioned; but it also sometimes forms
visible two-dimensional patterns and thus it foreshadows the
great domain of picture making and picture reading which lies
ahead of the learner. This is what Bruner terms the 'iconic mode'
of instruction – those instructional representations which help
someone to manipulate and internalize spatial experience. As we
shall see in chapter 8, this is largely, but not entirely, a power
which has its physiological basis in the right cerebral hemisphere.
There is also music and this too reverberates predominantly in
the 'non-linguistic', right half of the brain.

Janet Adler restricts her communication to the non-linguistic
modes of representation. She courts the child with a wide,
expressive repertoire – glance, movement, music and form – but
never has recourse to the most formal, most daunting and
characteristically human mode of language. We shall often return
to the five main modes of representation, the interpersonal,

enactive, iconic, musical and language-like activities with which human beings make meaning. They all support each other and they interact and make way for each other, just as, in our present example, dance and music are preparing the ground for future language. Music plays a crucial part in the time-patterning process of the dance and it goes far beyond this into worlds of pitch, harmony, mood and feeling.

All these modes are rooted both in the outer world of cultural 'things' and in an inner world of mental processes. To speak of an inner world of sound or an inner world of pictures is to refer to mental phenomena which we all experience; but it should be emphasized that current research is only on the very fringes of a scientific understanding of how such 'inner worlds' may function.[6] Nevertheless when we visualize a pattern – a coiled rope, say – something representational of space must be happening in the deep strata of our brains, and furthermore we can *do* something with such an image if we wish. That is what Piaget means by 'concrete operations' – mentally manipulating the images of reality which the brain presents us with. The word 'concrete' here stands in contrast to the more abstract term – 'the formal operations' of language – and neither term refers directly to the world outside. To turn a pictured cube around, thinking about it 'in my mind's eye', is such a concrete operation. To think of the notation $4cm^3$ is to perform a formal operation involving abstract concepts to do with measurement and with 'cubeness'.

Though there may be danger in over-emphasizing this separateness of inner and outer worlds it is something that we constantly experience. Models of reality can exist on the table in front of me or as an inner mental process. Piaget's theoretical account of what is going on in cognitive development – 'concrete operations', 'formal operations', 'schema', etc. – refers to inner mental activity. In contrast, Bruner's 'instructional' terminology matches this, but refers mainly to the outside world, to what we, teacher and learner, do about it as we try to facilitate the inner cognitive development. Instruction, then, could be described as helping someone to transform a pattern from an outward to an inward representation (see also pp. 135–7). I have laboured these distinctions in order to stress that all the basic modes of instruction which we have been illustrating in terms of a dancer – interpersonal exchanges, movements, pictures, music – all these form a hierarchy of experience in which each layer supports and intercommunicates with the others. It is on these foundations, by constantly drawing structure from them, that a learner comes to develop language and other more abstract thought forms.[7]

These main instructional modes which assist such development can be envisaged as five storeys of a house or as layers of a pyramid. We can think of education – straining the metaphor slightly – as the sustained and guided exploration of such an edifice. It is often an alarming experience for the learner, with constant ascents, retreats and rests; new phases of work start low down, perhaps at the enactive level, and then mount gradually so that more abstract representations are internalized. Many of our most difficult educational problems are to do with where a learner should start on this edifice. Far too often a sense of fear and failure accompanies the attempt to move from one stage to the next. An experienced secondary teacher will know, for example, that if a group of 13-year-olds is having difficulty with algebraic 'language' it is likely to be helpful for them to reinforce their sense of achievement, their competence, by playing and practising at the iconic level – the next level down – where they can use diagrams, graphs and other two-dimensional examples. 'Draw a picture of it', she will say, or 'show me how it might work in a model'. This counsel – *reculer pour mieux sauter* – not only takes away some feelings of fear and failure but it permits a strengthening of the foundations on which the more abstract thinking has to rest. It is a mistake always to assume that there is some special virtue in abstract thinking as opposed to more concrete thinking. There is a pervasive snobbishness about this. We need to be able to work at several levels. The most creative people in science or literature are those who can move readily from model building, to picture making, to turning an idea into mathematics or language and then back again into new models or experiments.

As teachers too we need to be imaginative and flexible in thinking about our subject at all levels of abstraction. At times, when great stress or discouragement faces our pupils, we have to revert, almost, to being 'mothers' – to the most basic interpersonal mode of culture; to giving a kind of wordless reassurance that the world is trustworthy. In most of our deliberate instructional initiatives we work at the upper levels of the pyramid. We set up games, problems or exercises which appear to be at about the level of difficulty suitable to the individual or group concerned. A new way of thinking about an old problem can be just as interesting as total novelty. We need, most of all, insight in to what it looks like and feels like on the learner's side of the interaction.

Approaching the frontier

A number of other aspects of education can be discerned in the model of the dancer and the frightened child whose potential space needs gradual expansion. Not only is there a big asymmetry in the way in which the two participants understand what is going on; one knows so much and the other so little. There is parallel asymmetry in their feelings. The teacher must be able to bridge this and to know, or guess, what the learner is feeling. That is, *she exercises her empathy*; she understands the child's fears or loves. Also, *she has an intention for the learner* – that the child should be healed of these fears, that it should respond, smile, talk, grow up. This is extremely important because the teacher's task is not only to make available some structured elements of knowledge (concepts, spatial patterns, relationships, etc.); she is also bound to sketch in, though perhaps only faintly and largely in terms of felt and intuited meanings, some of the main lines and future direction in which this assembly of structures may be developed by the growing child. Such intentions and directions are many, complex and will sometimes seem contradictory. The teacher, if she is wise, will not be too explicit about such hopes. She may revolve them in her mind and may discuss them with colleagues, but she must tread softly, for they are not her dreams underfoot.

Just as an imaginative teacher entertains intentions and hopes for her pupil so he (the learner) explores his own future in imaginative fantasy. Two points must be made here about the way in which each of us looks towards his or her frontier – up the beach. One of the characteristics of a maladjusted child, as of a neurotic adult, is that his fantasies contain relatively few elements of reality; they are inadequately rooted in real skills and coherent experience. Looking at the experience of some acutely unhappy children – Janet Adler's partner would be an example – one gets the impression that their space for play and fantasy is reduced almost to nothing by fear or by wordless anger. There are many possible causes for such impoverishment and these will be touched on in the next chapter.

Much depends on the mixture of feelings with which a learner approaches the frontier. Is fear or hope or curiosity or awe in the ascendant? Experience with 'normal' teenagers suggests that we need a special term to describe a learner's perception of future possibilities and pathways. These *vistas* of possibility, as I propose to call them, are much more diffuse than social ambitions or career goals. Yet they arise from real experiences and from a dawning awareness of the learner's own potential. Youthful vistas are unlikely to be a ready subject for conversation though children often travel down them in fantasy. An adult who initiates a practical discussion about 'your first job' or 'your career' is likely to find it a prickly topic. Why? Partly because the whole field of future possibilities cannot be clearly seen, let alone described in words; also, because the child's perception of a vista is itself a frontier experience and depends on many just attained or not-quite-attained skills and concepts, it is almost always a zone highly charged with feeling. There are occasions when a youthful vista does appear attractive and fairly clear. This is usually because of the influence of some admired individual or perhaps of a community embodying a desired way of life. In such cases we could properly use the word 'vocation', rather than 'vista'. For most young people such specific callings are unlikely to be strongly sensed; but vistas often will be, even though they are more fleeting and more open.

It is always good for teachers to have their own active, learning frontier because it helps them to enter, imaginatively, the child's potential space and to know how he feels and, perhaps, what his own frontier problems are. Each person's frontier exists where his or her competence is at full stretch, where, by definition, he knows that he can only just cope. So it is a place of acute feeling, of possible failure and of apprehension – apprehension in the double sense of both grasping and fearing the new realities. Most people do not enjoy such exposure for very long and soon turn back for comfort and reassurance nearer to base. Nevertheless these moves towards a frontier of novel and authentic experience are an essential ingredient of education. It is at such times that a person first sees significance and new form, first makes a discovery or glimpses some yet more distant vista of meaning.

Here, then, we have the elements of a theoretical model of education. There is a learner who explores 'space', moving towards a more or less dimly perceived frontier and thereby develops skills and competence. There is a teacher who not only sustains such learning space but who also enriches it by introducing appropriately structured things. The whole process, however, is dynamic and the things used for learning change with changing use and growing competence.

Notes

1 For an account of the origins of Dilthey's distinction see Sir Isaiah Berlin's *Vico and Herder* (1971, 66–7). John Searle, in his 1984 Reith Lectures, while not relating his ideas directly to Vico, follows similar lines. He stresses that it is man-made meanings and intentions – 'a constantly changing reality' – which are incorporated into the social sciences and which therefore make them different from the natural sciences whose reality is constant.

2 The phrasing has been slightly altered. One of the valuable aspects of Boden's introduction to Piaget is that she 'locates' him in regard to other philosophers, psychologists, linguists and biologists.

3 A central method of Zen Buddhism, which it probably acquired from Taoism, is to keep alive a creative sense of play. A *koan* is a special kind of spoken or acted joke. Some of the best eccentric teachers have the gift for making such jokes and these are often preserved in the folk-lore of schools. A *koan* has the opposite effect from that of a symbol which holds together and focuses different levels of meaning. A symbol throws you up the slope towards a more abstract grasp of meaning (see the next chapter); a *koan* trips you with nonsense so that you stumble and 'open your grasp'. What you then say should be precisely the opposite of 'Aha' or of 'Eureka'! For perplexity, not clarity, then breaks in. Alan Watts writes that a *koan* 'is concerned not only with the primary awakening to the Void but also with its subsequent expression in life and thought'. This is from his book, *The Way of Zen* (1962, 126).

4 It is worth noting, in this connection, a somewhat similar concept in the Japanese tradition of *Noh* Theatre. The final goal of *Noh* drama is termed *Yugen*, which means an emotionally heightened *readiness for feelings* and ideas. The emphasis is on *openness* to anticipated experience. Literally *yugen* means 'obscure and dark' but it can be better understood as 'suggestive' or 'implicit', a directional space which allows the imagination to move. Its opposite would be

'over-statement' or 'explicit'. The above remarks are based on Peter Hulton's notes on the display of *Noh* masks in the Dartington Hall Library.

5 'Colwyn Trevarthen . . . claims that evidence from films of more than 100 exchanges between mothers and their infants of two or three months of age forces us to conclude that a complex form of mutual understanding develops even at this age. He believes that this kind of early interpersonal responsiveness is the source from which the whole [?] of human intelligence springs.' This description of what I call 'The Interpersonal Mode' is from *Children's Minds* by Margaret Donaldson (1978, 29). The book gives a sympathetic, yet critical, account of Piaget's ideas and of how these have been modified in the 1970s. For another view see also Dunn and Kendrick (1982).

6 We discuss one aspect of this problem in chapters 8 and 9 – the interaction of pictorial imagery and language. But many other interesting possibilities are beginning to appear. There is, for example, the immense potential offered by educational drama and music and – more remote perhaps – the educational possibilities of exploring inner space through lucid dreaming and contemplation.

7 Bruner (1983) has coined the acronym LASS (language acquisition support system) to describe this patterned hierarchy of tacit knowledge out of which language grows. The initials are partly aimed at Chomsky who, for many years, has claimed that there must be a LAD (language acquisition device) which linguists will eventually identify as part of the innate circuitry of the brain. Though this argument may be partly semantic (e.g. what does 'device' mean?) it also reflects important philosophical differences. The emphasis on cultural things and interactions which Bruner makes is in line with the general perspective adopted here.

3 Things for use and things for meaning: tools and symbols

> Tools and machines do not merely signify man's imaginativeness and . . . creative reach, and they are certainly not important merely as instruments for the transformation of a malleable earth: they are pregnant symbols in themselves.
>
> (Weizenbaum 1976)

You are thrown on the beach, alone or with a few survivors, and in this situation almost anything that you find might be useful. There are less melodramatic experiences of such marginality: the migrant family on the edge of the great city, the new child at school or – as we suggested – the jaded commuter regressing to the relative simplicities of sea and sand. These are all situations in which either the play of fate or the play of our own choice presents us with the opportunity to regard whatever is lying about with new insight. The broken shell *could* be a knife; the sheet of rusting tin, a roof. It is the kind of situation where one considers not only what things are but what they might be, that open kind of space between two worlds, where tools are found. Or discovered?

A tool, properly speaking, is an object which has first been chosen, then adapted to function as part of a skill. Men have always used tools and so have a few animals. Chimpanzees, for example, use stiff grasses for probing termites' nests and they also use sticks as weapons, i.e. as special tools for use within a skill of aggressive intent. It is unfortunate that our linguistic watchdogs have not kept as close an eye on the vocabulary of tools and technology as they have on some more abstract pronouncements. Increasingly the word 'tool' is used when 'skill' or 'technique' would serve better. A recent newspaper headline, for example, was 'Study in prison: a tool for mental survival' when what was meant was strategy or means for survival.[1] These distinctions are important because one condition for the cultural survival and further development of free men is that we should understand more clearly the nature of tools and of 'technology' and their relation to ourselves and to science.[2]

How far should we carry this idea of a tool as something lying within a skill and taking its essence from it? One might, sometimes, say that a book is a tool if it forms part of an individual researcher's project: but, defined in a more public context, as within a reference library, the idea of a book as a tool begins to lose sharpness. If one pushes the use of the word 'tool' in the contrary direction, towards the micro-skills of language, an interesting set of meanings emerges. Spoken words themselves can then be seen as shaped, transient *things*, each differently fashioned of vibrating air, and collectively forming a tool kit (i.e. a vocabulary) for use within the fine skills of language. To call words 'tools' is a just permissible conceptual stretch, in my view, and it allows us to regard the use of a concept or the process of conceptualizing as a very fine skill – that of classifying and connoting. Both skills and concepts, seen in this way, are directional; they impose limitations and yet they are open-ended towards new meaning and to the frontiers of creativity.

Not only should a tool be defined as lying 'within' a skill but, because of this, we need to recognize that machines and tools usually embody principles which have been abstracted from systems of greater complexity – the probe from the finger, the camera from the eye, for example. There are important exceptions, such as the wheel, but these do not alter the general suggestion about use: that a tool should be definable within a specifiable skill which has a history and which points to a cluster of intentions. This means that a tool can always be thought about at two levels at least: first at the level of nature – what it is made of when found – and secondly at the level of culture, where it is incorporated into a skill and used or held in readiness for a range of human purposes. This is perhaps obvious but it leads on to further distinctions in the understanding of all cultural objects, including words and pictures: that they can be used with only slight intent (toys), with precise intent (tools) or to cope with ambiguities and with multiple levels of meaning (symbols). It is these distinctions and relationships, and particularly the dynamic yet complex meaning of 'symbol' which will now concern us.

Toys, tools and symbols

Donald Winnicott's ideas can lead to a new way of understanding the origin of 'cultural objects' and the three different phases in which these can be used – namely as toys, as tools and as symbols. He starts his analysis by discussing those well-loved bits of cloth, those tattered toys, those fetish-like shreds of culture, onto which an infant readily hooks. Sometimes parts of the body serve the same consoling purpose – the fingers caressing the hair, for example, or the thumb in the mouth. Together they calm the child for rest or steady it for action and in this, curiously, these objects, in their steadying function, resemble both cigarettes and prayers. Winnicott gives them the general name of 'transitional objects' and describes them as having a 'me, not me' quality (1971, 2–3, 96–103). They exist on the self's exploring boundary or frontier and that boundary is a shifting one. Transitional objects are sometimes part of me (hair, for instance) and yet they are also transitional towards – they point towards – the shadowy world which lies beyond me and beyond the safe 'space' which my mother and I have created.[3]

When Winnicott tried to become clear in his mind about the status of these transitional objects and where they should be conceptually located, he coined the phrase 'potential space' which we have already defined as the locus of play, and whose outer edge is the frontier of discovery. For an infant the well-loved and tattered piece of cloth *is* what it is, the comforter, and it exists in potential space. We, from a mature vantage point, can see that it points forward to much more – to future toys, to future tools and to future symbols and to all the ranges of action, reflection and confidence which these enable, hence the stress on potentiality.

The overlap between the three categories – toys, tools and symbols – never entirely disappears, even in maturity. Sometimes young adults – students at the secondary stage of education for example – display a powerful fixation on transitional objects which is reminiscent of childhood and yet which also foreshadows maturity. One 16-year-old youth whom I knew – Edward – was for a year or so obsessed with knives. They were his toys but they were tools and symbols too. He could whittle with great skill and he had to be discouraged from using his knife-throwing expertise in the vicinity of human targets. A Freudian will immediately recognize the symbolic, phallic reference of the knife. When thinking about symbols, however, it is a mistake to narrow their meanings down to 'nothing but' interpretations. The knife and indeed the phallus which it often signifies are symbols for a much wider range of possibilities and potencies than sex. When Edward showed me a specialist catalogue for knife-lovers this range was clear to see. Some of the knife associations undoubtedly had a touch of machismo and even cruelty about them. Others pointed to hunting, to the backwoods, to tropical forests and to the high seas; but always there was a suggestion of an adult person competent to adapt to a non-mechanical, 'natural' world, free, yet facing tasks and problems.

Seen from the viewpoint of 'things for use' transitional objects can be regarded as the juvenile source from which flows all the practical gear of a technical world; but from another perspective – 'things for meaning' – they are the beginnings of all our imaginative and intuitive dreaming, of poetry and of religion. This is undoubtedly an area of powerful ambiguity; yet Winnicott has pointed a way through. What is this relationship between things for play, things for skilled mastery and things we grope with? One might describe the topic as 'the phenomenology of tools': how can a stone or a chip of quartz become a play thing, then a tool and then part of my exploring imagination or, perhaps, a mere gadget? These are all questions which bear on our understanding of other cultures, on the development of children and also on the problems of our own technologically choked civilization.

As soon as an infant (or a shipwrecked mariner) picks up a natural object and starts to use it intentionally, a world of culture has been entered. And immediately the use/meaning paradox arises. However – and here I summarize the argument – these ambiguities can be resolved if we hold onto the idea that every man (or child) is potentially an explorer, and yet he cannot be exploring all the time. Sometimes he must play and sometimes he must sharpen his tools. Nevertheless if a thing is only played with, it remains a toy or a gadget. (A gadget is a special kind of toy – a tool made with high level expertise but played with by those who have little competence, or intention, to explore with it – a Porsche in the hands of a playboy!) In the transitional world of childhood it is clear that toys often become tools, as play turns into skill. If a tool is properly used, at increasing levels of skill, it becomes, through practice, an extension of the user – what Bruner calls 'a prosthetic device' – a wooden leg, for example, or a radio telescope. Polanyi looks at this from the other side and speaks of our 'indwelling', or pouring some of our life into such tools. Cultural objects, however, are not only for consolation and achievement. When a tool becomes part of me it also points to the frontier which is my special zone of problems, of danger, of ambiguity and therefore of *possible* achievement or failure.

In the example of Edward's knife there was a powerful non-instrumental usage where feeling and fantasy had rein. Similarly I have known a climbing rope become a focus of unrealized long-term meanings for a young man who spent most of his school life on the flat ground. (He is now a successful manufacturer of climbing equipment.) The knife and the rope, as well as being fascinating toys and, occasionally, useful tools, may also be symbols in the full meaning of the word. A symbol, in this sense, is not just a sign standing for something else, it is a focal, relatively clearly perceived image which, though part of a field of present experience, points to future possible acts and meanings. It is both directional and dynamic, for it is around symbols that our 'motivational' energies tend to gather. In terms of our Crusoe model, of the play space with the frontier ahead, *the symbol points to a vista*. The term 'vista' is used here in the rather special sense which was suggested earlier. The symbol → vista terminology can be useful in education and psychology because it links up certain complex experiences of development. A similar innovation was made in biology by Waddington (1957, 32) when he introduced the terminology of chreods. By 'chreod' he meant a fated or favoured pathway through a morphogenetic field. If we adapt the vista concept to educational psychology, it allows us to envisage a learner making his way through a field of discovery on his frontier. It is what enables an explorer to perceive openness on the frontier and to expect to find new structures there.

Seymour Papert is the only writer on education, as far as I know, to have seen the importance of transitional objects after infancy. He vividly describes his early involvement with gear wheels and how they led on to 'powerful ideas':

Piaget's work gave me a new framework for looking at the gears of my childhood. . . . As well as connecting with the formal knowledge of mathematics, [the gear] also connects with the 'body knowledge', the sensorimotor schemata of a child. You can *be* the gear. In a terminology I shall develop in later chapters, the gear acts here as a *transitional object.* (1980, viii)

Without such encouraging and comforting symbolic objects one can soon feel lost, and give up.

Why is novelty, frontier experience, sometimes so alluring – as with the gear wheels – yet sometimes so repellent? Bruner has given us the term 'pre-emptive metaphor' to describe how it is that at times of sharp developmental transition a boy or girl may be blocked from learning by a cluster of ideas which link associatively with one central focus of fear (1968, ch. 7). It is useful to have a similar but positive terminology for those objects and experiences which *foreshadow success in exploring.* It was when I used to think about the problems of frustrated, angry adolescents that I began to realize that we require a concept such as this to suggest the idea of an opening or an encouraging pathway perceived by a learner near his own frontier. A young man who seems to be the despair of his teacher, who has quarrelled with parents, who has low self-esteem, suddenly finds an 'outlet' in painting battle scenes. Yet it is not just an outlet for surplus energy, it points the way forward, for him and for his teachers, if they could but see. Such an opening is made available or entered into through the action of some transitional object becoming a symbol. Where education and development is happening in the process of apprenticeship, such a symbol may well be the respected teacher or, to use Bruner's term, 'a competence model'. But in the contemporary world of young adults, where breaking away from parents and involvement in the peer group have become important, some symbols of maturity will be rejected and others – often less human – will be sought.

The creative cycle: things for use

How are these concepts – toys, tools and symbols – related? This question runs parallel to the crucial educational problem of how play, practice and creative discovery merge into each other within a heuristic field. Each relates to the others in an apparently smooth transition but how does this happen? The philosophers of art and education have not yet provided adequate means for conceptualizing the problem. On the other hand a number of psychologists, George Kelly, Bruner and Liam Hudson, have developed a view of learning in which play *and* discipline, convergent *and* divergent thinking are seen as complementary. Kelly's personal construct theory describes the 'creativity cycle . . . as one which starts with loosened construction and terminates with tightened and validated construction'.[4] That is a useful beginning.

Play, practice and exploration: we need to hold these together in a model which is coherent and which matches our common experience of teaching. The easier part of this three-fold concept is the relation of play to practice (Figure 2, p. 46). Surprisingly little serious attention has been given to the concept of practice in education. It has, it is true, been studied in connection with high pressure training for narrow skills. Examples of this would be training of airline pilots by using electronic simulators which replicate the hazards of take-off, landing and navigation, and which allow for constant repetitions and refinements of skill. There has, till recently, been a widespread assumption among progressive teachers that drills and anything like rote learning for young learners are, somehow, retrograde. Yet there is a considerable body of research which suggests that the most effective teachers are those who manage to keep a balance between what are sometimes called free or creative methods and the more old-fashioned methods in which acceptable drills, mnemonics and success-biased testing play a part. It is not easy for a teacher to create such an optimal balance, especially if the learning group is large and of widely varying competence, but it can be done. Because teacher education and teacher evaluation tend to be thought about in terms of the false dichotomy of progressive *versus* traditional, the difficulty continues to be, in part, a conceptual and linguistic one.[5]

Educational researchers and teacher educators need to look closely at the question of what it is that makes practice congenial and effective. Enjoyable practice does not have to be lacking in rigour. Indeed it can be largely self-rewarding. Japanese children

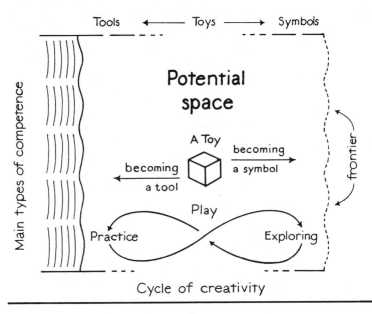

Figure 2   The creative cycle

The things a person plays with can, with practice, become part of some skill and thus eventually assimilated to a general area of competence. However, a toy or 'playwith' (Coleridge) can also be pushed out to the frontier and become what might be termed an 'explorewith'. Symbols (in this strong sense of the word) or an original hypothesis or a probe in competent hands would all come into this category. Learning – whether by a child or by an adult – can be seen as an oscillation between play, practice and exploring. In this and similar diagrams the teacher is only implied: he makes the space, sustains the dialogue and introduces structures, problems and evaluations.

of about 5 or 6 years old who learn to play the violin by the Suzuki method work in an atmosphere of sustained, vigorous enjoyment. Many little games and tunes are mixed with episodes of systematic practice. A group of four children, for example, share one violin and one bow. The tune is kept going and the children change roles, as in a dance. The constant exchange of function, the dance-like patterns, the unifying tune, the familiar and unfamiliar skills and the danger of possible breakdown – all go to the creation of a little work of art in which play, practice and tension are all embodied. Another important element in this approach is that wherever possible the mother is involved in the practice. There may be weaknesses in the Suzuki method but in many respects it is a great advance on traditional music teaching (Wickes, 1982 *passim*; Gardner 1984, 373–9).

In the example of the dancer it was clear that much could be achieved without talk. It is generally a mistake to explain the theoretical structure of a learning activity before the learner tries it. The teacher himself undoubtedly needs to be familiar with the grammar and other underlying structures but the learner should encounter them first in action, pre-theoretically. Ryle's dictum sums this up: 'efficient practice precedes the theory of it' (1949, 30). A colleague of mine in the Sudan who was a pioneer in teaching English as a foreign language taught almost all his grammar in this fashion. Much of the early part of the course was built around active learning games for 12- to 14-year-olds. A group would mime with a chair, for example, at the front of the class while the teacher orchestrated a continuous pattern of grammatical commentary. The chorus would go something like this: 'Adam would like to get onto the chair but Mohammed won't let him. I would like to get onto the chair but you won't let me . . .' and there was appropriate pointing. Nevertheless this teacher trainer was quite ready to encourage students to use grammatical terms retrospectively, that is, when they wished to consolidate newly acquired language skills or to analyse errors. This way of acquiring speech patterns in modern language learning is fortunately becoming more common than the premature learning of grammatical terms and rules. Its value lies partly in the fact that the activity of a pupil speaking or acting in a group is open to everyone's sensori-motor experience, partly that words and reality can be constantly linked, and partly that it is fun, i.e. it can be made sufficiently playful. And this helps the teacher too, because as soon as he senses boredom he recognizes the need for a change of method or tempo.

Piaget has been an admirable educational guide and prophet and his influence on education has been mainly salutary. Though details of his approach have been criticized (Bryant 1974, Donaldson 1978, Boden 1977), his emphasis on, and understanding of, active learning has been of enormous benefit to primary schools. His influence on secondary education, however, has been less, partly because most of his work was with younger children and with those not in a spontaneously active group. He has also been responsible for a one-sided view of play, which he sees as being essentially a kind of repetitive practice. Play, seen in these terms, as helping learners to assimilate new concepts or skills to existing mental patterns (schemas) is not enough. Piaget failed to emphasize the complementary direction in which play is also useful: that which leads learners towards exploration and to the more stressful and challenging processes of *accommodating* unfamiliar experiences and concepts. This failure of Piaget and other developmental psychologists to relate play sufficiently to exploratory learning may be connected with the fact that he also shows relatively little interest in feeling and emotion.[6]

The creative cycle: things for meaning

A probe or a stick being used by a sightless person is an example of a tool with a rather special function. The probe has been discussed by philosophers of science because it can be regarded as the very prototype of all experimental devices – as something especially chosen or made for exploring puzzling phenomena. So a stick, used in this fashion, is not a tool for making something or a weapon for hitting, it is first and foremost a meaning-seeking thing. In this it resembles all those other sophisticated extensions of the human senses with which scientists probe the universe – telescopes, spectroscopes, seismographs. We will stay a little longer with the blind man's stick, for it exemplifies certain essentials common to all of these and to hypotheses and symbols too. They are all 'discovery things' or, parodying Coleridge, who writes of toys as 'playwiths', those things with which we actively make discoveries could be called 'explorewiths' (Raine 1957, 143).

When a person first handles a probe or any other simple tool and then tries to use it, he will find himself thinking a good deal *about* the tool itself, feeling its pressures on his hand and looking at it. Then, when he has become more practised in its use, he ceases to do so much handling and thinks, rather, about what he is doing with it. Niels Bohr, when reflecting on the apparatus which he used in the early days of research in quantum physics, discusses the nature of probes and makes a similar distinction, between 'analysis' (of the tool, apparatus or experimental procedure) and of its 'application' (what you do and find with it). In the latter case the researcher is on the lookout for expected regularities as well as for anomalies and surprises. He is on the frontier.

Polanyi takes a very similar line and speaks of someone having 'subsidiary awareness' of the tool in his hand and of having 'focal awareness' of the task on which he is actively and skilfully engaged. In the latter case, if there is a tool – probe or chisel, for example – the skilled user's attention will go forward and will hover round some focus which lies just ahead of the tool in time and place. As a way of describing this focused unity of a person and his tool Polanyi uses that rather strange word 'indwelling' which we have already encountered; it is as though the user's mind flows through the tool towards the task. Polanyi applies this idea not only to probes but also to any hypothetical model or experimental procedure which an investigator has made his own. An investigator with such a degree of involvement in the material – whether it be a diagram, a model or a verbal construct, either externally or internally – 'in his mind' – can commit himself, for a time, to the focal action of exploring.[7]

Where does play come in? Consider the oscillation which goes on between a person looking *at* a tool and working *through* it with focal awareness, and compare this with the infantile origins of such actions. Winnicott (1971, 96) suggests that 'when we witness an infant's employment of a transitional object, "the first not-me possession", we are witnessing the first use of symbol and the first experience of play'. At this early stage toy and tool and symbol are the same thing and they only gradually become differentiated. The use of gadgetry – a new ego-boosting camera for example – is often a sign that such differentiation is not complete. Where a craftsman or an athlete has developed a high degree of skill, he or she will retain the capacity for play and in moments of relaxation will be able to look objectively at the tools and techniques involved. Part of the function of recreation is comfort and rest; but no less important is the chance it offers for the dis-assembly and re-integration of skills and the opportunity which this offers for improving the tools being used. The bad workman may either blame or unduly revere his tools; the good workman likes old ones and, when not hard pressed, may enjoy designing new ones. Tools, like words, are provisional and open-ended. What we play with we always might create with.

One of the weaknesses in much contemporary craft teaching is that it is so involved in giving a wide experience of materials and 'problems' that it only offers a shallow experience of tools.

Winnicott's theory about the origin of toys, tools and symbols converges closely on the Bohr–Polanyi analysis of probes. In using tools and in developing the technical skills in which they are embedded, a skilled person – rather like an infant – constantly oscillates between treating them as 'not me' – that is he objectifies them so as to analyse their faults and possibilities – and then treating them as 'me' again – applying them directly to the work on which personal knowledge and skill are focused. It is important to remember something else which Polanyi stresses: that at any particular moment such ongoing focal awareness is incompatible with subsidiary or analytical awareness. If our attention is focused on what we are doing we will be organizing and integrating, almost without knowing it, a great hierarchy of innate and acquired skills, experiences and sensibilities. It is this dynamic totality of relevant information which Polanyi termed 'tacit knowledge'. (See chapter 4 for a fuller definition.) While we are in the process of integrating such diverse tacit knowledge in a continuous complex act we cannot possibly shift into an analytical perspective without stopping the whole procedure. I would not advise anybody running down a steep hill, for example, to think much about exactly what his feet are doing. Alternatively, as Stephen Potter (1947) advised: 'Analyse your opponent's putting. . . . Ask him which muscles he brings into play and from what part of the body "the sequence of muscular response" begins' and he will certainly fluff his shot. Gamesmanship apart, however, there is often a place for analysing what we do *once the action is over*. Grammar and theory are mainly useful retrospectively when we reflect on experience and when we wish to diagnose failure and to improve tools and equipment. Theory and analysis of competence are also important for developing instructional methods and, when shared, they can form a powerful intellectual bond for the community which shares critically in such development.

The oscillation between familiar and unfamiliar

There is still a further subtlety about the Bohr–Polanyi model as it applies to frontier situations. Think of a probe in practical use. (It is a good idea to try this, blindfold, with a stick on an unfamiliar garden path.) You will find as you go forward, tapping, that a pattern of expected information comes up the stick as well as occasional unexpected bits of information. You tap along the grass edge to the path – tap, tap, tap, tap . . . then – nothing! There is a problem. The inference may be 'perhaps a step down' or 'perhaps a corner'. But when you began tapping, didn't you expect something like this? You started off with the definite expectation that you would encounter problems and ambiguities. Nevertheless as one pattern becomes more or less familiar, so you assimilate it to what is already yours. Then comes the anomaly. The skilful prober eliminates looseness from his grip but he transfers it to the distal end of his wobbling antenna. The yes, yes, yes of the expected finding is familiar and becomes assimilated almost as part of 'me'; the sudden gap of the anomaly demands a change. It is 'not me' and it requires a change in me and in my exploratory procedure. It may, indeed, continue to tease and draw me for days or for years. In terms of the competence-play-frontier diagram (Figures 1 or 2) the probe, in skilful hands, can be regarded as reaching right over the potential space to the frontier which is itself the interface between serious play and some yet-to-be-discovered orderliness. *All discovery things, from probes to hypotheses, involve this attribute of symbols, that they are intended to cope with ambiguity, with the tension which precedes surprise, with what you expect to find and also with what you don't.*

In trying to think clearly about the relationship between play, practice and discovery I found myself in a cul-de-sac. The reason was that I had imposed a mistaken sequence on the three kinds of artefact with which we act in these roles. Toys, I thought, were most primitive; tools must develop out of toys and then symbols must develop somehow out of tools. And yet that never seemed to be right. The relationship was not linear and sequential. Assimilation and practice implied a steady move towards efficiency, predictability and control; whereas exploration and the need for accommodating new experience through symbolism or hypothesis moved in the contrary direction – towards the frontier where ambiguity lurked and where doubtful competence and even danger threatened. So we seem to require a two-way oscillating and dialectical concept, more on the lines of Taoism's *yin* and *yang* and less like a linear progression. Play is there at the beginning, and it remains central – a springboard for two complementary kinds of action. We can either move from it in the direction of increasing efficiency and control, as we consolidate our competence, or we can move towards uncertainty and challenge as we stretch our competence.

Here then is the way the cycle of creativity generally seems to go – play-practice-play, then play-exploration and back to play again. Toys are what we play with; probes – in the broad, symbolic sense which I am using – may be pictures, poetic images, a work of music, a scientific hypothesis, a person or a ritual; all these may be what we explore new worlds and new meanings with. Yet to do so we must in some degree, be firmly committed to them. We dwell in them. Figure 2 suggests the oscillations which take place between play and the two quite distinct kinds of 'seriousness'. Play merges in one direction into controlled, instrumental practice; in the other it runs into frontier activity – to exploring, or sustaining attention to, what is problematic, ambiguous and, perhaps, dangerous. It should be remembered that play, in the rather extended sense which we are using (i.e. 'pressure off . . . for a purpose'), is the phase of activity in which reflection and self-criticism are likely to be effective, as well as the fundamental, pre-cognitive processes of rest and solace.

It is not uncommon to find these or similar ideas – the need for a balance between play and practice and taking risks – in the writings of practising artists and craftsmen. Here, for example, Peter Cropper, a violinist, describes the need to keep 'mechanical consciousness of the instrument' in balance with a sense of commitment and risk in the high endeavour to become an unimpeded channel for the music itself:

> The whole point of rehearsal is to dissect every single note, discuss its function, build up each phrase, and then gradually the sections of each movement. . . . This done, I believe the analysis must recede into the unconscious, and only thereafter can one start to perform. The instrument one is playing, one's

instrumental thoughts, must also recede into the background with technical problems swept aside. It is in this state that one can begin to communicate directly from composer to listener; but at what a risk.[8]

Such words echo the ideas of Polanyi. In many primary schools and in some teachers' colleges there is a tacit understanding of the importance of balance between practice, play and creativity; but it is rarely explained to teachers at a theoretical level. Among secondary teachers in general there is little coherent understanding of the interaction between play and practice or recognition of the need to face the risks of discovery.

The following educational maxims summarize the links between all three phases of the creative cycle and good teaching.

(i) Teachers should be able to initiate a range of activities for learners which covers the play-practice-play-discovery cycle.

(ii) The range needs to be wide enough to match and extend the different levels of competence of learners in a given group.

(iii) The quality of a student's action is a good test for the beginning of an educational episode or of a plan of learning. Similarly, the quality of feedback resulting from it – what he or she learns from successes or failures – is the crucial test for judging its conclusion.

(iv) The range needs to be sufficiently varied that, at any given level, allowance is made for some relearning and overlearning of skills, and for some analysis of error without producing boredom.

In our terms 'boredom' means moving out of the bracing and open tension of the competence-play-frontier continuum and into a mechanical mode of learning where there is scope for neither success nor failure, fun nor challenge.

Many experienced teachers will have already arrived at some such understanding as the above. Nevertheless, many fail, especially beginners, either through thinking that all learning ought to be at the level of play (the 'progressives') or – more commonly – through having an inadequate repertoire of play-practice procedures. Too often teacher education is planned, and teacher performance assessed, on the basis of a limited range of skills being deployed in an inflexible programme. 'You must never go into a lesson without a full plan,' students are told; but this is only a half truth, for to it should be added, '. . . and yet no lesson is likely to come alive unless you are ready to modify that plan as you go along'.

Initial teacher education should have two objectives: first to break up the student's usually conventional, adult view of the contents of the subject so that he can play with these contents and reflect on them without losing hold of their intrinsic structures and ethos; and, secondly, to introduce him to an initial kit of play-practice activities which will embody and make available these structures at the levels of ability that he is likely to encounter with pupils. Then the young teacher can start building up competence on the job, and can gradually push out to more demanding pedagogic frontiers of creativity, of discovery methods, of team teaching and of experimental curricula. The time for extensive philosophical and psychological analysis of education is, for most teachers, much later, when they need to clarify and give form to five or ten years of experience.

The symbol as a focus of meaning

The view of symbolism adopted here derives from a tradition going back through Susanne Langer (1957) to Ernst Cassirer (1953) and to analytical psychology. Yet it was Coleridge, drawing heavily on Schelling and Goethe, who developed the most extensive philosophy, or perhaps one should say, 'theology' of the symbol.[9] The crux of Coleridge's teaching was that a religious or a literary or a scientific symbol must be thought of as a lively personal creation or as an extension of our personal being. It is something not only which we grasp and use and make an extension of ourselves, it is also at the same time part of what we are exploring or creating. It has two faces. It is 'me' and 'not me' – part of the changing universe which I, through it, am disturbing. In this tradition, therefore, the symbol should not be thought of merely as a sign, which is what Piaget does when he defines a symbol as having 'some resemblance to objects or events (for example a stick used in a play as an umbrella)'.[10] Symbols do often have resemblance to what is signified but the profounder, more dynamic meaning of the word is properly stressed by analytical psychologists. Jung is emphatic that symbols are, metaphorically speaking, 'alive'; they have a transforming, retroactive effect on their users; though they can easily lose this quality and become moribund or inactive. A great deal depends on the context or, as we might say, on the heuristic field in which they are being used. Jung (1946, 601–2) amplifies one side of this:

> The concept of symbol should be strictly differentiated from that of a mere *sign*. Symbolic and semiotic descriptions are entirely different. . . . For instance, the old custom of handing over a sod of turf at the sale of a piece of land, might be described as 'symbolic' in the vulgar sense of the word; but actually it is purely semiotic in character. The piece of turf is a sign, or token, representing the whole estate. . . . The symbol always presupposes that the chosen expression is the best possible description, or formula, of a relatively unknown fact; a fact, however, which is none the less recognized or postulated as existing. . . . The explanation of the cross as signifying Divine Love is semiotic, since 'Divine Love' describes the fact to be expressed better and more aptly than a cross which can have many other meanings. Whereas that interpretation of the cross is symbolic which puts it above all imaginable explanations, regarding it as an expression of an unknown and as yet incomprehensible fact of a mystical and transcendant character. . . . The symbol is alive only in so far as it is pregnant with meaning.

Just why a symbol should possess this 'lively', motivating power begins to become apparent if we consider the probable etymology of the word. In origin the word 'sym-bol' appears to have referred to throwing the parts of something together: two broken bits of a pot sherd, for example, might have been used to establish the potential friendship of two strangers who, each carrying a fragment, would then meet and match the broken edges. Even in its origins, therefore, 'symbol' points to the integration of differences and to the creation of a new, larger relationship – in this paradigm case, to an alliance or friendship.

Whether a sign is 'mere' or whether it is *for* the discovery of some expected larger meaning depends on how it is used. If it is used with knowledge and commitment at the seeker's frontier it is symbolic. Joseph Weizenbaum (1976, 18, 140) develops the same idea, expressed in the quotation at the head of this chapter, that symbols are pregnant with possible meanings. He is discussing the nature of a scientific theory. Though he acknowledges that a theory is first of all a text (a series of signs) in language, 'it is also a symbolic construction in a deeper sense for the very terms which it employs are symbols . . . which grope for their denotation in the real world'.

Susanne Langer (1957, 109–10) suggests that true language may have been generated, or its early stages may have been greatly accelerated, by the workings of symbolic processes. There is danger in speculating about 'early man' but she puts forward her ideas not so much as 'possible pre-history' but more as a fable for illuminating what language *is*. This whole subject is fraught with difficulties. Nevertheless Langer's ideas are worth pondering. She speculates that groups of early hominids would have been more likely to share a joint response to rare but recurrent crises than to commonplace happenings or objects. Examples would be the return of spring, escape from danger or the discovery of water in dry terrain. It is on such occasions, she suggests, that the first seeds of true language started to grow. The group response might well have been in the form of a dance or in mime or in drawing pictures, or it might have been a pre-linguistic song – the ululations which still, in some parts of the world, greet the return of warriors or a successful football team. Such experiences are not everyday affairs but because they may be crucial for survival or for self-respect they are charged with strong feelings and backed up by effort and courage. They can, therefore, be considered as a collective version of what I call 'frontier' situations and the pictures or vocal ejaculations which marked them were truly symbolic. They celebrated and embodied pride in, or hope for, the achievements of a group.[11]

Picturing and story-telling may have evolved together

There is a further cluster of ideas about the origins of culture which illuminate our understanding of symbols. They have been explored by Alexander Marshack (1972) in his extensive research on the artefacts of early man. He accepts that critical events such as the finding of water in the desert or the making of fire may have formed symbolic focal points for early cultures. But he has opened up a further dimension to our understanding, by show-ing that paleolithic man was able to calculate times and seasons and to use 'time factoring' notational systems to a much greater degree than has been generally supposed. This research has also increased the time scale in which we can think of man's early linguistic, social and technical development. We no longer need to imagine, for example, that the first agriculture developed rather suddenly and mysteriously about 12,000 years ago, just after the last ice age. It now becomes reasonable to look for evidence of the systematic 'time factored' processes which pre-ceded early Middle-Eastern agriculture throughout Eurasia and Africa and to follow them right back through at least 100,000 years, ebbing and flowing with the ice ages. Furthermore these findings make it easier for us to guess the answer to a question which will concern us subsequently: how might it have come about that the twin brain hemispheres of *homo sapiens* developed their different but complementary functions over this distant, but geologically brief, period?

Marshack's discoveries came from examining the complex markings which are often found on palaeolithic bone implements but which seemed to be neither obviously functional nor decora-tive. He has now established, leaving little room for serious doubt, that although our palaeolithic ancestors were probably unable to count as we do, they did possess a notational system which enabled them to make lunar and solar calendars around which they planned their lives. Marshack has deciphered many hundreds of these notations and it is evident that the skill was widespread throughout Africa, around the Mediterranean and along the grasslands – rich in game but cold – which fringed the European ice sheets. His suggestions relate mainly to the de-velopment of palaeolithic man's accurate awareness of the main cycles of time which, he maintains, was acquired roughly in step with the emergence of symbolizing and linguistic skills, while technical and social activities formed the common ground where all these interacted.[12]

Marshack has not, as far as I know, related his discoveries to the problem of accelerated two-hemisphere cerebral specializa-tion. In view of the findings which will be summarized in chapter 8 about the close connection between fine manual skills and language in the left brain hemisphere – where man's most sharply 'time factored' activities are carried out – it is tempting to postulate a steady interaction between cultural and genetic evolution in these time processing functions. While the mainly diachronic mental processes – the planning and refining of complex sequences of action or of events – were developing, a corresponding development in the more synchronic skills of the right hemisphere – of recognizing faces, footprints and *gestalts* – can reasonably be assumed. Nor should we overlook such right hemisphere abilities as the almost instantaneous hearing of a tune or the moving of the whole body in a co-ordinated leap of action or of the mind itself in a leap of intuition. The origins of these powers must, surely, go back further, but the processes of their hominid and human refinement may have been intense and rapid. Yet, it is a common mistake to think about the left and right brain functions in isolation. Both kinds of mental activity would have developed in harmony. It looks as though visual imagery which we now 'do' mainly in our right hemisphere may have played a special part in palaeolithic psychology. This might help us to understand those marvellous dark cave paintings of Altamira and of Lascaux. Somehow those outward pictures, dimly visible in the caves, seem to have contributed to an inner, mental focusing and sharpening in preparation for future action. Marshack sees both the time factored, 'story-telling' representations of reality on the one hand and shared synchronic representations on the other – symbolism, exemplified predominantly by pictures but also by dance and mime – as together providing the cultural matrix in which tools and techniques were developed. So, when the ice finally withdrew, he suggests, in a powerful phrase, that 'Man retained the ability to function in a complex, time factored reality *by the use of symbol and the equations of story*' (p. 340).

The toy-tool-toy-symbol schema fits these ideas. Human artefacts should not be just for fun. There is always about them a desire for meaning and mastery and there is also a paradoxical desire for problems and uncertainty. Marshack requires of the human sciences far more adequate 'evaluations of human cognitive processes . . . in various cultures and at various stages' before we can speak confidently on these matters. Only by strenuous multi-disciplinary enquiry, he suggests, will such questions as 'what is man? and how did he get this way?' receive a satisfactory answer.[13]

What has all this to do with a classroom or a holiday or even with a survivor on the sea shore? It helps to emphasize that symbols are real and that whether we are concerned with advanced computers or with children or with art and literature they are not far away. As Jung said 'whatever acts is actual'; and symbols act. They are particularly potent in the lives of young adults who are often in the process of breaking away from what they regard as old models and old interpretations and are looking for new ones. The last thing which teenagers require is an inquisition into their dreams and yearnings or a pedagogue chattering to them about blocks and vistas; but they do constantly need our insight and co-operation. Nevertheless it is our business to respect the symbols of youth and also to remember that some are transient and that there may be more powerful ones on the way.

The growth of a young person's competence often demands from elders an effort of what Keats called 'negative capability' – doing very little, with faith.[14] It is not only the explorations of great artists, musicians and scientists which start with play, practice and fantasy and still, just occasionally, take off for higher things. That is how we all start. When the going becomes monotonous or dark, it is usually some cluster of not very logical symbolic objects, a focus of ideas – a diagram perhaps, a puzzle, some special person, act or icon – which points down the vista. By fits and starts, and sometimes by retreats, a person's competence to know and to do grows and is given direction.

Notes

1 Article by John McVicar, *The Times Higher Education Supplement* (22 September 1978).

2 This is one of the central themes of Manfred Stanley's *The Technological Conscience* (1978). He argues that only by developing a more discriminating linguistic consciousness in regard to tools and 'technics' will we be able to avoid a creeping subservience ('false consciousness') towards technology. He calls this cultural disease 'technicism'.

3 Since Winnicott's death few writers have discussed the link between comforting objects and adult behaviour. One who has is Paul Horton in *Solace* (1981). However, by focusing on the solace-giving function of transitional phenomena and excluding them from the

wider category of primitive cultural objects he creates needless difficulties. And what of transitional objects' capacity to irritate? The emotional charge attached to 'scabs' provides an interesting illustration. Scabs are transitional phenomena in Winnicott's sense (me/not me?) and also in the industrial relations sense (us/them?).

4 D. Bannister and Fay Fransella, *Inquiring Man* (1971, 206). This is a good introduction to Kelly's ideas; see p. 79n. See also Liam Hudson, *Contrary Imaginations* (1966, 119).

5 Neville Bennett, *Teaching Styles and Pupil Progress* (1976), and the controversy which followed are relevant. See Jane Hesketh's critique in the *British Journal of Educational Psychology* (June 1981).

6 For a discussion of these problems see R. E. Heron and B. Sutton-Smith, *Child's Play* (1971, chapter 8).

7 These ideas were sketched in Niels Bohr's *Atomic Theory and the Description of Nature* (1934). Polanyi's discussion of the idea – similar to Bohr's but with more emphasis on the knower – is in *Personal Knowledge* and also in *The Tacit Dimension*. A useful comparison of the two approaches has been made by Christopher Kaiser in his 'Niels Bohr and Michael Polanyi: some interesting parallels'. See also Torrance (1984), 124–35.

8 From *Scroll '79*, the newsletter of the International Music Seminar; originally a BBC talk.

9 For a study of *symbol* and of the vicissitudes of the word's meaning, from Coleridge to Dean Inge, see Jadwiga Swietecka, *The Idea of the Symbol* (1980). Coleridge, according to her, is one of the few writers to give the symbol concept its full meaning. Swietecka emphasizes that this meaning must be rediscovered and developed by future philosophers and theologians (pp. 177–8). See also Mary Warnock, *The Imagination* (1976).

10 J. Piaget and B. Inhelder, 'The gaps in empiricism', in A. Koestler and J. R. Smythies (eds) *Beyond Reductionism* (1969, 129). James Britton has pointed out the difficulties that occur if we use the word 'symbol' to denote language-like signs (e.g. words) as distinct from other signs, and he notes that Bruner falls into this trap (see p. 120). Though Britton follows Susanne Langer's usage of 'symbol' to denote pictures, dances and other representations of, or acts of, meaning, he does not stress their dynamic, heuristic function (Britton 1970, 193).

11 Both Jung and Langer were writing before the wave of structuralist thinking swept Europe. For a good summary of Lévi-Strauss's central position in this see Edmund Leach's *Lévi-Strauss* (1970), chapter 3, 'The human animal and his symbols'. Because his position is fundamentally reductionist, Lévi-Strauss has no need for symbols

of the kind which point to, or grope towards, unrealised possibilities.

12 The speculations of Julian Jaynes (1982) in regard to this problem are interesting but seem far fetched. His suggestion that there was a momentous dawn of 'consciousness' only five or six thousand years ago seems implausible in the light of Marshack's findings. For yet another perspective see Owen Barfield's (1952) study of idolatry.

13 These are two of the three questions which Bruner poses in his famous and undeservedly controversial *Man, a Course of Study* curriculum. See *Toward a Theory of Instruction* (1968), ch. 4.

14 'Negative capability, that is, when a man is capable of being in uncertainties, mysteries, doubts, without any irritable reaching after fact and mysteries and reason' (John Keats, *Letters to G. and T. Keats*, 21 December 1817).

4 Competence

Silas seemed to weave, like a spider, from pure impulse, without reflection. . . . His hand satisfied itself with throwing the shuttle, and his eye with seeing the little squares in the cloth complete themselves under his effort. . . . Now he had five bright guineas . . . but what were guineas to one who saw no vista beyond countless days of weaving. (George Eliot, *Silas Marner*)

Competence means the ability to cope – the ability to play, to practise, to discover and change from one strategy to another while maintaining overall direction. So coping always involves a person's will, as well as the mobilization of appropriate skills. Some of these skills are deeply ingrained, genetically programmed perhaps, or formed by habit; others will be open to careful, conscious thought. The more unusual the contingency the more must the person coping be deliberate and flexible in deploying his skills. Competence, then, is the ability to use our 'tacit knowledge' – all those complex programs and memory traces which can become focused in the performance of a task, but which may remain latent until the right time or until the right trigger operates. Language is the paradigm case: an extensive range of skills bearing on and responding to a vast but identifiable field of action. Linguists emphasize the extreme creativity of language and its generative power, as well as the necessary constraints which make this possible. A user of language has at his disposal a vocabulary and the choice of many phonetic, grammatical and stylistic patterns. All these innate and acquired, conscious and unconscious resources are creatively activated when his or her unique thread of speech is generated. Since competence involves many skills and attitudes of which we are not even aware it is not easy to replicate it mechanically. We would be wise, therefore, to treat with a good deal of scepticism those claims made by various experts – some surgeons, for example – that they have transferred their 'skills' to a computer program and that these can then carry out important teaching tasks. Even the most articulate teacher knows and teaches far more than he can tell.[1]

Competence and motivation

There is a further aspect of human competence which has been widely discussed, though perhaps not sufficiently in educational literature: what is often described as 'motivation' can be understood in terms of competence (R. W. White 1959). Briefly: 'If you can do something you will probably want to'. Rather than asking 'what stick or carrot will make children active in certain ways; or what will make them go in this direction rather in that?' we would do well to turn the problem round and to say: children will go in any case, for it is an expression of their being to be purposeful and energetic. So we may rephrase the question, in the terms introduced in the previous chapter, as follows: *what vistas of action do children perceive as available to be energetic in?* What helps them or hinders them in seeing such vistas? What kind of experiences do we have when we move into a field of enquiry and find ourselves involved in the struggle to discover form?

If I (as teacher or as parent) see that a certain 'good' line of action is being ignored I must wonder what the obstruction is – what sort of symbol or 'pre-emptive metaphor', up on the frontier of the learner's experience, is he or she finding repellent or frightening? It is quite possibly something to do with me. The parent's or teacher's task is to help such vistas or 'affordances' (Shotter 1984, 82–3) to become known; and they can only be known at first hand, by the learner-engaged-with-reality. It is his reality and vista, at his frontier, which you the teacher can only know by imaginative guesswork. And it is changing all the time. If we can free ourselves from the tendency to think of children instrumentally, as controllable extensions of ourselves or as passive victims of the system, and think instead that they are, in essence, autonomous, self-motivating explorers, makers and co-operators, then we begin to free them and us for education.

The psychological approach to man as an active, enquiring, meaning-making creature, which we are taking here, has been well mapped by George Kelly and by others who have developed his personal construct theory. This offers an empirical approach of great promise to teachers. Kelly questions the whole notion that people need 'motivating'; 'the thing about life is that it goes on,' he writes. 'The going on *is the thing itself*. It isn't that motives *make* a man come alert and do things; his alertness is an aspect of his very being' (Bannister and Fransella 1971, 19).

Kelly's personal construct theory also offers a wide range of systematic experimental methods for examining how individuals or groups make sense of the world, how they view it with shared or different 'constructs'. A construct, in the special sense used by Kelly, is the way in which someone sees things as being alike yet different. You, for example, might have a strong, central construct which tends to see the world in friendly/antagonistic terms. I, being somewhat prim, might tend to construe situations in terms of what is proper/improper. But we might both share a tendency to construe the world in true/false terms and this would enable us to sustain a somewhat prickly dialogue. So when people 'share a vista' in the sense in which I have been using the word, they could be said to share a sufficient number of constructs to make sustained co-operation possible. Kelly does not use the term 'vista' but the terminology which he has developed is similar to mine. What he says about symbols, as enabling us to be conscious of a direction for individual or joint action, is in line with the ideas set out below.[2]

A satisfactory definition of education must include the essential notion of enlarging a learner's competence and therefore his motivation. This involves skills as well as play and both, as we have seen, must be cherished by a teacher. But this is not enough, because neither of these two complementary attributes can be understood *in vacuo*. Skills and play are always partly directed to the future. So competence, which embodies them, is always *for* some broad area of achievement, for speaking a language, for practising an art or for survival in wild country: in short for making meaning where the ground may be rough.

Freedom from and freedom for . . .

A person who is involved in the process of discovery is likely to feel a sense of freedom, even though many rules and frustrations may press hard upon him. A creative act feels free partly because alternative ways of doing it are available and yet just one of these has been freely chosen. More fundamentally, however, it feels free because it results in a move 'upwards' into a more highly ordered state from a simpler one. To give a preliminary example: when we utter a spontaneous sentence we move 'up' *from* words *into* language.

Freedom, then, is experienced both *from* constraints and *for* a higher level. Popular reforming rhetoric generally emphasizes the first aspect – freedom from hunger, ignorance, oppression – and such rhetoric is certainly capable of producing initiatives for the relief of injustice and suffering. But the negative emphasis easily creates confusion. For example, people's need for food is at a different and more basic level from their need for justice or for literacy. This is not to say that food is of greater value than justice but to stress, rather, that biological needs should be seen as separate from, and prior to, social needs. A well-fed prisoner might be said to enjoy freedom from hunger, and this would be a debased sense of the word compared with the higher freedom which he desires. Phrases such as 'freedom from hunger' tend to make charitable people focus on supplying food and to evade the complex technical and political problems which generally link oppression, ignorance and hunger (Sen 1981). And further, such talk obscures the essence of freedom's meaning which is to do with action – by people, who may even be the hungry ones – towards some higher level of achievement, towards something new which cannot be adequately defined in terms of the removal of constraints. The truth of this can be seen most clearly in what is sometimes described as 'creative work' by artists or writers but also by people who struggle to understand and to improve their own lot.

Clifford Ellis, when he was head of the Bath Academy of Art at Corsham, provided an example in training artists for freedom. Many of his initial projects for art students were aimed at loosening the prejudices and inhibitions which tied up their talents and imagination. So they were encouraged to paint with big brushes on newspaper. They acted and mimed and learnt to play with colour, shape and movement. This was the playful part, but it was only half the battle. I remember asking why a group of students at Corsham had to spend so much time in laboriously regrinding the surfaces of stone in preparation for studying lithography – why not cut out the tedium and teach them to use easily processed zinc plates? No, said Clifford Ellis, that would not do; and he then explained that for students to come to terms with the hardness and the grain of stone is a fundamental element in the craft which should not be skipped. The young artist must assimilate many of these real and diverse components of the art – tactile impressions, skills of hand and eye, timing and spacing of tasks, the nature of the material – before gaining the artist's freedom of putting all these together in flexible, creative action. This does not mean that short-cuts should never be taken, but rather that the educational value of any chore or exercise can only be properly assessed when we know what place it may take in the building up of some larger, all-embracing competence.

Competence in any complex task comprises a great range of minor sensitivities and skills. Some of these, especially ones which have been recently learnt, will be open to conscious analysis and monitoring by the performer. Others – those which were acquired long ago or which were part of a person's genetic inheritance – may be so deeply embedded that they cannot be consciously examined by the user even if he wants to. Nevertheless all these component skills and sensitivities contribute to competence and are focused or integrated by the performer. In action we do not think about these subsidiary elements. The focused mass of relevant conscious and unconscious information is 'tacit knowledge' and in action we have 'focal awareness' of it. On the other hand when we do stop and think and analyse what we have been doing, only a few bits of this total knowledge will be readily available for reflective examination. This truth is summed up in Polanyi's oft-quoted maxim that 'we know more than we can tell' (1966, 4).

These ideas are important and in tune with commonsense, but there is more to it than untellable or unconscious knowledge. Polanyi offers a partial explanation of how the groping processes of intuition work in practice. If I were a poet, struggling with words, or a scientist attempting to integrate diverse and perhaps contradictory clues in a new explanatory model, I would, in some sense, be very un-free. I would be constrained by all those habits and patterns of my tacit knowing *and* by the intractable material which I am trying to shape and integrate. It is within such a straitened personal and existential context that tacit knowledge works. Polanyi preferred the use of the participle – 'tacit knowing' – to 'tacit knowledge', because it allows the concept to cover the unconscious store of personal knowledge that we bring to a task.³ So we integrate an already patterned array of partly conscious, partly unconscious knowledge in a creative act of knowing or doing. Polanyi claimed that such patterns in ourselves and other patterns in the extensive array of material that we work with all play a part in guiding our discoveries. This does not deny that something new and important may be emerging under our thinking eyes and hands. Towards this new picture or poem or theory all our efforts are tending and when the new artefact eventually appears it will give those efforts their meaning. Yet the form of the poem or picture is not entirely your creation or mine. Even less is the form of a theory, especially if it is one for which others have already recognized the need within the general body of science. Here again we encounter Polanyi's theme, that a person making meaning at a higher level – in art or science – from ingredients gathered at a lower level is, *a priori*, committed to values, and these are implicit in the initial effort long before the person is ready to reflect on them or to give them names such as truth or beauty or justice.

Polanyi calls the later stages of the movement towards an achievement or towards meaning 'a semantic relation', for the paradigm case is in language when a person moves from using words alone towards grasping their collective meaning in a whole sentence. He also illustrates this idea in regard to the manner in which sounds are integrated as a word, and how it is that we come to *mean* a statement or an action. Polanyi often uses the simpler example of sense impressions – how a multiplicity of separate sensory signals must be skilfully integrated if one is to understand the world. He slows down our conceptualization of such processes by considering how a blind person or someone in a dark room gropes forward, and this is why he frequently returns to the example of a probe or stick. In reading the following passage it is worth remembering how strange words feel if you think about them as things, if you make them the centre of focal awareness and savour their different component sounds; compare this with how they feel in familiar, fluent use, when they are subsidiary to the focused act of communicating.

A *set of sounds* is converted into the name of an object by an act of tacit knowing which integrates the sounds to the object to which we are attending. This is accompanied by a characteristic change in our impression of the sounds. When converted into a word they no longer sound as before; they have become, as it were, transparent: we attend from them (or through them) to the object to which they are integrated. Current theories which would explain meaning by the association of sounds with an object, leave unexplained this vectorial quality of meaning which is of its essence.

There is a parallel to this transformation of sounds into words in the conversion of an object into a tool. Someone using a stick for the first time to feel his way in the dark, will at first feel its impact against his palm when the stick hits an object. But as he learns to use the stick effectively, a transformation of these jerks will take place into a feeling of the point of the stick touching an object; the user of the stick is no longer attending *to* the meaningless jerks in his hand but attends *from* them to their meaning at the far end of the stick.

. . . Once established, this from-to relation is durable. Yet it can be impaired at will by switching our attention from the meaning to which it is directed, back to the things that have acquired this meaning. By concentrating on his fingers a pianist can paralyse himself. (Polanyi 1969, 145–6)

Polanyi is here developing the distinction which we have already encountered. When I am thinking about the meaning which is being generated by my probe or about the work of my instrument or tool or the meaning of some word or phrase then my awareness is focal, out there. Yet at the same time I do have subsidiary awareness – unfocused – of innumerable pressures in my hand, mouth or body, and of information coming into my senses. If, for some reason, I switch my focal awareness away from its point of attention and think focally about certain of the subsidiaries – my fingers for example – then, as in the case of the pianist, I will break up the total act and will probably falter. Even in sustained and difficult tasks it is, nevertheless, sometimes necessary to withdraw attention from the main focus and to direct it to particulars. For example, someone might have to locate an error or re-tune an instrument. Nevertheless a good performer has to be able to commit himself, for long periods, to action on his frontier and to the largely uninterrupted 'focal awareness' which accompanies such action.

When a learner has mastered a serious problem, integrating into its solution a diversity of skills and perceptions, he moves into a higher level of performance and feels the new sense of freedom and satisfaction – at least for the time being. We know this mainly from our own experience. It should be clear that 'higher' and 'lower' are used metaphorically and that reference is being made to superordinate and subordinate systems of skill and sensibility, operating within a hierarchy. Nevertheless there are scientists who, while not denying this, would claim that a downward, atomistic and reductive explanation is more true and more scientific than the others. There is a widespread, powerful resistance to any explanations which are suspected of being even faintly goal-seeking or teleological. Such an attitude may be appropriate to the physical sciences; but a reductive, one-way explanation ought to be critically questioned in the psychological and social sciences and perhaps in biology too. In studying living things we are not confronted with the simple alternatives of chance *or* necessity. There is a vast range of directional or goal-seeking phenomena which cannot be accounted for by reference to predictable, mechanical behaviour in living nature. While at the human level, though there are immensely complex causal sequences which may be unravelled, there are also tensions, fields of influence and 'catastrophic' changes which always involve more than reductive explanations can encompass.[4] Nor are we postulating magical states or powers if we speak of 'higher and lower levels of being' in the universe or take seriously the notion that people often strive for a higher, more comprehensive view or mode of experience. The ever-present example of such upward, 'from-the-parts-to-the-whole', vectorial movement is to be found, as Polanyi stressed, in language itself. The phonemes, words and grammar of English are certainly more fundamental, in the sense of being more elementary, than are, say, the sonnets of Shakespeare; but the poems themselves cannot be explained simply in terms of the phonemes or of the grammar which comprise them.

The making of meaning, in language and in all other creative activities, is always a putting-together, an integrating; and it is a putting-together not under the pressure of one or two simple principles of action, as though we were machines, but in a context of limited freedom. Great artists have sometimes managed to secure such a sense of freedom in situations which to others might seem desperately un-free – when in prison, crippled or blind. The complex working of the whole heuristic process, this discovery of meaning, is undoubtedly hedged about with problems and constraints but it is not a total mystery. It is constantly being opened up to comprehension and it has an ever-present bearing on the processes of education for it is precisely such well-rooted knowledge which can issue in competent action. The experience of that is what young adults most need.

The act of discovery in slow motion

In a collection of his essays entitled *Knowing and Being*, Polanyi summarizes and develops his central ideas about discovery, first expounded in *Personal Knowledge*. What he offers is a partly psychological, partly philosophical analysis of intuition, and he claims that it works in much the same way as other creative, meaning-making acts, including even the everyday working of our senses. 'The structure of scientific intuition', he writes, 'is the same as perception . . . it is as fallible as perception, and as surprisingly tending to be true. . . . It is rooted in our natural sensibility to hidden patterns' (Polanyi 1969, 118). Many crucial educational processes depend on this same tendency and it matches the skill-play-frontier model which we discussed in the preceding chapters.

Complex and difficult creative acts can rarely be accomplished under pressure. They need reduced drive or – in terms we have been using – they need potential space, especially for their initiation.[5] Once a breakthrough has been achieved, however, the subsequent consolidation and validation of a discovery may often be done at much higher pressure. Under these circumstances a certain amount of competition and awareness of deadlines have their uses. Here we are concerned with the initial creation or breakthrough, something which, on a small scale, children need to be constantly experiencing. All creative action displays what Polanyi calls a 'from-to' structure. We have already encountered this in the examples of a probe and of language, where the seeker, or speaker, moves from working with particulars at one level to integrating them in a more meaningful form at a higher level. This is the same phenomenon as the second half of what I described as the cycle of creativity – the movement from unpressurized play towards the frontier of discovery. It is not difficult to think about such a transition, from subsidiaries to wholes, when it takes place at a relatively simple level – a child, for example, gradually assembling the movements and judgements which make up a skilful achievement, such as that of using a cup; though even the acquisition of such elementary skill can be a long drawn out business. The blunderings and gropings of adult explorers are less easily studied, except perhaps in the analysis of our own errors and short-sightedness.

Polanyi, who was an outstanding research chemist, knew about the labour of scientific discovery from inside. He became a philosopher by way of an interest in economics and politics but it was his own deep involvement in medicine and then in physical chemistry that provided the scientific experience on which he later reflected. He was able to think about discovery in prospect, in retrospect and during the hard labour itself. Only in his later writings did he use the term 'phenomenological' to describe such a many-dimensioned approach. We can now see that it was just such a multiple viewpoint which he had been expounding and that he was probably unaware that continental philosophers, particularly Maurice Merleau-Ponty, were going the same way.[6] An essential element in phenomenology is that our perspective, from which we view phenomena or appearances, changes and *yet we assume that a certain underlying structure is constant and that this is discoverable* (Pivčevič 1970, 13). We must be prepared, therefore, to adopt a variety of viewpoints – as outside observers, as beginners and as subjects passing through the experience, and as members of a community reflecting on common experience. This requires flexibility and a measure of humility too. Whether or not we, ordinary teachers, use such philosophical terminology is unimportant but there is no doubt that we have to be phenomenologists in practice.

When Polanyi slows down and analyses the discovery process he is attempting to open up what we have called a heuristic field and to see it phenomenologically. If we are to understand the groping explorations of children we will do well to follow him through his analysis, for it applies to all exploring. You, the reader, should imagine yourself confronting some new conceptual model or, which is perhaps easier, some unfamiliar implement or machine which you intend to use – a loom say, or a lathe. Several perspectives now become available: first you have, immediately ahead of you, 'a child's view' as you face new problems and new materials with feelings of apprehension, but you also possess a generalized sense of some rudimentary competence; after all you have dealt with tools and machines before and have survived. Secondly, you can soon become an actor or participant, trying out the machine, fitting unfamiliar material into it and shaping this as you judge best. Thirdly you can, if you try, achieve a crude, but complete, piece of work. And finally you can look back at the whole process, objectively, as 'a scientist' and attempt to place yourself outside the whole episode. At this stage, discounting your feelings of frustration or pleasure, you try to see in your achievement some generalizable quality or pattern: has it integrity? Is it true to relevant areas of art or science?

According to Polanyi's analysis the knowledge you will get as you work through these stages towards discovery is of four kinds which approximate to these four viewpoints. Let us stay with the example of a hand loom weaver because it is easier to illustrate the four aspects of meaning-making or discovery if we think about a craft which actually results in some unique object being made rather than considering inner, mental operations. There are four stages to the weaver's active knowing, and we shall find that these approximate to the four sources from which form comes in to the process. Polanyi (1966, 9–20) describes these stages as follows.

(i) There is the *functional aspect*. Information, from tradition and from experience, is embodied in the weaver's skill (or functioning) and it will show in the relationship to the tools and materials which he is using. This is the specific competence which the weaver brings to the task and it includes both inherited and acquired powers.

(ii) As he works, a patterned something begins to appear on the warp. This is what Polanyi calls the *phenomenal aspect*. If our weaver has already planned the work, on paper or in his head, this phenomenal pattern will have already made a preliminary appearance, but in a relatively abstract, imagined form. The full appearance which accompanies the doing of a task is manifested diachronically – over a considerable span of time. This is characterized by bursts of skilled activity and also by flexibility as to the sequencing of the performance.

(iii) As the completion of the task approaches, the meaning of the whole becomes apparent. There is a sense of release, of surprise, both to the craftsman and also to those who, subsequently, respond to the work. This is when sense is first made and that is why Polanyi calls it the *semantic aspect* of the process.

(iv) But the new 'whole' will embody forms and relationships which belong to a newly attained level of being, to tapestries or textiles in this case, but not yarn or looms. If the work of art is original, some of these new forms will come as a surprise to the artist for, in addition to the initial feeling of novelty, there are also likely to be new constraints and structures which provide new intelligible meanings – unexpected rhythms and relationships – which were only vaguely apprehended while the work was in progress. These constitute what Polanyi calls the *ontological aspect* of the discovery or creation – ontological because they characterize the very being of the new thing itself. In a major work of art or in a comprehensive scientific theory a whole army of commentators and investigators in the years following its appearance may examine and expound these ontological structures, and may indeed get to know them much better than the genius who first embodied them in wool or words.

George Eliot's account, quoted at the head of this chapter, of Silas Marner's weaving, when he had lost sight of any vista of love or purpose in his life, is a fine description of the kind of servile craftsmanship which is based only on the first two stages; on skill and putting together but not on meaning. It is also a prophetic epitome of the alienating possibilities of large-scale industrial organization.

In Polanyi's essay, 'Tacit knowing', he summarizes the fourfold analysis as follows:

From the three aspects of tacit knowing that I have defined so far – the functional, the phenomenal and the semantic – we can deduce a fourth aspect which tells us what tacit knowing is a knowledge of. This will represent its ontological aspect. Since tacit knowing establishes a meaningful relationship between two terms [the 'from parts – to wholes' relation in all search for meaning] we may identify the ontological aspect with our understanding of the comprehensive entity which these two terms jointly constitute. . . . So we comprehend the entity by relying on its particulars for attending to their joint meaning. (1965, 13)

Whether we are working with the raw sensations of perception, with paint or thread or words, or with that subtle combination of words *and* images which characterize so much sophisticated culture, this kind of meaning-making is uphill work. Though it cannot be forced from outside it must be willed. It happens on those existential boundaries or frontiers where we see vague, often ambiguous symbolic forms. If we do not, at least in some degree, yearn for them and welcome such encounters with the unknown, we shall probably fear them.

Feeling

A brief comment must now be made on *feeling* and I am assuming that not only is some freedom necessary for all creativity but also that in any thorough-going expression of our competence we are likely, from time to time, to feel free, happy and apprehensive at the same time. In our teaching too, especially if it is open and oriented towards exploring and making we require an appropriate grasp of the nature of feelings, and of how they initiate or reflect processes of discovery and achievement. Here Susanne Langer's analysis is helpful.[7] Feeling, she claims, is our awareness of action or of patterned 'act-like' processes – either of such an 'act' or happening within us or of external action on us. By 'act' she does not only mean consciously directed deeds but also those other organized unities of activity such as the beat of the heart or the slower rhythmical tides of endocrine activity, of sleep or the reproductive cycles. Susanne Langer is not denying the enormous complexity of physiological processes and interactions but she is making a philosophical claim for us to regard our inner feelings as our *awareness* – a very partial and unformulated awareness – *of these changing physiological states*. She writes: 'An act engendered predominantly from within, such as the "firing" of an assembly of neurons as a result of organic processes without specific external stimulation, if it *is* felt, is differently felt from a response to environmental impact' (p. 28). And later she sharpens this distinction when she stresses that 'by "subjective" I mean whatever is felt as action, and by "objective" whatever is felt as impact' (p. 31). Whenever we are aware of these internal or external changes ('acts' on the one hand, or 'impacts' – in her terms) we have feelings. We may respond to such processes in various ways – 'expressing' them perhaps by some immediate reaction or harnessing them in some delayed, large-scale project (Freud's 'sublimation') or by interpreting them, giving them a name and a meaning, and this is what we call 'having an emotion'. 'Feelings', writes Margaret Boden, 'are cues to emotion' (1977, 441). To have an emotion is to recognize and to categorize such a state of ongoing arousal and activity in ourselves. Empathy, on the other hand, is the imaginative, intellectual understanding of someone else's feelings; as opposed to sympathy which is feeling for their feeling – for their changing inner states.

Feelings of fear, hunger, sex, comfort or pain can be considered in the above, subjective sense, but what about those feelings of freedom or anxiety which occur in the kind of creative or exploring act we have been discussing? Here, it seems, we are aware, though not analytically aware, of an on-flowing total process, of the complex integrative endeavour in which various subsidiary skills and judgements are brought together in one conscious achievement – in making a sentence, a picture or a textile. We know that this process of action is, somehow, ours. It takes on a different emotional colour depending on whether our feeling is before, during or after action; hence apprehension, exhilaration, relief. Here I am using the language of emotion and introspection to describe the subjective experience of the play-discovery-play arc of the creative cycle.

There is a paradox, however: up to extreme limits, our feeling of freedom mounts with the narrowing and sharpening of the surrounding contingency. One can see this zest for astringent freedom developing in adolescents. A young mountaineer, for example, approaches an unknown climb. He sees a tenuous, hopeful line, which he projects ahead of him, onto the rock face.

The immediate prospect which he faces is one of uncertainty, of constraint and hard, skilful work. Yet, aware of his own competence, he still feels free. Subsequently the feeling of freedom is reinforced or reinterpreted when the act has been completed. Whether in prospect or retrospect, however, we must not allow these pleasant feelings to obscure the other half of the cycle: that pattern of rules and skill which constitute competence, that mass of tacit knowledge which the child or artist or explorer needs for his task, and with which he works towards its achievement.

Competence and tacit knowledge

We need to sharpen our understanding of what should be the educationally central concept of competence, especially in its relation to Polanyi's somewhat similar concept of tacit knowledge. Both are to do with consciously known ingredients of knowledge as well as with unconscious ones. Both are dynamic and constitute those energizing and directional processes which are sometimes spoken of in terms of motivation. Yet the two concepts need to be distinguished from each other.

Polanyi certainly gave tacit knowledge a very wide connotation but he was at pains to protect it from becoming a portmanteau term for all sorts of mysterious and inexplicable powers. One may think of the phrase as denoting *all that inherited and acquired information in an individual organism which can be brought to bear on an act*. Both Piaget (1978) and Popper (1972) use a similarly extended and biologically rooted concept of knowledge. Polanyi's 'tacit knowing', however, is distinguished from Popper's 'knowledge' by the way in which the former insists on the personal knower as the agent who brings the process to a focus and, as we have just seen, Polanyi is also intensely interested in the groping and intuitive stages of discovery. Popper is more interested in that 'objective' knowledge which a group or community may share and he pays less regard to the actual process of discovery. How, then, does the concept of a person's tacit knowledge differ from his competence, for both seem to be made up of a flexible bundle of skills and of inherited and acquired information?

The most satisfactory answer is to regard competence as a *recognizable, educationally accessible part of tacit knowing*. We may conceive of the latter as resembling the total root system of an ancient but living tree, a tree which constitutes the information patterns comprising you or me or a learning child and which includes our genetic inheritance. Most of the 'root system' is deeply hidden but it is not, in principle, inaccessible to scientific enquiry. Like the roots, tacit knowledge was laid down in the past and yet it has a bearing on the future shape and health of an information-rich organism. A similar picture is given by Douglas Hofstadter in his book *Gödel, Escher, Bach* when he discusses the hidden springs of action in the deep strata of our brains:

> It seems that a large amount of knowledge has to be taken into account in a highly integrated way for 'understanding' to take place. We can liken the . . . thought processes to a tree whose visible part stands sturdily above ground but depends vitally on its invisible roots which extend way below ground giving it stability and nourishment. In this case the roots symbolize [!] complex processes which take place below the level of the [conscious] mind – processes whose effects permeate the way we think but of which we are unaware. These are the 'triggering patterns of symbols'.[8] (1980, 569)

When Hofstadter speaks of the 'triggering patterns of symbols' he is referring to assumed neurological patterns which correspond to some of those powerful transforming experiences in the world of culture which are of such interest to poets, analytical psychologists and theologians, as well as to teachers.

If, in our analogy, we move to the surface of the soil, and call to mind the base of our imagined tree – an old gnarled tree – we can envisage a few main roots coming together at the trunk. It is these main roots which are analogous to the principal, identifiable clusters of skills which I am designating 'competences'. They are certainly nourished by tacit knowledge and yet they are now united in large recognizable bundles, and they are more open to instruction (or damage) by parents and teachers than are the deeper layers of knowledge.

It is interesting to notice how these concepts, both tacit knowledge and competence, have gained currency amongst scholars in a number of different fields, all of which converge on the central idea of creative flexibility. For example, Polanyi in his essay 'Sense-giving and sense-reading' (1969, 181–207) shares the problem of competence-for-language with Chomsky but he answers it

differently. He speaks of language as an instance, a very sophisticated one, of the intelligent exercise of tacit powers and so, 'the
meaning of language arises, as so many other kinds of meaning
do, in a person tacitly integrating hitherto meaningless acts into a
bearing on a focus which thereby becomes their meaning' (196).
He should perhaps have added 'or acts hitherto meaning something else' for in language, above all, we often integrate old words
into new meanings. Then, in phrases which foreshadow more
recent biological theory, Polanyi adds 'I would try to trace back the
roots of this faculty to the primordial achievements of all living
things'[9] (p. 156).

In the example of the dancers I sketched the general idea that
five main competences for culture may be identified – the interpersonal, enactive, iconic, musical and language-like levels or
'highways' into culture. One can cut a cake in many ways and it
will be obvious that within these overlapping competences lie
many subsidiary competences or skill clusters. To understand
any of these – rock climbing or singing or teaching for example –
we need to bear in mind not only the way in which skills from
different levels all grow in the play-practice-exploration cycle
and that they support each other, but also that all of them have
an ancient history in our individual and biological development.

Margaret Boden steps firmly across a biological/anthropologi-
cal divide when she stresses the common ground between
Piaget's discussions of language development in children and the
way in which living cells can grow along different morphogenetic
pathways in developing organisms or organisms regenerating
damaged tissue. Speaking of the fruitful comparisons which can
be made between higher cognitive activities and biological processes, she uses words which bring together several important
trains of thought:

> The word 'competence' is deliberately reminiscent of Chom-
> sky's postulation of the adult's tacit knowledge of grammatical
> rules and the baby's innate language-specific learning system,
> and highlights the structured and creatively generative poten-
> tial of . . . 'knowledge'. (1979, 124)

Boden is here construing 'knowledge' in the wide, biological and
cybernetic sense of information systems which bear on antici-

pated future achievements and which are also open to constant modification and feedback.

What then of teachers whose task it is to be both crucible and alchemist, to contain the space for learning and to speed up the metamorphoses which learners are ready to undergo there? It should scarcely surprise us to find that if the process of discovery does, as a rule, pass through recognizable stages, then those whose task it is to enter that process and to monitor it, to protect and to stimulate it – that such teachers cannot remain in only one stage of the teaching-learning process with one unyielding persona. They too have to show creative flexibility, to draw on ancient patterns, to play for time and to be open to someone else's future.

Notes

1 Daniel Dennett, the authority on artificial intelligence, sounds a warning about the new 'expert systems'. 'Doctors', he claims, 'are prone to taking advantage of any short cuts that they can convince themselves are authoritative. They are apt to be suckers, in short, for expert systems. Will their own diagnostic skills, their deepest understanding of medicine, be jeopardized by the wide adoption of [such] systems? There is reason to fear it. . . . Those who rely on such systems are paying a heavy cognitive price.' Quoted in *Computing* (13 October 1983), 28.

2 See Bannister and Fransella's *Inquiring Man* (1971, 19). I am not entirely clear about the sense of their definition of symbol (p. 204). But I think if personal construct theorists could take the notions of a heuristic field seriously they might open up a useful extension to their theories. For a most valuable definition of 'construct' which distinguishes it sharply from 'concept' see D. Bannister and J. M. M. Mair, *The Evaluation of Personal Constructs* (1968). M. L. Pope and T. R. Keen, in *Personal Construct Psychology and Education* (1981), describe a range of empirical investigations, but fail to present a corresponding theoretical analysis of the process of education.

3 The best introduction to the idea of tacit knowing is chapter 4 in Polanyi's *Personal Knowledge*. His first essay in *The Tacit Dimension* explores the process of discovery more succinctly and introduces the terms we use here.

4 For an example of the reductivist viewpoint see Jacques Monod, *Chance and Necessity* (1973), and R. W. Atkins, *The Creation* (1982). An extensive rebuttal of such views is to be found in A. R. Peacocke, *Creation and the World of Science* (1979). He draws heavily on the work

of Prigogine and Eigen and develops a sophisticated view of chance: life-like processes constantly play against chance dicing, as it were, for more and more unlikely patterns – and thus producing super patterns, such as DNA which themselves have stability and power to survive and generate.

5 There is a well known psychological version of this called the Yerkes Dodson Law: 'In complicated tasks . . . as the stress in a situation mounts, our performance deteriorates' (Dennis Child, *Psychology and the Teacher*, 1973, 54). In a letter to *The Times* D. C. Damant writes: 'The fact that professional skills are dangerously diminished by threats of punishment in the event of failure was recognized by Napoleon, who advised the doctor attending the Empress at the birth of their child that she should imagine herself delivering a slut in the backstreets of Paris'.

6 In Polanyi's paper, 'The structure of consciousness', ch. 13 in *Knowing and Being* (1969), there is clear acknowledgement of the influence of Merleau-Ponty's *Phenomenology of Perception* (1962) and of other phenomenologists.

7 In *Mind, an Essay on Human Feeling*, vol. 1 (1967), Susanne Langer develops this concept. It is unfortunate that she did not find, or coin, a word to cover the great class of act-like, systematic happenings which are *not* the intentional doings of humans or animals. We need a wider, less purposive word than 'act' to refer to all these discernible cyclical *ongoings* in nature. Such 'acts' always, according to Langer, begin small, reach an organized climax and then fade away – cumulus clouds, for example, or influenza. Perhaps 'ongoings' should be the word.

8 In this passage Hofstadter uses the word 'symbolize' where 'signify' would convey the meaning which he seems to intend. However, his reference to 'the triggering patterns of symbols' shows that he is aware of the wider, more dynamic connotation of the word.

9 To trace back the causal roots into the biological past or to draw on earlier stages of evolution for *models* to help our understanding of the present is not to say, as do some sociobiologists, that social behaviour can be explained in biological terms.

5 The four roles of a teacher

The aged gentleman was staring at him with a kind of unwinking and benevolent curiosity which made him feel that it would not be at all rude to stare back. (White 1938)

When young teachers start their professional training they quite rightly assume that integrity is a central quality which they must hold on to. But it is easy to move from this to thinking that integrity implies treating children 'just as I treat my friends'. Inexperienced teachers do not realize that their pupils will not appreciate this and will not expect them to be predictable or to present an entirely consistent persona. So a teacher has to learn to change gear; and, as in the old-fashioned double de-clutch, the trick is to make sure that both sides of the interaction are turning at about the same speed.

The roles which a teacher has to learn are best understood if we begin with the idea of making and using potential space, which we discussed in chapter 2. To create psychological space, to hold back some of the pressures of the world in order that many kinds of learning can take place, is the first requirement of education. Michael Marland (1978) puts it well when he describes the head of a department in a secondary school as being 'responsible for creating the space in which a subject can flourish'. The school institutionalizes this and such personal space for the purpose of growing and exploring should spread throughout the whole organization – not uniformly, but like air in a crusty loaf. For whatever age of learner a school is intended, it has two essential functions – first to protect and secondly to instruct. The protective function – holding back the more pointed pressures of the world – creates the space in which instruction can take place. In this way the concept of potential space and play are related, the one being a necessary condition for the other. Play is the activity which most strongly characterizes such space and so the most fundamental role of a teacher, both actively and passively, is that which relates to play. His other, sterner roles, are all dependent on, and develop out of, this one.

All learners, whether they be children, adolescents or adults, tend to move out from play in two contrasted directions: towards repetitive patterns of practice – the aspect in which Piaget was mainly interested – and towards further explorations of their own frontiers. So, on the one hand, we see moves towards the consolidation of competence; on the other, the movement is towards stretching competence – sometimes to the limit. Teachers help to initiate and to assist both kinds of movement and the roles which characterize their work can be roughly classified according to when and how they enter the cycle of creativity and exploration.

If you take a group of children out on a field-trip you will probably share with them a strong feeling of new energy and new interest. This is brought about partly by the shared consciousness that there is, quite literally, more space than there was in school. As we think about such a change theoretically, this sense of physical space can be seen as concealing a more important, underlying openness; and it is this which lends importance to the first word in the term 'potential space'. In educational talk, the whole bias of our language and of our technological world view tends towards dead and static models rather than live ones. This is the difficulty with the bread metaphor which I have just used. Bread, when we come to eat it, has ceased to be alive. The holes, whether small or large, have been fixed. We should have been thinking about the bread when it was rising; but that is a process which we rarely see. So in thinking about education we need to try to correct this tendency, by turning our thoughts away from mechanical models and towards processes which go on through time and where many causes operate synchronously. 'Potentiality' is such an idea and refers *from* the present *to* what is emerging; it shifts our attention towards processes which run on into the future.

The trap of dead metaphors is particularly strong in secondary education. I remember one school governor, facing a minor drugs crisis and saying, 'sorry, we must sack that boy; one bad apple will corrupt the lot'. But then the head, who must have been brooding on this, replied, 'Ah, but in your barrel all the apples are dead; on my tree they are all alive'. We meet the same problem in my own metaphor of children crossing the great 'developmental watershed' of adolescence. This too, at first sight, is a non-living spatial metaphor. It has the obvious features of being topographically 'given' – by nature, and further a watershed is the place where, almost imperceptibly, great rivers start. Though suggestive, these ideas were not my original intention. A watershed is also something *we experience as we travel*. We cross it gradually yet decisively in a time dimension and, as we do so, new prospects and new problems open up.

Teachers in secondary schools assist in the transforming journey of adolescence and they take a part in it indirectly many times over. As they travel, the balance of their role-playing changes. One cannot help wondering how well the conventional comprehensive or high school pattern meets the emotional as well as the intellectual needs of learners and teachers – the need for real, shared problems, for joint enquiry and for some shared risks of error or mishap.

The protective function of education, though it continues to be discernible in every teacher/learner relationship, becomes less and less evident as the learner matures; while the other functions – those which relate to the introduction of more and more structured and challenging experiences – become increasingly important. The play-leading and play-creating role of a teacher diminishes with older pupils, but while there is an educational dyad of any sort some scope for shared play must be available.

Role theory

Sociological theory about the roles which a person plays has undergone many changes. One authority has even argued that the whole concept of role is obsolete.[1] A hundred years ago the word 'role' was occasionally used to denote a mode of expressive human acting, as if society were a spontaneous drama. From about 1880 till 1950 sociology and social psychology became more and more functionalist and mechanistic, and role theory developed with an increasing emphasis on the idea that society shapes people, and this has had a lasting effect on educational thinking. Roles came to be seen as ready-made moulds into which young people had to 'be socialized'.

By the 1960s and 1970s the tide was beginning to flow the other way. An early and powerful move in this, contrary, direction had taken place thirty years before when George Herbert Mead (1934) developed his theory of symbolic interactionism. He worked out a cluster of highly original ideas about how people relate to each other, and how they progressively find themselves through 'significant others'. The theory was the source of many subsequent non-mechanistic ways of thinking about social psychology. The basic 'dyadic' model which we have been using, of a teacher who knows more, interacting with a learner who knows less, and with both contributing and both changing, comes indirectly from Mead.

In essence the contemporary and revived interactive view of role is that two or more people negotiate a mutual channel of communication appropriate to a recognized social pattern and to shared intentions. They do this largely by non-verbal methods – by choice of context, by gesture and action and by facial expression. Along the resulting role channel flow feelings and empathy (rational insight into another's feelings) and then, by degrees, more explicit ideas can begin to shuttle back-and-forth. *'My' perception of 'our' channel and the way in which I try to adapt it and create it for traffic in feelings and ideas is the role which I play.* With this more active and interactive view of role has arisen new interest in what is called the 'dramaturgical model' for understanding small social groups. The idea is that we are all acting an unscripted play, taking parts, donning masks, and thereby creating and exploring meaning. The dramaturgical view has value, provided that we remember its limitations: first, that we are all authors as well as actors and, secondly, that there is usually no passive audience; we have to be audience as well as co-authors of the play.[2]

Bruner commented on an earlier version of this chapter in a way which links it to his own studies of infant/mother interaction and to the problem of language acquisition. It is worth noting that when he writes of 'involving some universals in the human cognitive domain' he is referring to inherited patterns – active, motor patterns as well as to acquired interpersonal and social patterns and rule systems. Language evolves from both.

> Learning a role . . . is like learning a language or learning a set of rules (generative and transformational, both) that permit one to construct appropriate reactions in social situations and

to avoid generating inappropriate ones. . . . One cannot . . .
fully understand the nature of this kind of 'learning the rules
that permit one to fulfil functions' without invoking some
universals in the human cognitive domain. The first of these is
to have and to carry out intentions and to interpret the behaviour of others in terms of their intentions. Learning to
interact with somebody else (from one's own culture or
another) is, at base, dependent upon having a theory about the
other person's intentions. And all such private theory building
. . . is the result of negotiation between two people; negotiat-
ing in the sense that I behave toward you as if you had a
particular end in view, as if you also had certain means to
deploy, and above all, as if you were operating within certain
knowable bounds of legitimacy given by 'the general culture'.[3]

Where Bruner writes about 'learning the rules which permit one
to fulfil functions' he is overlapping Polanyi's 'functional' phase
in a person's approach to discovery (see pp. 72–3), but in this
case 'the problem' – the discovery to be made – is not scientific
or technical but social. The aim is a workable relationship. Bruner
also reminds us that the cognitive and motor skills which we
bring to such problems are partly innate and partly learnt. His
emphasis on shared intentions is also important: a failure by an
adult or child to know the other's intention and to allow for it in
communication is a frequent cause of educational failure. I would
argue, further, that only minor 'intentions' are communicated
explicitly, and that in education and perhaps in culture generally
we need to understand how lively symbolism and ritual can
generate strong directional currents which are part of the educa-
tive influence of a community in the longer run, and these may or
may not include conscious intent.

If we transfer the interactive role theory to education a rather
special version of it emerges – special because the teacher/learner
relationship becomes the characteristic and defining one. A
teacher and a learner are, together, trying to discover and to
create order out of various contrived and unexpected elements
which might otherwise be dis-ordered. I suggest that if one looks
at any reasonably open and varied educational situation four
main teaching roles can be distinguished. There is overlap and
transition between these roles; but a teacher's competence de-

pends, to a large degree, on his or her ability to change gear (or role) among these.

My reasons for putting forward a variant on role theory in regard to teaching are as follows. The general idea grows from Polanyi's analysis of what goes on when an exploring individual struggles through a heuristic field; and from asking in what ways teachers become involved in this. Secondly, if I look back on my own experience and, even more if I recall a few really good teachers whom I sometimes tried to follow, the common pattern of diversity is clear. Thirdly, sociologists and social psychologists have not yet moved far enough in studying the complexity of parenting and teaching. Perhaps they need to be stimulated in this direction. And finally, the question is beginning to gain political importance. The convention that there should be a 'life-long', more or less unbroken work pattern for most people in affluent countries is almost sure to be undermined in the next few decades. Nor should teaching generally be a forty-year career. We need, increasingly, to understand that education – both the learning and teaching sides of it – is a process which should flow in and out of life continuously. It should flow through in-service courses and industry, through churches and holidays, through great cultural enterprises and through old age. A number of critics of our present system have touched on this question of excessive professionalism (Illich 1973; Nuttgens 1977; Hargreaves 1982). The following ideas about the many-sidedness of teaching are offered as a contribution to a debate which may have to go on for a very long time.

The four roles which can be seen as constituting a teacher's repertoire, and which a child also comes to participate in are: (1) that of play – in its more or less pure form, that of fool; (2) that of judge, or evaluator of standards; (3) that of instructor or fellow explorer of hidden structures; (4) that of prophet – one who foreshadows meaning by pointing to problems and profound ambiguities. It is important to remember that these four roles apply at every level of education. A mother has to play, instruct, judge and prophesy in her relations with her infant. A university teacher need not be so serious as never to be light; if, on the other hand, lightness comes too easily he may have something to learn about judgement and structure. Though here I am concentrating on teachers rather than on learners, if I were to classify the four corresponding learner roles, the following terms seem to fit: fool, skilled person, maker/explorer and hero.

Playing the fool

Even the most dignified teachers will not be highly regarded unless, sometimes, they are able to play; not merely to smile and laugh, but on special occasions actually to play the fool. The schools and colleges of the Sudan, which I knew during the 1950s, provide an example. They were not unduly solemn places but there was a strong traditional respect for all teachers which had not been much eroded by western influence. The teachers of Islamic religion and of Arabic were spectacularly dignified. They wore special turbans and flowing robes. They were spoken to in phrases of great respect – 'Oh revered one', etc. The educated Sudanese intelligentsia, in one way, and the foreign teachers in other ways, also generated messages by their styles of dress, greeting and manner. The predominant message of the *Sheikhs* was, without a doubt, that of tradition and dignity. Yet, just occasionally, at a staff football match, for example, or at the annual festival of the rural Institute of Education, even the most dignified sheikh would be prepared to change gear. Flowing robes would be hitched up and held in the teeth. Camels or donkeys would be ridden at a gallop. The expert in *sharia* law would win the back-to-front donkey race by a short head and the wild cheers of two thousand onlookers would rend the air. Next day his demeanour would be restored to all its former gravity (Griffiths 1976).

The same lesson was demonstrated more recently by a highly dedicated headmaster of my acquaintance. When I was last at his school the town was buzzing with talk of his masterly performance as the police sergeant in *The Pirates of Penzance*. His own spartan standards and courage, his optimistic requirements from pupils (and he is one of those comprehensive heads who still teaches in class and insists, among other things, that some French vocabulary must be learnt by heart) and his high expectations from colleagues – all this must have become just a little more acceptable as a result of that 'cat-like tread' and that bull's-eye lantern.

I remember also a teacher in Africa who had a hole in his

old-fashioned plywood blackboard. From time to time it would become a volcano or a well or an eye, and sometimes the chalk would be passed through to the back where 'secret' messages would be written.

These are homely examples, but they illustrate the point, that the playful role must be available to a teacher, sometimes tentatively, sometimes wholeheartedly, if his credibility in other roles is to be sustained. To put it in terms of our basic educational model the teacher has to be able to survive and cope in the play space if he is to be acceptable when he moves, as he often must, into more austere roles of judging competence or of going to the frontier. The fact that the world's greatest teachers are only recorded as using rather specialized kinds of play – jokes, *koans*, parables – does not invalidate the general claim.

How are we to see the three other roles in relation to the primordial role of play? They can best be thought of against that same cycle of creativity which we imposed on the basic competence-play-frontier model. The terms which I use for the other three roles – judgement, instruction, prophecy – have a rather Old Testament ring. But why not? The playful, foolish role always stands alongside each of the others. Once again there is nothing very special about there being four. Elements from each can be combined. One might, for example, speak of a diagnostic role when playfulness, judgement and a questioning search for structure are combined; and, as we shall see, the judging role can also be blended with others.

Judging

Just why this word should be suspect in the 1980s is hard to say. Judgement does not have to be 'judgemental'. It is true that in many psycho-therapeutic situations a hasty private judgement, or even *any* spoken judgement about right conduct, may do harm, but a person who claims competence in any field of action must be prepared to judge and to be judged. There is a widespread but misguided notion, resulting from our extending science beyond its bounds, that we ought to be able to devise impersonal scales of measurement which would spare us the apparently unseemly task of deciding how and why one person's achievement is better or worse than another's. When such 'objective' tests are fashioned and widely used, however, they too become suspect, and often with good reason. Measurements of mental speed or of bodily strength or skill undoubtedly have some value, but only if the results are used as ingredients in a wide, connoisseur-like estimate of a person's total competence and of the many factors and circumstances which affect it. Again, it is often assumed that judgement is negative. On the contrary, in education, most spoken and written judgements of learners' achievements should issue in intelligent appreciation. If a student has good grounds for welcoming and respecting a teacher's judgement, then occasional, penetrating negative judgements will be all the more acceptable.

Judgement presupposes the possibility of both achievement and of failure. A legal judge, though he confronts human failure and defeat more frequently than does a teacher, will do his judging better if he assumes that even a 'hardened' criminal has the capacity to perceive some values and to achieve some good. In education there can be no doubt about this sense of personal worth and dignity.[4] Unless teachers maintain respect for the essential competence and dignity of all their pupils – acknowledging the capacity of every one of them to cope and to achieve goodness in some field – then they themselves will achieve little in the field of education, and the margins of pupils' exercise books will continue to be filled with teachers' depressing blood-red 'corrections'.

The teacher as judge, therefore, is mainly concerned with assessing how competence has been exercised. As his pupil moves away from play towards practice and to the enlargement of competence, so the teacher turns away from play to judging the skills which constitute competence. It must be remembered, however, that all teachers exercise judgement at several levels. They must have some appreciation of the possible innate limitations in their pupils – slowness of response (IQ for example), or possible sensory defects (e.g. deafness) or cognitive defects (e.g. dyslexia). Most of a teacher's judgement will be directed towards the vast range of acquired skills which make up the main armoury of his pupil's communicative and expressive competence – language, for example, or music. In addition to these communicative competences there is another which looms large in most teachers' perceptions – the learner's basic interpersonal and social competence. It is here that most so-called disciplinary anxieties gather. Is this particular child coping with the rules, routines, customs and expectations of the educational community? Simple measurements or tests can often be designed to assess the constituent skills or subsidiary information components (facts) involved in the exercise of competence. What such mechanical instruments cannot evaluate is any substantial exercise of a learner's competence – an extended essay for example – in which personal style and originality are important. We need, therefore, to take a much broader view of the teacher's judging function and to regard him more as a connoisseur of performance and of achievement and less as a pass/fail expert.

Educational judgement should be on a wider footing than that of decisions by the bench. A teacher is deeply concerned, not merely with recognizing achievement and failure, but with identifying their reasons and causes. This requires insight into the structure of skills and of the achievements they enable – how the bits all hang together; and sometimes don't. In this diagnostic and therapeutic function the two roles of teacher as judge and teacher as instructor frequently merge. However, the transition from one to the other is neither as easy to attain nor as common as it should be, because the teacher as judge tends to be institutionalized in the guise of external examiner. This applies also to our private judgements. Mary Midgley, in her *Wickedness* (1984, 49), expresses the idea well when she stresses that 'the function of moral judgement in our inner lives is to build up a store of cases approved and disapproved for various reasons – a map by which we can orient ourselves and plot our own course when we have to make decisions.' The more 'external' a teacher is the less will he be able to diagnose causes of failure or to apply therapeutic assistance. The ability to understand the nature of mistakes or shortcomings or successes is essential both for proper judgement and for proper instruction.

It may be useful at this point to set out in the form of a table the approximate relationships between the four main teaching roles and the other terms which we have been using, and to place it alongside my competence-play-frontier model and the parallel Polanyi model of the four sequential and cyclical aspects of discovery.

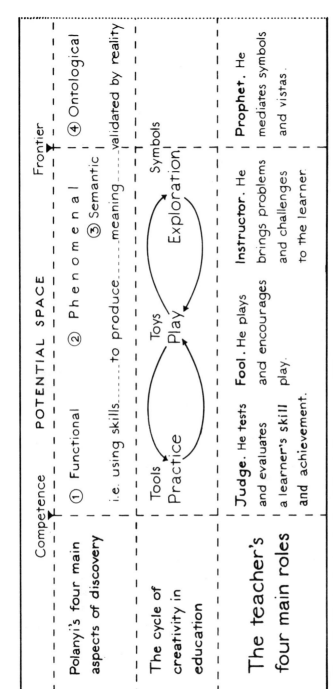

Figure 3   The teacher's roles in relation to the process of discovery

In-structing

The case for rehabilitating and sharpening the concept of instruction is strong and I have argued it elsewhere (Hodgkin 1976, 73–8). Learning is, to a large extent, concerned with how an organism develops and thereby internalizes new (to it) representations of structures in the world outside. This idea underlies Piaget's (1971a, 1979) genetic epistemology and psychology. On this basis instruction should be understood as the positive action of one organism helping a less mature one to achieve more adequate representations of the structures of the universe. The rest of education is to do with making a favourable space for autonomous learning or for assisted instruction to happen in.

The word 'structure' may, loosely, be applied to skeletons or frameworks but its more precise meaning concerns non-material *relationships* – between two or more bits of some larger whole which is made up of such bits. Before we can speak of structure we must recognize a system, the larger 'whole'. If, for example, we look at the constellation of Orion we see ten or so bright stars which form a figure; but we now have reason to believe that these are not related to each other in any sort of system. The stars just happen to be in that pattern as seen from the Earth. If, using binoculars, we observe the planet Jupiter and its moons we can check by observation what we have heard from other, authoritative astronomers that these are satellites, circulating around the central planet. Galileo recognized this as a unified system as soon as he turned his telescope to Jupiter. He and Kepler assumed that there were structural relationships between the planet and its satellites and began to direct their questions at that and similar problematic systems. So to say 'there is a structure' always implies that 'there is a system' and it also implies that there may be scope for making models of that system which will help us to understand, i.e. to internalize, that structure (Boudon 1971).

A language is another example of a highly complex, many levelled system which we only partly understand. In it, words, phonemes, pauses and stresses are regulated and related to each other by structural patterns which are by no means entirely rigid. This flexibility allows different levels easily to interact with each other. We can attempt to analyse the whole construction at different levels: in terms of phonetics, syntax, euphony, rhythm or, which is even less rigid and predictable, in terms of style.

Order is a more universal term than either form or structure. Form generally presupposes that there is someone who might perceive the order. Structure is more specific and presupposes a system whose parts are potentially understandable as being in relationship to each other. So both structure and instruction are terms which should imply that there may be knowledge to be gained by the investigation of some system. I often wonder, for example, whether the constellation of stars which we call the Pleiades is a system or an accidental grouping. Clearly I have still not been, or become, sufficiently 'instructed' in this matter.

There are philosophical and practical questions about where such orderliness is. When we learn to add 2 and 2 to make 4 are we taking into ourselves a structure of the universe or were we programmed, as it were, to do such sums? Deep questions; especially in regard to mathematics. If we follow Piaget and other 'realists' we get a useful both-ways answer which relies on the idea that human and animal bodies have been in an evolutionary dialogue with the universe since life began and that therefore many fundamental patterns are already within us. Undoubtedly a learning child *does* take in or discover new structures (and is often helped to do so by kindly instructors). But also such a child becomes ready for language, ready for visual or musical or kinaesthetic knowledge by virtue of all his or her inherited 'experience' and subsequent development. We shall return to these questions in the next chapter.

Instruction involves bringing a learner confidently up to his frontier so that he begins to ask interesting questions, finds some answers, creates appropriate models or pictures and, perhaps, does some experiments. Such activity will only be appropriate and interesting if there *is* a hidden structure on which the learner's probe can touch. The teacher will often know that this is so. In which case we have a conventional picture of what is called 'enquiry learning'; but the problem goes a good deal further. The crux of the matter is that teachers are not only concerned with closed and logically answerable scientific questions, that is with *Naturwissenschaft*. They must also be concerned with what is pre-theoretical (because they are teaching inexperienced children) and also with what may appear to transcend theory (because they are teaching potential explorers who will have to cope with obstinate puzzles and mysteries).

So we face the question of how teachers can encourage learners to step out from their assumptions about relatively 'hard' knowledge of nature to the more problematic and open knowledge of value and spirit. How can they steer with confidence from the largely explainable structures of *Naturwissenschaft* to the largely non-explainable, but nonetheless real, structures of *Geistwissenschaft*? I suggest that elementary instruction in sociology or politics or philosophy is *not* the way. Too often these subjects are offered to young adults with strong but false assumptions about their logical or factual status. What students need is to appreciate the ambiguities, the problems and the risks of all lively knowledge and this they can best do by handling enquiries which are not too abstract. Their primary need is to build up a tacit base out of which, at a later stage, more theoretical knowledge may, or may not, be developed. Just as small children begin to assimilate the concepts and problems of physics to their tacit store of knowledge by playing with sand and water, so older learners need to become familiar with the deep problems of society and culture by social and cultural action, and this means not only play but pre-theoretical practice and pre-theoretical exploration in the school. Producing an Arthur Miller play, for example, might offer more powerful instruction in social psychology than half a dozen text-books.

So coming to terms with structure is not only a matter of asking answerable questions. There are many structures which a learner needs to confront, knowing well that no amount of enquiry will yield more than a shadowy answer. He may perhaps gain an authentic emotion or a powerful intuition in the process. For example: what *is* time? – gravity? – or life? Or – to take a question at the unanswerable limit – what is God? The universal vistas of meaning onto which such words open are not to be regarded as 'containing' structure, in the sense of being ultimately explicable. Some questions have to be left open, perhaps for ever, but they may still require an enquiring and active response. As to gravity, much of our pattern of response is learnt in infancy or is inherited, and yet the reality continues to be mysterious. In religion the response usually seems to be a matter of will and choice – to pray, to praise, to worship. We do not know if there is an innate preparedness for this in human beings, though there may be. Nevertheless there is a relationship to various dimensions of infinity which can be explored, pondered or rejected by a child. So there is fundamental justification for a certain amount of theory, implied by the chilling phrase 'religious in-struction'. But it must be a small part only of that potentially all-embracing, difficult, life-long business of pondering and telling religious stories.

Nor must we overlook the context of feeling which ambiguities or puzzles may evoke. The ethos in which a difficult problem is encountered or in which a paradox is faced or rejected has a powerful bearing on a learner's future encounters with hidden structure. This helps to explain why it is important for children to learn that most adults are trustworthy, even though they will often seem enigmatic. The child is fortunate who develops a hunch that, behind those masks of his teacher, there *is* some integrity even if he cannot put a name to it. There are many symbolic ways in which the depths of possible meaning can be kept in sight – riddles, myths, rituals or mandalas are examples. Nevertheless it is people themselves, more than any of their symbolic artefacts, especially people to whom children are linked by interest and affection, who keep open the idea that perhaps there is more to the cosmos than meets the explaining eye.

Prophesying

> We are saved by making the future present to ourselves.
> (George Eliot, *Felix Holt*)

The overall pattern of a teacher's life up to the present, and what he or she seems to be aiming at, can be a powerful unspoken influence on a learner. In the heat of the moment children often misinterpret the messages of the daily drama in which they find themselves, but in the longer run those messages and the under-lying quality of remembered teachers remain potent. As Alasdair MacIntyre has argued, we are part of a world shot through with stories and biographies and so 'mythology, in its original sense, is at the heart of things' (1981, 201).

It is hard to find the right word to describe the foreshadowing, myth-making role of a teacher. Sometimes 'charisma' comes near to what is needed; but in its common use that word carries a sense of power and of overt leadership which is not what we need. Some teachers, and they are very often not those who carry the marks of authority, have the gift of helping children to see into their own and into other depths – into the potentialities of things; and that means becoming aware of unexpected possibilities. This is the non-magical function of a *guru* or wise man, and in religious as in educational terms that is what 'prophecy' should imply. Thor Coade (1966) of Bryanston School was a headmaster with this quality and he exercised it largely behind the scenes, especially in the way in which he produced plays, and took risks and demanded excellence in all the dramas which he staged. Or I recall just one phrase, from a teacher called Bill, which I overheard as we walked through a wood when I was about 13: 'a good chap deRadowitz!' was what he said. But deRadowitz was very wicked. He made colossal explosions at night with sodium. He gave most of his teachers a bad time, looked ugly and, which was not altogether on the debit side, he could always raise a rude laugh. Why did Bill say he was a good chap? And did he say that kind of thing about us to other teachers in staff meetings? Such questions continued to perplex me mildly for quite a while. It was only decades later, after Bill had died, that I realized that he *was* a very special kind of teacher, who saw much further into deRadowitz than most of the others did and saw beyond him too. I still do not know whether that remark, which I overheard in the wood, was intended to be heard.

It will be obvious by now that the phrase 'prophetic role', when applied to a teacher, is not meant to imply an ability to mouth Jeremiads or to foretell the future in any but the most general terms. It is meant to suggest that there is an art in making the future more real to a learner. A teacher does this by asking big questions at the right moment, by generating myths, by turning accidents to good effect, by being sensitive and imaginative in regard to symbols, especially the learner's own symbols. He also does it by persuading impatient people to let time operate, and sometimes by challenging deeply-engrained prejudices.

There are many examples in literature, especially in the biographies of childhood, of the ways by which wise teachers help time to loosen the chrysalis of youth. Below is an example by an author who knew a great deal about the practice of education –

T. H. White. Merlyn has become involved in educating young Arthur – the Wart. The young prince finds that he is being treated with a certain lack of dignity by his old teacher and he learns that sometimes a person has to doff old hats and don new ones.

He found he had no clothes on. He . . . had tumbled off the drawbridge, landing with a smack on his side in the water. He found that the moat and the bridge had grown hundreds of times bigger. He knew that he was turning into a fish.

'Oh Merlyn', cried the Wart. 'Please come too.'

'Just for this once,' said a large and solemn tench beside his ear, 'I will come. But in future you will have to go by yourself. Education is experience, and the essence of experience is self-reliance.'

The Wart found it difficult to be a fish. It was no good trying to swim like a human being, for it made him go like a corkscrew and much too slowly. He did not know how to swim like a fish.

'Not like that', said the tench in ponderous tones. 'Put your chin on your left shoulder and do jack-knives. Never mind about the fins to begin with.'

The Wart's legs had fused together into his backbone and his feet and toes had become a tail fin. . . . He was a beautiful olive-green colour with rather scratchy plate-armour all over him, and dark bands down his sides. . . . He did jack-knives as the tench directed and found that he was swimming vertically downwards into the mud.

'Use your feet to turn left and right with', said the tench, 'and spread those fins on your tummy to keep you level. You are living in two planes now, not one!'

The Wart found that he could keep more or less level by altering the inclination of his arm fins and the ones on his stomach. He swam feebly off, enjoying himself very much. (1938, 63–4)

Notes

1 Margaret Coulson, 'Role: a redundant concept in sociology? Some educational considerations', in J. A. Jackson (ed.) *Role* (1972).

2 E. Goffman is the best known exponent of this view: see his *The Presentation of Self in Everyday Life* (1969). For a development of similar ideas see also Rom Harré, *Social Being* (1979). An important concept

of Harré's is that the motive behind all social drama is closely connected with the participants' sense of personal dignity. I think that he pushes the 'dramaturgical' model too far, and also the centrality of dignity; but see note 4 below. A thorough discussion of the status of role theory can be found in Hinde (1979), ch. 13.

3 Personal communications from Bruner in 1973.

4 Manfred Stanley also takes human dignity as a central concept in his important book *The Technological Conscience* (1978). He broadens the concept however by an arresting and ingenious definition: 'Human dignity is the respect-worthiness imputed to human kind by reason of its ontological state as creator, maintainer and destroyer of worlds (p. 63). We are, he says, inevitably moral agents, 'thrown' on a steep and dangerous shore. Because Stanley sees human beings in this almost Manichean, good-versus-evil, conflict his overall diagnosis is extremely gloomy. He leaves out the possibly redemptive elements – play, contrition and re-birth.

6   Embodied form

> The pattern to which things are made is embedded in us; we do not find the universe wholly alien; we are of a piece with the nature of things. (Clark 1984)

Standing upright is a moral as well as an athletic achievement for a young human. Yet a child's sense of uprightness (or, for that matter, a fish's sense not to swim down into the mud) must go back in diffuse but powerful ways, to the fertilization of an embryo and far beyond that. An innate awareness of up and down can be regarded as a line running through evolution and through individual development. Such underlying lines or polarities – awareness of male and female would be another example – are formative in the development of consciousness. Human culture has many ways of making us aware of, and of refining, such awareness of – such preparedness for – the grain of the universe. I shall not say much about the virtues though they too display (or *can* display) a similar vectorial character, patterning both past traditions, which as a community we may enjoy, and marking out the future as a creative yet directional field which we explore (MacIntyre 1981).[1]

Where did such inner order come from? That sense of uprightness – was it really there from the beginning? Such questions are partly about the potentiality of things. Many Oriental and Greek thinkers have been exercised by this problem which is still being debated by scientists, linguists and philosophers. Aristotle spun it fine and Thomas Aquinas re-wove the ancient threads in a Christian fabric. According to Anthony Kenny (1980, 76) the contemporary view about a human being's rich innate competence for language and other complex achievements involves this concept of potentiality in a sense very similar to that used by Aquinas. Spontaneous use of language is the paradigm case of what we are discussing. Those partly ordered bits (phonemes or words, for example) are put together to make a meaningful whole that was not there before. Kenny reminds us that 'It is because of Aquinas' Aristotelian comparison that to this day we speak of being *informed* about a matter and call the gaining of knowledge the acquisition of *information*' (Kenny 1980, 77). Being informed or instructed, then, is not a question of putting in some new 'spiritual stuff' but of building up familiar words, numbers and shapes in new ways which, nevertheless, often embody universal patterns. At the highest, most abstract levels of mental life such putting together is achieved by our two slightly different brain hemispheres in their joint activity of thinking, envisaging, imagining and 'minding'.

There are strong reasons why educational philosophies should accommodate to such holistic, constructivist ways of thinking. Western society is becoming more and more diversified, with many cultures, languages and religions, working together and often clashing. If a more fruitful dialectic could become habitual between all these different systems for comprehending the world, then 'cognitive respect' between the proponents of one belief system and of another might become the common way, rather than confrontation (Berger 1980). And yet this does not imply the insidious corollary that we can dispense with personal commitments and critical judgements about what is better and what is worse and about why we are loyal, but not blindly loyal, to what we love.

Robinson Crusoe's predicament is a caricature, an extreme instance, of life at the margin, between two worlds. He, however, had to make almost everything from scratch, using fragmentary memories and trial and error to give form to grass, stone and driftwood. He also had to take account of universals – of gravity as shown by a plumb line or of the knots with which he tied his thatch.[2] In addition he had to make allowance for unpredictable hazards such as typhoons, and in this way chance and the future also came into his calculations.

In attempting to answer questions about the sources of orderliness we come up against a problem which affects our judgement about the rationality of different cultures. For any unfamiliar object that we find (a curiously carved stick, for example) there are some ways of understanding it which are locally contextual (Where and how did you find this? What do these people do with it?), and there are other questions which are set in a more universal framework (How long is it? What is its specific gravity?).[3] The more one tries to make statements of the latter kind, which may be open to universal checking, the more one will be trying to make scientifically rational claims. However wide and coherent our central belief system may seem it is always ringed around with a penumbra of incoherence and doubt – those typhoons, for example. So the competent castaway, like many another primitive, like many another sophisticate, takes practical precautions *and* crosses himself or says '*b'ism illahi*'. Richard Rorty puts this succinctly and with irony when discussing Dilthey's two kinds of knowledge:

> Nature is whatever is so routine and familiar and manageable that we trust our own language implicitly. Spirit is whatever is so unfamiliar and unmanageable that we begin to wonder whether our 'language' is 'adequate'. (1980, 352)[4]

Leaving on one side some deep problems about 'ultimate' reality and about where one should draw the line between real science and other locally coherent belief systems, we may persist with our relatively simple question about young learners. Where does this sense of the vertical – which seems to be both in the learner and outside – where does it come from? The importance of the question lies in the fact that many educational problems – the nature of the curriculum, for example – cannot be approached without some assumptions about the answers. Yet there is often no simple answer. Whatever it is it must be to do with distant past, with the present and with what might be, with our private, inner images and with our outer acts of knowing. For these reasons we are forced away from a naive view of knowledge as 'facts', or from regarding judgement as 'knowing what I like best', towards wider and more universal frameworks. A sense of beauty or truth may have many local contextual elements mixed with it but it is not just a matter of taste and custom. Our capacity to value things, like our capacity to recognize what is vertical, derives not only from what we do and whom we meet, not only from our resonance with nature, but also from the widest frames of understanding and interpretation that we can competently use.

When you or I find ourselves stranded, for a few hours, as a replacement teacher perhaps, with the limited chaos and the many cross currents of somebody else's 'C stream' class, we begin, if we are fortunate, to create or to discover little patches of order. One or two ideas catch on to someone's interest. Yet if the interest, the orderliness, the in-formation, do not really come from us, there remains the question – where do they come from? When, in short, we discover order, where *was* it?

The sources of orderliness

In the person

One of the common demonstrations of innate knowledge in the very young is to place an infant gently on a 'visual cliff'. A sheet of glass (warmed, so the psychologists assure us) is arranged so that it covers a table and extends well beyond its edge. The infant is then placed above the edge of the table, overlooking the apparently dangerous drop beneath the glass. Even a newly born infant recognizes that this is a nasty situation, protests and will try to move its head away. There are many other procedures for demonstrating the mass of innate knowledge which new-borns possess. Unless psychologists intervene, most of this knowledge is hidden and it may have to wait for months or years before it is manifested at the developmental stage appropriate to its use.

There is also evidence from another direction as to where such inner order is located in the brain itself. Physiologists have discovered parts of the brain cortex which contain some of the actual cells responsible for basic knowledge about spatial orientation. The work of David Hubel and Torsten Wiesel has now become well-known, partly through the writings of Colin Blakemore (1977) who has himself done important work in the field.[5] The research involved placing fine electrodes in the brain cortex of cats and monkeys, and it was discovered that certain regular layers of cells only fired strongly in response to a limited kind of stimulus, for example when a light/dark edge *at a particular angle* was being scanned by the eye. These brain cells have now been called 'orientation detectors'. It is, therefore, assumed that some parts of the brain are specially tuned to 'up', 'down', 'vertical', 'oblique', etc. and, presumably, to innumerable other elementary patterns of information received by the eye and from all the other sense organs. But from this it certainly does not follow that every human memory, power or concept has one specific cerebral location. Memories, as we shall see later, are retained in both brain hemispheres, in the cerebellum and elsewhere. Though the problem is still obscure, there is undoubtedly great redundancy in the storage systems as in the other functions of the brain (Rose 1976, 250–60).

The origins of sensory organs and of the corresponding specialist brain cells in vertebrate brains go back to the early evolution of single-celled creatures. Primitive animals and plants came to terms with the realities of space, gravity and light in many different contexts and the anatomy of their descendants now reflects these early adaptations. The roundness of the eye, for example, can be regarded as 'an image of the sun and of the physical properties of light which are present, irrespective of whether the eye is there or not to see them' (Lorenz 1977, 6).

There is a great range of sensory and motor reflections *of*, as well as readiness *for*, the universe in the human embryo. There is also 'openness' – readiness to learn new patterns. John Macmurray was one of the first philosophers to look closely into this – the apparent vulnerability and unpreparedness of human infants who, nevertheless, are born with preparedness and potential for learning. In *Persons in Relation* he puts it this way: the human infant 'is "adapted" to being unadapted, "adapted" to complete dependence on an adult human being. He is made to be cared for. He is born into a love relationship which is inherently personal' (1961, 48). That relationship, that field of love, is where education begins, where – in our example – the person's innate sense of the vertical is nourished. Such endowments can be developed in a great manifold of possible applications, including, eventually, moral ones.

Orderliness from experience

Seeing with our eyes is far from being the camera-like registration of whole scenes or images which some people suppose. From an early age children display a powerful appetite for order, for discerning new patterns of meaning and they create such patterns when they can. Just as an infant learns to discriminate with regard to food, so he/she gradually learns to build up a stable picture of the expected world and adds to this all the information that eyes and ears and other sense organs can contribute. So it is the see-er who is active, learning to make more and more accurate searches, guesses, hypotheses about what is out there, in order to infer how the incoming information may be best interpreted. Occasionally there may be serious contradictions between alternative inferences and then people are liable to suffer from optical illusions – or from sea-sickness. When someone looks at a Necker cube (Figure 4) there are two equally possible hypotheses as to what the diagram represents, and our inferences then oscillate between one interpretation and the other. Sometimes we intentionally set out to discover or create a novel view of the world – to participate in what Kuhn (1962) calls a paradigm shift; then we will be attempting something different. In general, however, we progressively synthesize a coherent set of representations of the world based on regularities which we expect.[6]

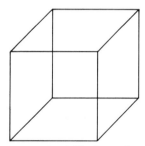

Figure 4   A Necker cube

Immanuel Kant stressed that much of our knowledge and all our perceptual knowledge is inherently synthetic or built up. He can thus be seen as the forerunner of these 'constructivist' theories of perception. His idea was later developed in the mid-nineteenth century by H. von Helmholtz. Then, as Richard Gregory points out, the whole notion that we see by making inferences was forgotten for nearly a century. Kant also regarded certain basic categories, such as space, time and causation, as being *a priori* in a strong, transcendental sense. Our understanding of the slow evolution of sense organs has made it easier for us to understand how some innate knowledge of causation or verticality, for example, could have been gradually acquired and transmitted by genetic inheritance. Konrad Lorenz's example (taken from Goethe) of the sun-shaped eye is a famous though, as regards the sun, a slightly questionable example. There is still a good deal of debate about this, especially in regard to the degree to which we are genetically 'prepared' for acquiring language. In any case it is reasonable to assume that human beings are heavily programmed at birth and that these neuronal and other programs have a phylogenetic history going back many millions of years; but also – and partly because of the long period of unprotected mother-dependence which is our lot – humans have a quite exceptional degree of openness to learning and experience. So, along with all the 'wiring', there is freedom too; freedom, in our example, to explore and experience 'the vertical' in many ways – on sandy beaches, in mountains, in mathematics and in the metaphors of poetry or religion.

So far we have been thinking about a learning child confronting problems and about castaways enjoying comparable experiences. We have stressed that both child and castaway have much in common with an exploring scientist or artist. They all search for order, meaning and control. Using Polanyi's analysis we have seen that order makes its way into such a search both functionally (from the tacit knowledge which 'the explorer' brings) and phenomenally – the bit-by-bit order which appears before a person's eyes as he proceeds with the exercise of his competence or with his experiments. If we press the same analysis a little further it will come as no surprise to find that a sense of completion or wholeness may sometimes crown such creative striving.

Discovering new order

The steady, unspectacular consolidation of experience is what Piaget calls 'assimilation' and this would apply to a good deal of what has been described above. But learners, young or old, sometimes make quite drastic changes in the way they perceive the world. We make a new 'inner' map of some bit of our surroundings and perhaps we give it a name. This is what Piaget means by 'accommodation' – when we change our own sense-making patterns rather than accepting patterns from the world around. Such accommodation evokes a new schema or inner pattern and this is often what happens as the culmination of Polanyi's gradual groping towards discovery. The explorer was already aware of being near a frontier problem and this led him or her to work at it, until the moment came when mentally an appropriate model or diagram was created or some verbal formulation of it. A new concept was born. Such a semantic, meaning-yielding breakthrough often involves a mental combination of words and images – what Rom Harré calls a 'statement-picture complex' (1970, 12). This idea of an inner, two-stage mental representation or 'operation' – word and picture being active together – has great importance for our subsequent discussion of visual aids. This third, *semantic stage* resembles a landmark – a point where outer terrain, inner map and public naming all come together. It is the moment of 'Eureka' and it terminates the private groping towards discovery while often initiating a more public phase of discussion and debate.

There are risks of error in all inferences, especially when the imagination has been ranging freely. If the discoverer's statement-picture is a correct inference, that is if its public manifestations (statement of principle or of theory, or a new work of art) are comprehended by other people, and if its form fits in with the experience of those who have tackled similar problems, and if it withstands their very proper attempts at refutation and criticism, and if, further, it is enriched by their usage, then it will be in the process of establishing itself as part of a far wider representation of reality than its creator's initial formulation. Here we move into Polanyi's final *ontological* stage. Such a confirmatory orderliness is *not* rooted in other people's judgements, though it is mediated by them. It is the reflection of real but still only partially fathomed patterns of a many-levelled universe. These ontological patterns reach far beyond our present powers of assimilation and it is they which ultimately reject or validate those intuitive guesses and experiments about order which first appeared in human consciousness as, for example, the inward mental operations of a Kepler or a Newton. Newton, with all his achievements behind him, could still see himself as a little boy, playing on the seashore, with the ocean of truth lying undiscovered ahead.

It should now be clear that none of these manifestations of order really begin with us; though sometimes our characteristic muddles and quirks may leave a finger print on them. We first drew order into ourselves, or rather, we were given it, at our conception. We have subsequently exploited our own unique version of that order (our particular genetic inheritance) by learning and being in-structed – that is by taking in additional structures of orderliness as we grew and gained knowledge. We progressively discover, through science and art and especially through social living, how the patterns which constitute us and the patterns of nature and society all around us interact and correspond and enhance each other. So life is a continuous finding of order, creating of order, assimilating of order, passing on of order. Death and decay are the reverse: a losing of order and sometimes a destroying of it; yet also, as in compost, decay may be a condition of new life. (See Capra 1976, chapter 15, 'The cosmic dance'; Bohm 1980, chapters 1 and 7.)

George Eliot's weaver, quoted at the head of chapter 4, was experiencing only the first two aspects of creativity. He was a skilled craftsman but he was locked to mechanical manufacture. Though he was his own master he had become alienated, to use the Marxist phrase; but he was alienated not for economic but for psychological reasons. He had skills, independence and a loom, and he used these to make patterned linen. No exciting discoveries clicked in his mind, nor was he himself developing as he worked. So he perceived no vistas of long-range meaning. His golden coins (and coins, note, are designed to be neither toys, nor tools nor symbols) were themselves symbols of this deadlock. Eventually, like the Ancient Mariner, he escaped; but only by learning to love once more.

Checking it out: the ontological verdict

In the scientific enterprise it is not love which breaks in to crown or judge men's patient efforts but a sense of truth – and beauty too. The verdict that a man's work is true and harmonious is that which the evolving universe passes on his creation, working through the critical minds of men, and the verdict may be given long after the maker of the work is dead. In Polanyi's slow-motion analysis of discovery he adds this long-range, ontological aspect of the creative process, but it was not a metaphysical after-thought. He knew, from Einstein's extraordinary epic and from the work of many lesser scientists, including himself, that though discoveries are ours and local, in the sense that we commit ourselves to their making, they also have a rightness of their own which (provided they *are* true) becomes increasingly apparent.

All discovery is not only judged by, but to some extent it is also guided by, the obscure, high-level patterns which are being investigated. Nevertheless there are many examples of brilliant intuitions that 'felt' right but were eventually judged wrong. This leads to a key question in the philosophy of science: what is the nature of this arbitration process which may force scientists to scrap one theoretical probe and to look for another? Polanyi argues that the crucial judgement is not given by the established authority of science, though this may be important (for other reasons), or of the state, though its pressures may be hard to escape, nor is it the neatness of the fit of the new hypothesis into the coherent matrix of world-wide 'objective knowledge' (*à la* Popper). It cannot, either, be adequately envisaged as a *post hoc* verdict after a revolution in basic concepts (Thomas Kuhn's paradigm shift) though such do happen (1962, 1974). Polanyi goes beyond all these and stresses that it is reality itself which subsequently judges the probing act or, rather, it is that newly emerging aspect of reality on which the 'probe' of continued experimentation and search has touched.[7]

It is partly Polanyi's emphasis on this ontological dimension in discovery which makes him unacceptable to Marxists, combined with his stressing of free, unplanned enquiry and the risks and personal commitment which all exploring entails. Marxists tend to ignore, or make light of, the guiding and judging function of the grain of nature and retain an exaggerated view of man's own autonomy and control. It should be said however that there are many non-Marxist scientists who are also suspicious of this aspect of Polanyi's philosophy. They are motivated, I believe, more by intellectual caution than by error. 'Stick to what we might measure or refute', they say, or 'minimize the fancy hypotheses and let us get on with the experiments and the statistics'. But if we reject the possibility, or rather the likelihood, that ordinary people are, occasionally, able to glimpse fragments of truth far beyond the grasp of measuring or common sense, we may find ourselves belittling what is best about people – their conscience and intuition, their virtue and vision – those very properties which make them stay upright and human.

A problem of contingency: 'Did you create that or find it?'

There is another complex, connected issue which has a long history. As this book is about exploration and the discovery of order we must at least take note of the problem. It is an aspect of a larger cosmic puzzle or mystery – that of *order versus chance*.[8] 'Contingency' originally meant things coming together; in the philosophical sense it means more, for the implication is that though the coming together is by chance, yet the result is likely to be significant and, in a new way, ordered.

Marjorie Grene, in her *Portrait of Aristotle*, shows that many of Aristotle's ideas, especially in regard to the orderliness of living things, should still be taken seriously. The main way, according to her, in which Aristotle went wrong was in regarding the various animal and plant species as fixed and final embodiments of form. This failure, and the dogmas which flowed from it, must have done much to delay subsequent evolutionary thinking. One might now say, with scientific hindsight, that Aristotle placed undue emphasis on visible geometric shapes but was insufficiently interested in the material which form embodies. Here is an extract from his *Parts of Animals* which shows his position:

> No one can look at the primordia of the human frame – blood, flesh, bones, vessels and the like without much repugnance. Moreover, when one of the parts . . . is under discussion, it must not be supposed that it is its material composition to which attention is being directed but the relation of such part to the total form. Similarly, the true object of architecture is not bricks, mortar or timber, but the house; and so the principal object of natural philosophy is not the material elements, but their composition, and the totality of the form, independently of which they have no existence.[9]

'The true object of architecture is not bricks'; but is that right? Should not an architect develop a deep interest in bricks and mortar, in stone and timber – the material of his art? Nowadays we would say that he should be concerned with such things as well as with the form and function of buildings. This brings us back to the desert island house – the desired vertical alignment of its pillars, the vertical circularity of its walls and to the knots tying the thatch. These are our examples of universals. Wherever in the universe there are planets which can sustain living, intelligent beings who build houses, surely such verities will maintain. It was such phenomena, considered in their abstract 'ideal' form, which so fascinated Aristotle and, even more, Plato. Yet in the main Western Christian and scientific tradition there has developed a crucial understanding that we can best know these if we are ready to soil our hands and to work with the material all around us. What should be our view about all the contingent material available on the island – the trees that happen to have fallen, the driftwood on the beach, the lianas and dry grass? According to Aristotle these are much less worthy of interest than the formal patterns which they might be made to embody. But then Aristotle never had a microscope. He never saw a cell or the incredibly complex patterns of its inner architecture.

It has been argued that it was precisely because the Judeo-Christian tradition *did* give honour to the earthy as well as to the divine, to human clay as well as to 'The Temple of the Spirit', to contingent substance as to universal form, that science was able to grow in Europe when the right tools became available. One should be cautious about such simple explanations when complex phenomena are in question. Nevertheless there was often in the West a fruitful balance between interest in form and interest in contingent matter.[10] When we have swung away from that balance in education it has usually been in the direction of overemphasizing the wordy and the theoretical. On the other hand, the so-called 'progressive' movement has at times gone too far in the opposite direction, almost idolizing the individual child and the expression of its personality, yet failing to explore the forms of community which can best sustain a child's development and all the external harmonies to which a human being must become attuned.

Despite such swings, however, the last four centuries in Europe and America have produced a significant number of scholars who have been prepared to get their eyes tired and their hands dirty examining blood and tissue, mud and clay, as well as hypothesizing about the abstract patterns which relate these. Scarcely less important, there have also been craftsmen able to look around, to love stone and wood and to make new objects of ingenuity and beauty. Here again we are close to that creative cycle of play, skill and exploring, but on a larger scale. We may recall how Clifford Ellis insisted that all his students should strengthen the roots of their competence in the hard texture of stone before they were ready to step out to their own creative frontiers. The skilled use of simple tools involves dirt and shavings *and* precision. Full competence requires a capacity to push our skills towards invention too.

I am uncomfortably aware that throughout this chapter I have been sitting on, and scanning two sides of, a famous philosophical fence. If we transfer our initial question 'was the order there before you found it?' from considering an object such as a stick or a stone to the possible orderliness which we make manifest by using it (e.g. the 'verticalness' of the walls) the two alternative views become sharper. The critical realist says: that order was at least potentially there all along. The constructivist says: order was nowhere till this newly invented hut was made, and that true theory about trees (or anything else) was nowhere until you, for the first time, constructed it. My difficulty is that I like both views. *The first seems to fit better if I'm doing the exploring; the second if I'm thinking about someone else doing it.* Stephen Clark has similar problems and some consolation to offer when he writes:

> My provisional conclusion is that our choice is . . . between theistic realism and atheistic constructivism. (1984, 156)

> Until that high moment [of God-like vision comes] we must often accept antagonistic theses, each of which seems true and good-to-be-believed but whose conjunction poses a riddle we cannot resolve. (1984, 180–1)

A bent for achievement: the upward slope

One reason for reflecting so long on an almost Brahminical notion of form is to emphasize that, though the whole cosmos, the many-levelled universe, may be intuitively perceived as a great and often mysterious whole, our perspectives on it change and give an impression first of oneness then of multiplicity – first we see with faith, then with scepticism. At one moment we find ourselves analysing the parts which constitute some phenomenon; at the next we are looking, with reverence, at some majestic unity. We judge, we play, we enquire, we dream – all, at first sight, appropriate activities for academic élites or Brahmins.

But there are other, powerful reasons for emphasizing the idea that universal formal patterns are made manifest through practical activity. We shall subsequently be exploring an un-Platonic and un-Brahminical notion, that mind only blossoms when it is working outside the skull, when the hand is involved, when speech is involved and where there is community. The case for a new down-to-earthness and openness in pedagogy becomes increasingly urgent as certain monopolistic cultural tendencies increase – those by which more and more information is held by so called professional groups or by commercial corporations, valued as private property, concentrated in magnetic tapes or in slices of silicon hidden away in black boxes.

Though Aristotle was not able to see that form and all its embodying materials can work together in an evolutionary dialectic he steered early science towards a unitary, monistic view of the world – to the understanding that forms and ideas do not reside in some heavenly domain, but are embodied in contingent stuff. The subsequent vicissitudes of this idea make up a strong, twisting strand in the history of thought. Just why a countervailing dualism of mind and body became such a pronounced feature of western thinking after Descartes is a far from simple tale. I propose to take a short-cut by jumping to the later stages of that story and to Charles Taylor's book *Hegel and Modern Society* (1979, 154–65). Hegel, like Aristotle, was one of those seminal philosophers who had some ideas which, to us, seem very dubious, and others which are both relevant and powerful. A concept which Taylor finds especially useful is what he calls 'situated' or contingent freedom. He has been discussing the same kind of exploratory zest for breaking out of our present straits into some higher viewpoint or higher domain, which we have already mentioned. Taylor argues strongly against the illusory Utopian freedoms of communism and equally against that other progressivist freedom – the urge for self-fulfilment and self-expression as an end in itself – which has often been proclaimed in the west since the Enlightenment.

In the quotation below, Taylor is protesting against this second, illusory freedom. He claims that such 'self-realization' or 'self-dependence' is not an adequate basis for either culture or education unless it is for some achievement beyond and above the self or at least above today's 'instrumental egotism'. His message is one of great importance for present day education and he develops it from a standpoint which is grounded in the whole sweep of western philosophy.

> [We have to recover] a conception of free activity which [is seen] as a response called for by the situation which is ours in virtue of our condition as natural and social beings, or in virtue of some inescapable vocation or purpose. What is common to all the varied notions of situated freedom [e.g. that of craftsman or explorer] is that they see freedom as grounded in the acceptance of our defining situation. The struggle to be free – against limitations, oppressions, distortions of inner and outer origin – is powered by an affirmation of this defining situation as ours. . . . The notion of a freedom rooted in our nature and yet which can be frustrated by our own desires or our limited aspirations, requires a more articulated, many-levelled theory of human motivation. It is very doubtful whether any theory which recognizes only efficient causation can do justice to it. We need the notion of a bent in our situation which we can either endorse or reject, reinterpret or distort. (p. 160)

While Taylor recognizes the pervasive danger of totalitarianism, he identifies, with equal clarity, that other danger of self-expressionism and relativism. His 'bent' is a similar concept to Waddington's chreod or 'fated path' in embriology, or Polanyi's freely accepted 'heuristic field' or the existentially perceived 'vista' of hope which we have noted in George Eliot. Taylor makes a very similar demand on us to that which Alasdair MacIntyre makes when he roots each virtue in its history and tells us to follow it into the *telos* of immediate and future action: the value-laden, directional slope on which we find ourselves. Both are saying: take time – past and future time – more seriously.

Biologists are traditionally suspicious of anything which smacks of teleology. Yet there has been an explosion of interest in guided or 'telic' phenomena in systems thinking and cybernetics (Buckley 1967; Bertalanffy 1968; Laszlo 1972; Weiss 1975; Capra 1982). The notion of 'equi-final field' where many synchronous influences and ordering principles push steadily in one direction has become almost a commonplace. Many other critics of the present state, not only of biology but more especially of the social sciences, would argue that it is essential that we extend our conceptual range in regard to *processes* of change so as to allow for more thorough discussion of pathways, thresholds and fields of change in which we work, as well as of the occasional 'catastrophic' crises which interrupt them. Chance certainly comes in; but the life game – bidding always for new levels of orderliness – goes on being played against chance, and people, whether they like it or not, have to play it, at every level of competence (Peacocke 1979, 106–11; Eigen and Winkler 1982).

When the world is propitious for putting two and two together and making four, someone will probably do it. When most roads lead to Rome, or Mecca or Benares, the faithful don't *have* to go, but they tend to get there in the end. We may assume that all people possess a bent for creativity, a bent for discovering form at many levels and for asking questions which lead them to relate these levels and to recognize that some are higher and some are lower; and to act in this knowledge.

Notes

1 Alasdair MacIntyre's account of the west's loss of a strong feeling for, and understanding of, virtue re-establishes that concept partly by embedding it in a time dimension. Like Polanyi, he suggests that we share a traditional 'practice' of doing things with others, and thereby create a common field of explicit and implicit aims, i.e. a *telos* (*After Virtue*, 1981, 169–89).

2 'The persistence of knots in three dimensions so closely resembles the persistence of particles, that it suggests that particles are *nothing other* than knots in space time' (P. W. Atkins, *The Creation*, 1982, 87). The God whom Atkins progressively dissolves by finding him infinitely lazy, is the old God-of-the-gaps – outside particles, outside knots and, presumably, outside everything else.

3 The distinction between contextual criteria of rationality and universal criteria of rationality is clearly presented by Steven Lukes in his essay 'Some problems of rationality', in Wilson (ed.) (1970). See also Lukes, 'On the social determination of truth', in Horton and Finnegan (eds) (1973).

4 For a different and subtle distinction between knowing natural truths and knowing social or cultural ones see Berlin (1976) and Shotter (1984, 129–51) on Vico's teaching.

5 A useful general source is *Illusion in Nature and Art* edited by R. L. Gregory and E. H. Gombrich (1973). As in Gregory's other books, there are good examples of visual illusions and explanations of how

these come about. Searle (1984) is also relevant. And see Blakemore (1977).

6 There are interesting differences of opinion amongst the experts in this area, and a rich research menu awaits further theoretical and experimental study. J. J. Gibson's 'ecological' view is that the whole of a person's 'visual array' – all the detail coming in to his field of vision – plays some part in the integrative meaning-making process which happens around the point of attention or action. This resembles an externalized version of Polanyi's subsidiary and focal awareness. Gibson's account can be harmonized with Gregory's more analytic one on lines suggested by Ulric Neisser in *Cognition and Reality* (1976, 20, 24). John Shotter takes Gibson's ecological and holistic theory of perception as a model for his own view that a learning child (or adult) is embedded in a uniquely personal learning environment and that one cannot adequately think about learning in terms of any learner in isolation. Following Uexküll, Shotter calls this total and personal learning field an *Umwelt* (1984, 94–100).

7 The above paragraph is, in part, quoted from Wigner and Hodgkin (1977). For a fuller treatment see 'The place of Michael Polanyi in the modern philosophy of science' by T. F. Torrance (1984), or Gelwick (1977).

8 A. R. Peacocke, *Creation and the World of Science* (1979), part III, 'Chance and the life game', is of interest and gives a useful account of the work of Prigogine and others concerning the possible 'upward' emergence of primitive life. See also Eigen and Winkler (1982).

9 Quoted by Marjorie Grene in her *A Portrait of Aristotle* (1963, 57). The source is *De Partibus Animalum* An.645a, 4–37 (Oxford edn).

10 On pp. 9 and 10 of Peacocke's book, cited above, he quotes at length from Michael Foster's article in *Mind* 43 (1934), 'The Christian doctrine of creation and the rise of modern science'. However, there are other opinions on these matters. See, for example, Joseph Needham's *Clerks and Craftsmen in China and the West* (1970), ch. 2, 'The unity of science; Asia's indispensable contribution'.

7 Many-levelled theory

> It may be that our thought on one level can only be understood by
> its relation to the other levels; in particular our 'higher' more
> explicit awareness may always repose on a background of the
> implicit and unreflected. (Taylor 1979, 163)

Teachers are involved continuously in a movement and counter-
movement of thought as they swing their attention up and down
a hierarchy of less abstract and more abstract representations of
the world – maps, for example, or myths. The many-levelled
representations which teachers handle must, in the first place, be
adequate to their own understanding. Appropriate representations must then be chosen so that at other, 'younger' levels, the
same essential ideas will be accessible to learners whose perspective towards the hierarchy is more naive than the teacher's. Yet
educational thought lacks what Charles Taylor calls an adequate
'many-levelled theory' to make sense of such multiplicity. This
theoretical deficiency is one reason why teachers, and others who
think about education, readily fall in with those false dichotomies
on which we have already touched. They assume that the
'academic' really is opposed to the 'practical'; thus fostering a
popular misconception which may be one of the causes of
Britain's industrial decline (Nuttgens 1977). They slip into the
facile assumption that what is free is antagonistic to what is
responsible and disciplined, or they concur with that demeaning
view of education which sees pupils as receptacles, and knowledge as measurable material for filling them. Most teachers
know, in their hearts, that none of this is so, that children are not
things to be filled, moulded or sieved. Nevertheless the system of
organization and of thought which teachers find themselves
supporting and which, in turn, supports them, tends to generate
all these messages.

Some people would argue that nothing short of a total, catastrophic revolution can change all this, and yet it may well be that
a quieter revolution is already afoot and our task may be to push it

and ease it along. Some of the writers quoted here – Polanyi, Shotter, Taylor, Winnicott and others – have been creating a new, more hopeful, intellectual *milieu* for thinking about education and culture. Franz Capra's *The Tao of Physics* (1975) and *The Turning Point* (1982) or David Bohm's *Wholeness and the Implicate Order* (1980) suggest, speculatively but persuasively, that our most fundamental ways of thinking about nature and human nature are being drawn into a process of profound reappraisal. The purpose of this chapter is, in similar vein, to bring together some of the basic educational concepts which we have been discussing and assemble a unified model of the process. This may go some way to meeting Charles Taylor's requirement for a 'many-levelled theory'.

A two-dimensional model

Up to this point we have tried to keep apart two essential dimensions of education which will now be brought together – see Figure 5.
These are:

(1) the play-practice-play-exploration cycle, which we have also called the cycle of creativity. It can only be understood from the kind of existential, active-person-centred perspective which we established by using the examples of the castaway and the exploring infant. All such explorings are powered by the individual's innate and acquired action systems which we designated 'competences'.

(2) the hierarchy of cultural modes, the networks of social and cultural representations and expressions in which competence grows. These are the main high roads by which adults help children to come to terms with order and disorder in the universe and so to enter their own heritage of culture by many kinds of play and practice.

The total process which the diagram represents is to be seen, therefore, as one learner among many, being helped to make discoveries at several levels of culture. The process is complex and takes place in all the dimensions of space, as well as drawing on time past and anticipating time in the future. We need to bear

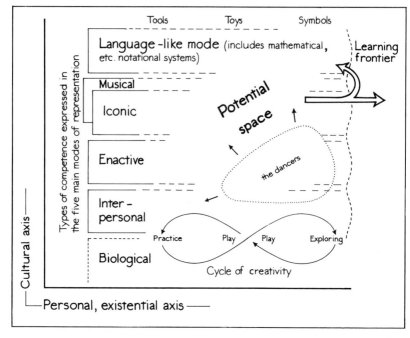

Figure 5 The process of education

The idea of a competent (sometimes playful) explorer is relevant to all cultures. Culture itself may be thought of in terms of five main modes of representation. It is important to remember that all these modes or levels form an open, interlocking hierarchy. Iconic (pictorial) competence, for example, relies on more basic 'enactive' and interpersonal skills. This interdependence of modes is not a one way affair – downwards: a child may know and use an abstract word or phrase long before he or she is ready to fill out its meaning with active practical use. The branching arrow suggests that an iconic symbol may be used both to explore with (art for art's sake) and to discover with – expressing one's findings in some more abstract form. 'The dancers' refers to an example of wordless education cited in the text.

in mind too that this model, though it refers primarily to cultural events and to an individual exploring cultural modes of representation, also refers to processes going on in the brain and body of that individual.

The division into cultural modes which I have adopted is not arbitrary, though there will always be overlap between the modes and there is scope for subdivision within them. Important evidence has been accumulating that there are subsystems in the brain which are largely isolated from each other and yet they appear to act and learn together – synergistically – in different but complementary types of mental activity (Fodor 1983; Gardner 1984). If mental unity and coherence are to be maintained, how are such relatively isolated subsystems of the brain capable of harmonious, purposive knowing and making? This is the question for which an answer will be suggested in the next two chapters. It will not be the whole answer but educationally it is of great importance.

We have already encountered the germ of this idea when we considered the dancer and the isolated, autistic child. The therapist was not trying to help the child by directly communicating to her about what she lacked, but was getting her to act – to 'do knowing' and to discover meaning – at the level where joint action was possible. They were playing and exploring the two basic levels of culture – the interpersonal and enactive modes – with a hint of iconic play just beginning to come in. The important points to note are that they were acting together and that they were exploring across modal boundaries. The unwilling and unspeaking learner was being lovingly lured, first into the simplest level of wordless, interpersonal communication and then into the world of co-operative bodily movement. Both were experiencing the results of action, and together knowing what it meant.

The general idea of a hierarchy of modes of representation was sketched out by Bruner in *Toward a Theory of Instruction*. He was turning Piaget inside out, taking all those supposed internal stages of a child's developing thinking – from the concrete to the abstract – and asking what outward, cultural things must teachers create and select *for learners*, and with what timing and degree of challenge must these be offered, if we are to optimize children's development. But he did not go far enough.

What Bruner suggested was that we all learn about the world – that we represent it to ourselves and share these representations with others – at three main levels or in three main cultural modes. We do this, he says, first in the intentional movements of our whole bodies as we refine the whole sensorimotor apparatus for the attainments of more and more specific skills. The patterns of these give rise to our own inner representations of the world and they are constantly being shared with others, as in the dance. This is what, with Bruner, we have been calling the enactive mode. Notice that he did not speak of an interpersonal mode but seems to have taken it for granted. The second mode which he named was the iconic mode – all those representations of experience in the form of maps, pictures, graphs and diagrams. Here again there is a vast cultural domain with outward as well as internal, mental representations. Thirdly, Bruner discussed the uses of language. In this mode, either precisely and perhaps mathematically (as in science) or symbolically (as in poetry) people learn to describe, classify and explore. A brief verbal-visual example of all three would be this: we dive into a pool or dance on the river bank trying out skills and so 'represent' the world in our movements. Then, rather more systematically and abstractly, we draw a sketch or a map of the river and its pool and then, using language, we 'explain' the existence of the pool or the erosive power of the waterfall or, perhaps, we write a reflective poem expressing our feelings about them.

Here we come up against a serious difficulty which makes it necessary to modify and develop Bruner's terminology. The difficulty hinges on the divergent meanings of the word 'symbol' (see pp. 54–5). Bruner, along with many other authorities, generally uses the word 'symbolic' to connote the language-like sign systems of speech, literature and mathematics. He is following a widely accepted Franco-Swiss tradition (from deSaussure to Piaget).[1] The Germanic usage which I advocated in chapter 3, however, gives symbolism a deeper meaning which is more appropriate to an understanding of exploration and of the feelings which go with it. It insists that the concept of symbol should keep its original probing, ambiguous and search-sustaining meaning. It also covers the other non-linguistic uses of symbolism, as when we dance or paint or act symbolically in order to enlarge our field of meaning. This connotation has respectable literary and philosophic antecedents, going back through Coleridge to Goethe (Swietecka 1980).

If 'symbol' is best reserved for those representations which, in some way, cope with paradoxes and problems and with exploring, there arises a question as to what alternative term we should use for the whole category of everyday communicative signs, for all those abstract, linear representational systems of coding which include spoken and written language as well as musical and algebraic notations. I propose to use the term *language-like* to refer to this general class of abstract, potentially discursive and sequential systems of representation. Newly minted symbolic words tend, with frequent use, to become ordinary – mere, useful signs. It looks, therefore, as though words and other signs generally start life in some extraordinary situation as symbols, and then by degrees become more common coin. So, though the distinction is important, it cannot be a sharp one.

Whether a verbal representation is to be treated as a 'mere' linguistic sign or as an active symbol is mainly a question of context. Some words might seem to be endowed with symbolic status just because they form part of a poem, but the context of living literature runs beyond print and paper, and involves people. The degree to which words are functioning as symbols depends on certain competences and sensibilities in the person who reads or hears them. These personal attributes in the reader of a poem will, to some extent, match similar qualities that were present in the poet who first wrote the words.

The Chinese ideogram for knowing is, in part, formed by the sign for 'heart' and perhaps we, in the West, need to recover something of that element of warmth in our understanding of the meaning of knowledge and of its representations. Yet what, after all, does 'heart' mean? It implies a quality of personal involvement, much deeper than logic and the ability to handle words. Everyone is now aware that speech is generated in one half of the brain. However, as we shall see in chapter 8, the left hemisphere language processing system need not, indeed it should not, act in isolation from the rest. When 'heart' and feeling are involved it is probable that other parts of the brain and other parts of our bodies will also be activated: tears may come, the heart beat faster. In the West we face a deep and pervasive problem at all stages of education about how we should keep this affective or emotional aspect lively, sensitive and disciplined, rather than allowing it to atrophy (Jones 1973; Holbrook 1979).

Two additions to the original Brunerian scheme have a bearing on the education of the emotions. They are both indicated in Figure 5 and have already been touched on: one is the interpersonal mode and the other is music. The interpersonal mode is more fundamental than Bruner's enactive mode. Though Bruner did not name it in his seminal books on education (1960, 1968), he and others working in the field of infant learning are very well aware that children do begin to make sense of the world *through their interactions with other people*, especially through their mothers, and that this happens long before language and at least a year before they start to explore their surroundings actively and independently. The interpersonal mode seems to dominate a child's learning from about the time of the first smile (round about the age of 3 months) until the age of about 15 months. This is the period when the mother and her infant live in that state of deep mutual interdependence which John Shotter describes as 'psychological symbiosis' (Shotter 1984, 60–5; also Spitz 1965). During this period the mother is, to the infant, alternatively and overlappingly, a plaything, an instrument and a symbol. The 'representations' or meaningful acts which structure and punctuate these early exchanges – facial expressions, gestures, pauses, absences and embraces – all belong, in the proposed terminology, to this most basic interpersonal mode by which the world beyond the mother and child is given its first comprehensible shape.[2]

That this *is* the fundamental level of education sometimes becomes clear from quite a different perspective – when a teacher has to deal with an emotionally disturbed child in a tantrum. At such times all sorts of high level considerations have to be put on one side: 'did you understand me?' – unimportant; 'was it yours or his?' – for the moment, unimportant; 'who hit whom first?' – leave it on one side. A teacher may sometimes just *hold* a young and violent child in an embrace of loving firmness while the storm subsides. Such measures will not work, however, unless the interpersonal bond has already been established. We saw aspects of the same process in Janet Adler's dance therapy. She was working mainly at the two lower levels of education – interpersonal and enactive. She used music, certainly, and traces of visual design, but she never spoke a word. She was preparing the essential foundations for any human culture and especially the pacing, timing and 'punctuation' of it.[3] The language level can only be confidently assembled and inhabited when the others are built up.

Figure 5 sums up and unites these two main perspectives. Here we can see the main dimension of our model which represents the *totality of a learner* and the cultural spaces in which such a learner operates:

   (i) the cultural dimension which is broken into five main representational modes or levels;
  (ii) the existential dimension in which is located the cycle of personal exploration and creativity.

I believe that here we have an outline model which contains all the essentials of education. It can be used as a means to review critically any major field of teaching and learning – from physical education to religious education, from science to literature. It also points to a more fundamental epistemology than the conventional 'subject' divisions of the curriculum. Of course there are omissions. There is no mention of the modalities of the palate or of touch, for example, and innumerable overlappings and subdivisions are taken for granted.

A simple example of how the diagram can be applied is to look 'through' it at Janet Adler's dance therapy with the withdrawn child. I have dotted in an area which represents an estimation of their joint educational interaction, which is mainly at the enactive level. One might be wondering what should be the next stage in the education of such a withdrawn learner? More of the same kind of 'courtship' in dance and music is likely to be needed by the child, and indeed, attachment through movement might well become a continuous strand in its subsequent life. And the child's frontier? There would be considerable risks and tensions from any pronounced movements in that direction while the child's foundations of competence are still so narrow. Its present insecurity suggests that frontier experiences will have to wait a while. So too will any demanding commitment to language, even to the initial stages of playful talk. On the other hand practice in the development of interpersonal skills, play and practice in the music and movement modes are likely to be immediately rewarding. The small arrows suggest these developments.

The reader may view his own experience of a particular educational activity through the same schema. Someone who has knowledge of an experimental science curriculum, for example, or of traditional and 'new' mathematics might plot a corresponding space (or spaces) of active learning which their pupils enjoy. In mathematical or scientific subjects learning extends more into the iconic and language-like levels than our last example and in their revised forms they will probably include more problem-centred, frontier experience. The model might lead one to ask whether the current fashions of the new maths or of new science curricula overemphasize discovery and frontier activities and underemphasize the importance of playful beginnings and of consolidating manual, iconic and linguistic skills by practice. Such lack of balance has sometimes been evident in recent curricular developments and it can be useful to have a conceptual scheme which keeps play, practice and discovery in the critic's or reformer's mind. If, in addition, Figure 5 raises unexpected questions about, say, the aesthetics of physical education or the skills of religion or the myths of science, so much the better. Its main aim is to suggest educational possibilities and to facilitate thought about the interlocking of all levels of the educational process; about cultural levels as well as personal or existential states.[4]

Any model or metaphor breaks down sooner or later. The most obvious weakness of this one is the distortions that have had to be introduced in order to show that music should be represented at much the same level as the iconic mode and should extend up into its own language-like (notational) mode. Music can be regarded as a conventional school subject but there is a strong case for it being given a more basic place in education, analogous to the iconic, enactive or interpersonal domains of experience. Both iconic and musical skills seem to depend largely on right hemisphere activity in the brain and yet both can be enormously enriched when access to language-like systems of representation is available. Further, as we shall see (p. 162), some fine musical skills and the very finest manual skills of humans appear to be the special concern of a particular lobe in the left (linguistic) hemisphere.

Another purpose of the model is to encourage teachers or others concerned with children to relate every problem to a wide field, to stress the holistic nature of the educational process. Not only do words, pictures and rhythms depend on each other in many subtle ways; they all depend on simpler, more basic activities and on interpersonal exchanges; and all these, in turn, depend on a great pyramid of biological information and activity. Here is a further example: a teenager has suddenly discovered the profound and durable joy of extending himself or herself in some exacting activity such as long distance running. An athletics coach might think about such an achievement somewhat narrowly, along the play-practice-frontier (i.e. 'personal best') dimension and with regard to its physiological foundations. But an educator (which should include many, if not all, coaches) will also think about how a physical achievement (exploring the enactive mode) links up with other modes, how it might enrich the young athlete's basic personal relationships – for example – powers of love and empathy, or his or her potential in related aesthetic, scientific or literary fields.

The model reminds us too that all these things need to work together. The various modes are hierarchical, yet not rigidly so. They depend on each other, not only in their origins but in their continuings. A teacher of drama, to take an extreme case, has both the opportunity and the difficulty of working in four, or even five modes simultaneously. And a scientist – teacher or researcher – no matter how abstract his theorizing, should never lose interest in making things, in models and in ordinary phenomena. The roots of a successful writer are sustained by memories of parents and forerunners, by his friends, by the tools of his trade at every level of action and by a vivid visual and aural imagination. To use such gifts in practice generally involves forgetting about analytical divisions and getting on with the job. If, however, we are trying to improve education by giving it critical attention we need a way of thinking about all its dimensions and parts, as well as about its wholeness. An old headmaster used to say 'you can't begin to understand the curriculum until you grasp its "hang together" '.

Moving from one mode of representation to the next

In the two following chapters we shall be considering the upper levels of our model, and especially the processes by which pictures and words can work together in creative thinking. The problem is fascinating and complex and it branches into many intellectual disciplines. It is central to pedagogy and yet educational research has given it remarkably little attention. What has been done tends to focus on learning difficulties or on educational technology in a purely instrumental way.[5] Answers to more far-reaching questions about optimizing everyone's general intellectual functioning will have to await experimental and theoretical probing. What follows is a reconnaissance of this largely uncharted domain.

The difficulties of the subject are partly semantic. The word 'representation', for example, can refer to things in the outer world or to inner mental operations and experiences. Or 'representation' can refer in a third sense to some supposed underlying neurological pattern which records our experiences in the brain. I doubt if it is possible to comb out these three semantic strands and keep them entirely separate in use. Nevertheless, anyone discussing these matters needs to be constantly alert to the way in which words and language can apply to different fields of reference. In a note at the end of this chapter I include a diagram of Gazzaniga's which illustrates the three kinds of language which we commonly use when discussing representations and similar phenomena – inner, outer and physiological language. I suggest that just as we are well advised not to talk of 'homunculi' or hidden agencies inside our brains, so it is probably best to avoid speaking of other inner entities such as 'the subconscious' as though it were a thing or a region of the brain. When we do use such words it is best to remember that the terms refer to processes or phases of activity: hence Piaget's 'concrete *operations*'.

A friend with whom I was discussing the way in which the model claims to represent the whole process of education remarked 'why don't you indicate that real education always follows an oblique direction – like this ⬈ i.e. towards exploration *and* abstraction? Essentially he was correct, though perhaps his arrow should have been more like this ⬈ ; for educational development of a learner cannot be understood in simple linear terms nor in terms of the exploration of one mode. It must involve both regression to, or reliance on, lower, more concrete modes *and* progressively more confident moves upward into greater abstraction.[6] This is the meaning of the two-way arrow which I have placed at the upper end of the frontier in Figure 5. It could, equally well, have been placed on the frontier lower down. For example, on the interpersonal frontier it would have represented some of the explorings of a new-born infant (or Janet Adler's problem child) establishing its first social contacts and competence. The arrow stands, in summary, for what I called 'an explorewith', i.e. it represents a probe in skilled hands or a hypothesis or a lively symbol or, sometimes, a person whom the learner has temporarily appropriated and with whom he or she is prepared to work at the frontier. Then, sooner or later, there will arise a crucial option: am I, a learner, going to continue exploring just at one level or can I move up?

There are many examples from the history of science and technology of creative thinkers holding on to some anomalous finding or to some problematic diagram or to some combination of picture and statement which becomes, for a time, a seminal focus of their exploring. Then they move 'up' and discover its meaning in a more abstract, communicable mode. Occasionally such symbolic seeds of discovery appear in dreams – Kekulé's famous ring of atoms for example. More often they seem to be consciously held and worked over in the explorer's 'inner eye'. Galileo's or Einstein's thought experiments are well known instances.[7] I believe, however, that essentially the same frontier processes can be the experience of every child, of every learner, facing the need for an educational breakthrough from one representational mode to another. But notice, and we shall return to this later, the elements of such symbolic discovery processes, and their enigmatic quality, arise from two distinct but interacting levels of meaning. The broken sherd (in our suggested etymology of the word 'symbol', p. 55) was not a mere sherd; it sustained a quest for the other half and for the meaning which the whole symbol – 'thrown together' – implied. Kekulé's dream of a snake eating its tail was not about 'mere' snakes; it became a hint about circularity and the explainable transformations of molecular structure.

In introducing his concept of modes of instruction, Bruner (1968, 10) started by explaining them as systems of representations – enactive, iconic, etc. He speaks of 'a child get[ting] free of present experience and conserv[ing] past experience in a model'. It may help the mechanically minded reader if we make one more explanatory suggestion. Keith Oatley in his book *Perceptions and*

Representations gives the cybernetic connotation of the word 'representation'. He stresses the triggering, energy-releasing-at-the-right-moment aspect of all representations and this in turn is reminiscent of the symbol which holds some tension till the time is ripe. Oatley explains this by citing the classic example of a thermostat in a central heating system. The setting of the thermostat *represents* some future, expected state of the world – e.g. a drop in temperature – to which the system will adapt. So here, as in all systems of representation, there is the same element of purposiveness, of energies conserved until the right moment.

When I was a schoolmaster I used to be puzzled by the way in which a 14-year-old might be making great progress in the art room, say, yet seemed to be getting nowhere in English or mathematics. Sometimes a breakthrough to active confidence in the language-like mode would come quite suddenly; sometimes it would be distressingly slow or never come. Why was this? What should one do to help? I do not know a simple answer but the kind of answer one should be looking for becomes apparent when the situation is thought about in terms of our model.

The problem appears to be that of a learner who is competent and motivated at one relatively abstract level of action – the iconic – but who is jibbing at the next stage – that of developing his or her language-like competence in fluent literacy or in mathematics or both. In Piaget's terms one would say that such a pupil is hesitating at the move from 'concrete operations' to 'formal operations' and this is indeed a common and intractable predicament which many adolescents face. Consider our example of the young man who has the skills and motivation to press back his frontier 'horizontally' in the art room, i.e. at the iconic level. He can also regress, as in recreation, to simpler modes, but he cannot, for some reason, commit himself to the upward arrow and to the high wire of sustained abstract thinking which the practical application of logic, say, or algebra require. In some ways he resembles Janet Adler's child who was unable, at first, even to exchange glances with her teacher.

The solution, according to the line of thought which we have been following, is likely to be something to do with such a student perceiving a vista and doing so by way of an appropriate symbol. But the symbolic key will have to be of his or her own finding. One can also be confident that the process will start in potential space; that is, with pressures being taken off – with this kind of purpose in mind. But what immediate purpose? It might be that of identifying and remedying some recognized technical fault, or of acquiring a new tool or skill which is relevant to the learner's frontier. What about trying Letraset, for example, or calligraphy? In general terms one can say that the most promising line will be for this learner *to develop his language around his art – in a context of feeling* – reading about artists, drawing according to the precepts of artists whom he admires, giving striking titles or explanations to his own pictures or illustrating myths or other stories which he has already latched on to. The last proviso is important for it suggests why the key is often so illusive. A learner cannot use a tool or a symbol with the courage required for frontier work unless he has made it his own, by practice or by dwelling in it mentally. That is why a teacher's or a parent's suggestion will rarely do, for teachers can only have a vague idea as to what symbolic seeds are already germinating. And anyway, the time may not be ripe; even though important examinations are just round the corner and make the matter appear urgent.

These problems are undoubtedly difficult to speak about in the conventional language of educational psychology. Nevertheless they are extremely common, especially among adolescents and young adult learners for whom a move 'upwards', beyond concrete (iconic) imagery, is often of crucial importance. The best short term prospect for any widespread extension of self-motivated, free-feeling education at the secondary level would be for a majority of teachers to understand these highly charged processes better *and* to have examination pressures on them reduced. In the longer run there will have to be radical changes in the whole educational system – spreading it out and mixing it more with service and adventure – if it is to offer the majority of young humans both the freedom and the sense of reality which they yearn for.

The potency of words and diagrams

Interesting lines of enquiry open up for anyone who is prepared to follow this new tack, to experiment and to think about education from the kind of perspectives which we have been sketching. I propose to concentrate on two promising questions: first, the interaction of the iconic and language-like modes in learning or, to put it in another way, to ask what is the significance, for education, of all the recent research on the interaction between man's right and left brain hemispheres? Then, secondly (and this is also speculative but has urgent relevance to problems and priorities in education), to consider what might be the result of putting competence and the five main modes of representation at the centre of our thinking about the curriculum instead of predominantly verbal knowledge. All this has a powerful bearing on the ways in which we relate to the technology which surrounds us. Are we to fear it, idolize it, or master it?[8]

There can be little doubt that the quality of children's early play and of all their explorations with the stuff of both nature and culture has a far-reaching effect on their subsequent capacity to enjoy and to learn and to think. Despite the teachings of Piaget and Bruner, there is one area in which conventional early education is frequently impoverished. One reason for educational inertia here may have been that we venerated Piaget too much. His teaching about a preordained order of cognitive development has now been questioned by many researchers (e.g. Bryant 1974; Donaldson 1978; Harré 1983). We fail conspicuously and for many reasons to lay down adequate foundations of play and practice in the experience of our young. This lack is especially marked in regard to computing and mathematics. Seymour Papert's experimental work has been particularly interesting in the way it has focused on these early needs, and he is not unduly concerned about what a child is theoretically 'ready for'.

Papert, in his book *Mindstorms*, lays great emphasis on these active roots of mathematics and technology. He stresses the obvious importance of 'babytalk' in opening up for a child the wide and early experience of his mother tongue. He also points to the absence, for most children, of something equivalent to babytalk in music as well as in mathematics and technology. The extent of the problem is evident if one considers the superficial way in which older children engage with electronic machines. They watch and watch the cathode screen. They tend to see calculators and computers as *gadgets*. The majority of students, even though they may possess a calculator and often play with electronic games, have little or no understanding of the computer's inner workings and little relevant tacit knowledge – no childhood experience of the babytalk – which lays down the necessary groundwork for an understanding of binary arithmetic, of electronic control systems or of information technology. Occasionally one result of this is that young adult learners become obsessively hooked on a computer, almost as though it were a drug (Weizenbaum 1976; Shallis 1984).[9]

Papert and his colleagues at the Massachusetts Institute of Technology set to work to design electronically controlled robots, and also a suitable language by which children could begin to relate to these tools of the twenty-first century – at the level of serious play. The best known of these robots were 'turtles' – vehicles with transparent shells which would follow complex instructions given by children and then trace corresponding patterns on the floor. These turtles were in one sense toys but they were also much more than toys for, in the perspective of our creative cycle, they were also tools around which skills develop. One could say too that they had some extra 'symbolic' value in the sense that children sometimes used them creatively, as 'explorewiths'. The children, through their turtles, were able to acquire tacit knowledge about underlying principles of cybernetics, feedback and control systems. They were undoubtedly experiencing both freedom and fun, yet this should not lead us to overlook the vast amount of structure which was made available to them (instruction) through their use of the hardware itself and of the programs on which they were constantly at work. All this was happening well before the children were ready to think about theoretical explanations. Yet, whenever possible, children should be given inklings about what is going on inside – the switching and storing and the tree-like structure of information which they control.[10]

Papert's interest in children's experience of dancing and juggling attracted less attention, but it is clear that he saw such demanding activities in the enactive mode as contributing to the enlargement of each learner's frontier. Such experiences are important, not only in themselves, but because they enrich the tacit foundations out of which higher levels of thought will subsequently grow – literacy and numeracy, and musical literacy too. Piaget, Bruner and Papert all agree that mature artistic and intellectual achievements are rooted in the first-hand exploratory activities of childhood.[11] The big educational problem, however, is still about how we facilitate this, how much we let it happen for many, not just for a few, and how we reinforce success. The next chapter will suggest that there are persuasive and newly discovered grounds which support the view that non-verbal and verbal experience must be allowed frequent and fluent interaction, even in the most sophisticated forms of education. My model attempts to stress: (i) the need for interaction between the modes in which we learn; (ii) the complementary importance of play and practice; (iii) the challenge of frontiers at all levels. Papert uses similar concepts and, in an important passage in *Mindstorms*, he points to the crucial boundary between the iconic and language-like modes:

> No knowledge is entirely reducible to words, and no knowledge is entirely ineffable. . . . An important component in the history of knowledge is the development of techniques that *increase the potency of 'words and diagrams'*. What is true historically is also true of the individual: an important part of becoming a good learner is learning how *to push out the frontier of what we can express with words*. (1980, 96, my italics)

This problem is summarily located by the forked arrow in the top right-hand corner of Figure 5. It refers to the question of doing more of what you feel good at *and* trying to express it at levels of abstraction where you do not feel at home but where other people will listen and criticize. At the heart of both approaches is the concept of a person as an exploratory, social, language-using meaning-maker.

The crucial question of how pictures and diagrams help a person to think with words is matched by the reverse – the 'downward' question – of how language helps someone to be inventive in their use of pictures – both outer and inner ones. Each kind of activity is dependent on the stock of words and images that are already accessible, and together they affect a person's readiness for action. For these reasons the educational problem of what visual aids *are* and how they function, is crucial – a keystone in the wide arch of human knowing.

In the late 1970s some neuro-psychologists were moving towards a radically new way of thinking about these matters, and I believe that they point the way for education. They developed the idea that the left and right brain hemispheres were not only different in their capacities for processing information but that each side of the brain is normally involved in co-operating with the other in a dynamic and integrative process. It is this, I believe, that can now lead us to a deeper understanding of the complexity of visual activity. Ultimately it may enable teachers to get more practical purchase on the varied processes by which pictures can enable everybody to think about what seems new and strange. Further, if this approach is correct, there could be great parallel educational advances in the teaching of music and of dance and movement, as well as in the teaching of social and fine manual skills.

Notes

1 In *Toward a Theory of Instruction* Bruner certainly seems to restrict the meaning of the term 'symbolic' to language-like notational systems and does not concern himself with the wider dynamic connotations of the word which I believe we ought to preserve. On the other hand, in his essay 'Nature and the uses of immaturity' (Bruner *et al.* 1976, 49), he follows Vygotsky (ibid. 537–54) in giving the word 'symbol' a wider meaning, much nearer to that which I have been advocating. The whole essay is interesting and touches on several themes discussed in the final chapters of this book.

2 The child begins to establish autonomy when he or she chooses to break the 'symbiotic' relationship. He or she crawls away from mother, for example, just when she had beckoned. This inaugurates the phase when undifferentiated play begins to turn into games with rules. 'The notional end of the period,' writes Shotter '. . . is indicated by the development of the children's ability (around fifteen months) actively to deny their mothers the option of influencing them, in other words, by their learning in effect to say "No". They are now beginning to move around. . . . Thus the period of social games . . . begins. For, if one is to play one's part in a game properly . . . one must be able to cut onself off from others. . . . [So children learn] as their first social skill how to open or close the social link at will' (Shotter 1984, 64–5). Shotter's whole chapter 'The development of personal powers' gives a more finely grained picture of play and early rule-learning than I do.

3 The suggestions put forward by Hamlyn (1978, 76) about speech origins are also relevant here. He makes the important point that long before language has developed in a child 'there may be *propositionally styled thought*'. All the give and take, the time factoring (e.g.

'punctuation') and 'logic' in the patterns of mother/child interaction can, in these terms, be seen as laying down an intricate structured foundation on which subsequent social and linguistic behaviour may develop.

4 This diagram emerged while I was trying to bring various loose ends together at the conclusion of *Born Curious* (1976), 116.

5 The American and British indexes of current educational research (1980) offer only one or two examples of investigations into the general significance of hemispheric specializations. There are a number of studies of 'handedness' and of various forms of writing handicap, but very little of the overall connection between visual and linguistic performance in education.

6 Even people born blind, who then learn to explore the interpersonal world and the world of bodily activity and of sound with especial sensitivity, are programmed to rely on some inner, map-like representations. A study of children, blind from birth, shows that they possess marked innate preparedness for using maps and diagrams. They respond enthusiastically when given a chance to draw on plastic sheets on which they can feel patterns. It would seem that they cannot make full and analytical and reflective use of their three-dimensional bodily experience without some use of inner two-dimensional representations of that world. See John Kennedy and Mary Heywood, 'I see what I feel', *New Scientist* (7 February 1980), 387.

7 The idea that discovering is the process of exploring *and* of transforming one's findings into more abstract and communicable modes was developed in my *Born Curious* (114–15). Columbus's discovery of America was taken as the paradigm case. The crucial work of a discoverer is to *represent an exploration in abstract form* for the (scientific) world to understand and criticize. The crucial work of a teacher is in the opposite direction – to make the world of ideas more concrete for learners themselves to explore. See also Polanyi (1958, 310–11).

8 There is not space to relate these ideas to the acute educational problems of non-affluent countries though some pioneers have already been moving in that direction. Gandhi was an example and so was Ivan Illich, though both took too little note of practicalities. Paulo Freire, on the other hand, both in his theoretical ideas and in his practice, seems remarkably on the ball. See pp. 176–7.

9 Papert's use of the term 'babytalk' was not in *Mindstorms* but was in a television programme on his work. Shallis (1984, 72) is unjustifiably dismissive of Papert's approach.

10 These turtles were some of the first of such robotic toys in which the

technology was open to children. The BBC in the early 1980s developed a similarly mobile and exploratory 'Buggy'. It too had the advantage of having most of its works exposed and yet it was criticized for that very virtue. 'The complete circuits are exposed to spilt coffee and other hazards' (*Practical Computing*, August 1983, 101). I should have thought the exposure was well worth the risk.

11 Dorothy Hodgkin, the discoverer of the structure of insulin and of Vitamin B12, relates how her early interest in crystalline forms was 'seeded' at the age of about 12. First she learnt to grow crystals at home, then she and her sister tried panning for crystals in the irrigation channels in their Khartoum garden. The varied interests of her Crowfoot parents, the one an archaeologist and the other a botanist and authority on textiles, must have provided an open and varied soil for subsequent germination of that seed.

Note on the problem of mental 'contents' – outer and inner speech and outer and inner pictures

Figure 6 is from Gazzaniga and LeDoux's book *The Integrated Mind* (1978, 18). It summarizes the system of inputs and links by which each brain hemisphere has access to the whole sensory environment. There are, first, the direct inputs which, in the main, cross over left to right and *vice versa*, and secondly, the system of commissures which allows all the sensory information coming in to one side to be carried across to the other side. Such a system is common to most vertebrates. This symmetrical arrangement and certain language-related asymmetries are discussed in the next two chapters.

The diagram, and particularly the 'thought balloon' at the bottom, highlight a philosophical problem which we have touched on in our discussions of representations: *where do mental events such as inner speech, acts or inner visualizing actually happen?* The question cannot be confronted adequately in this book but readers should be alert to it. To what extent, for example, are we speaking metaphorically when we say that the mind or its thoughts are 'in' the brain, or that feelings are 'in' the gut, or heart? Though I do, from time to time, refer to 'inner' speech or 'inner' representations, the reader should assume that these phrases imply secondary and often metaphoric meanings. Words and pictures are conceived socially – out there – though *they are stored privately* and are often re-used privately – in the head.

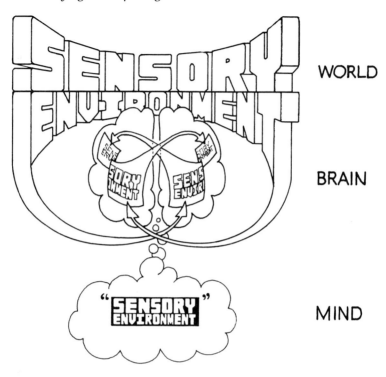

WORLD

BRAIN

MIND

Figure 6   Words referring to the world, to the mind and to the brain (after Gazzaniga and LeDoux 1978)

In the past two decades there has been a notable swing against reliance on in-the-mind terminology. The principal initiator of the trend was Ludwig Wittgenstein in his *Philosophical Investigations* (1968). The trend has been reinforced by many philosophers and other thinkers since. Richard Rorty's *Philosophy and the Mirror of Nature* (1980) is an example. An examination of this problem's bearing on social psychology, and therefore on education, is to be found in Rom Harré's *Personal Being* (1983). Harré makes an important distinction between what he calls subpersonal psychologies and personal or suprapersonal psychologies. In the first, certain subpersonal entities, such as brain hemispheres, cells, hormones or computer-like systems, are seen as acting on each other along chains of causation. These chains, when analysed, provide explanations for the larger systems. In personal and suprapersonal psychologies, higher entities such as persons, families, societies or species are the typical units of interaction and we use these in making our explanations or interpretations. The one kind of explanation tends to be reductive, the other tends to be holistic and interpretive.

In the succeeding chapters, which I wrote before reading Harré's book, I use the analogy of a conductorless chamber orchestra for coping with this problem. The various subpersonal faculties of a mind-body – our five (or more) intellectual competences for example – can be seen in the orchestral analogy as semi-autonomous members of a larger whole. The parts co-operate, as an orchestra or as a mind, in order that music, in the one instance, or mental activity – thought, or speech or visualizing – should happen.

Harré stresses that the main unit of social psychology should be conceived of as being *fully personal*. Persons, he goes on to say, are not only aware of their identity, they can also reflect consciously on themselves and on their actions. He then stresses that there is a third, crucial component of personal being, namely, *agency*:

> To be an agent is to be something more than a creature with a subpersonal psychology of active components like drives, motivations, intentions and desires. To be an agent is to conceive oneself as (hold a theory that one is) a being in possession of an ultimate power of decision and action. A pure agent . . . can adopt new principles and . . . can curb its own desires. (Harré 1983, 29)

From this follows the idea that it is primarily in the public domain – in conversation or in exploration of our environment – that we do all our important learning. Having once learnt a new usage in language or a new section of a map we will have these available 'internally' in diverse memory stores. We can then use them again and again for private thought. In this connection Harré quotes a telling passage from Luria which comes close to being an adequate definition of what 'instruction' is:

> what the child first does with help, and on the instructions of an adult, he later begins to do by himself, supporting himself with his own speech; that speech as a form of communication with adults later becomes a means of organizing the child's

own behaviour, and that function which was previously divided between two people later becomes an internal function of human behaviour. (Luria 1977)

Karl Popper's idea of objective knowledge can be conveniently fitted around this way of thinking about learning. By objective knowledge he means all that knowledge or language, theories, stories, pictures, etc. which has been detached from any particular knower and yet which, with appropriate effort and competence, can be available to any human learner (Popper 1972, 106–90).

8 Divided brain, uniting mind

Something I owe to the soil that grew –
More to the life that fed –
But most to Allah Who gave me two
Separate sides to my head. (Rudyard Kipling)[1]

We think and act, dream and believe by integrating the neuronal processes of different but complementary parts of our brain. The joint activity of the two brain hemispheres, which normally involves both internal and external communication going on between them, is a striking example of such synergy: in this case of two parts working as one.

The general idea that there is a basic two-sidedness in mental activity was familiar in antiquity. Taoists recognized it as an instance of the *yin* and the *yang* which constitute 'the way of knowing and being'. In the west there grew up an unfortunate tradition that the left side of a person was more furtive, devious, 'sinister' than the right. During the nineteenth century many studies of brain injuries made it clear that the left cerebral hemisphere is, for most people, the seat of language. Hence came the somewhat misleading use of the term 'dominant' for the left side of the brain which has direct control over the right side of the body. The general layout of the main nerves and the fact that they mostly cross over from right to left and *vice versa*, just before they reach the brain, has also long been known. Only since the work of researchers such as Roger Sperry and Michael Gazzaniga in the 1960s has the complexity and complementarity of certain cerebral asymmetries begun to be appreciated. Since then the notion of left hemisphere dominance has receded though it has not disappeared. In many activities the left side certainly does take the lead, but in others people are most effective when the right hemisphere takes over. We are now beginning to have an understanding of the important functions not only of the right hemisphere, but also of the subtle ways in which both halves can help each other in a co-operative search for order and meaning.

It has sometimes been assumed that man is the only species which shows this lateralization of function to any marked degree. This is not so. There is evidence for some lateralization in the brains of the more advanced apes and, to a marked degree, in some birds, especially those, such as chaffinches, whose group behaviour seems to depend on a great deal of singing (Springer and Deutsch 1981, 155–6). Nevertheless this kind of specialization is rare and man is the only mammal with pronounced cerebral lateralization. It can be regarded as one of the most important anatomical changes which made possible the evolution of human beings during a period of several million years. In all probability upright carriage, co-operative foraging and hunting, tool use, social feeding and the sharing of skills and language were not separate stages of development but were all aspects of a highly resilient general pattern of adaptation.

The integrative mind

Despite the great advances in neuroscience which have been made in recent years, we are still extremely ignorant about how the brain functions. Enough has already been discovered to make it possible for people seriously interested in education to attempt to understand a crucial paradox: that the mind often works as a unity and yet this unity relies on the workings of subordinate systems – of the two hemispheres and also of some less well understood and more 'ancient' systems such as the thalamus and hypothalamus. The central, 'constructivist' theme of this book could be summarized by saying that smaller bits (of matter or information) are brought together and embodied, by living processes, by evolution, by inquisitive animals, to make perceptual, cognitive and social *wholes* in which new forms are realized, forms which, before such integration, were only possibilities.

There is an extension of this line of thought, speculative but important, which we will now follow. It can be outlined in a manner similar to the above: where there are asymmetries in man's brain and in his motor or perceptual systems, as in his two fields of vision or in his two brain hemispheres or in his left and right handedness, *this gives rise to asymmetries of experience whose very ambiguities are themselves opportunities for realization of higher order patterns of perceptual and cognitive activity.* Binocular vision is the simplest example, though the emergence of sex, perhaps 1000 million years ago, seems to have been a much earlier example of evolution exploiting complementary differences. The integration of pictorial patterns with verbal patterns (both inward mental patterns and outward ones) is, I shall argue, a crucial and illuminating example of this integrative process. It is subtle, hidden from normal introspection and not easy to recognize or to analyse. Nevertheless it may prove to be an important key to understanding many of our more complex experiences of creativity. As children learning what is new or as adults creating or exploring, our actions frequently culminate in combining pictures and words – sometimes in fruitful unity, sometimes in absurdity. This is the key process whose nature I believe we are now in a position to understand.

A useful way of conceptualizing the mind is first, resisting the tendency to regard it as a single *thing* or organ, to think of it as the orchestration of a number of creative processes. The total mind process can then be seen as resembling a string quartet or quintet. There are one or two dominant 'instruments' and several extremely important less conspicuous ones. The functioning of the whole undoubtedly depends on much simpler processes: on mechanical and protective skeletons, for example (understandable mainly in terms of physics), on blood and neurons (understandable in terms of biochemistry and physiology) and the whole system constantly responds to environmental and endocrinal changes. But this extraordinary 'thing' – the brain and all the systems which support it – is not just an efficiently organized and centralized hierarchy. It seems to be more like a co-operative or team and is made up of several high level neuronal systems working in concert and sometimes slipping out of harmony. We shall be mainly discussing the two dominant systems – those two hemispheres – but we should remember that these and other physiological systems have evolved together and have shared in the co-operative aim of survival for hundreds of millions of years. In its outward, human aspect this sharing process has often involved the generation of patterns of information which were communicated in a social group – through patterns of dance, music, pictures and language. Culture is not only about communication between people; it is sometimes about communication between the parts of people.

Education is concerned with helping in this two-fold search for shareable patterns. It is about *co-operation within the brain as well as in the community*. Norman Geschwind was one of the first neuroscientists to bring to popular attention what I call the 'chamber music' view of a multiple brain striving for unity and for shareable meanings; and quite often failing. In the passage below, Geschwind describes a severe case of conflict in one person's behaviour – a woman who had suffered brain damage and whose left hand would sometimes attempt to injure or even to throttle herself. When such violent forces can occasionally be loosed how, he asks, is harmony normally maintained?

> What are the parents' main teaching activities in the first six years of life? No one teaches a child how to talk and no one really teaches a child how to walk, and most people do not teach their children how to read. What they are doing most of the time is teaching the child how to respond to all sorts of emotional impulses – teaching him not to bite the dentist, or to wolf his food, or to kick his sister. . . . The difficulty arises because the parent is trying to bring the many parts of the system under some kind of reasonable control without destroying the pieces. . . . The point to stress is that the events which go on after brain damage demonstrate the surprising fact that *thinking may go on in different places, and that each of the different regions may not be aware of what is going on in the others*. In the same way you may have emotions . . . in several different places in the brain, each of which may not be directly aware of the emotions at the other locations. . . . When someone tells you that he is in two minds about something, he may not realize that this apparent metaphor may be an unwitting statement of fact. (Jonathan Miller, ed., 1983, 124–5, my italics)

Here Geschwind is overemphasizing the negative, judging and constraining roles of parents or teachers and he underestimates both the creative competence of learners and their need to be confronted with appropriate levels of instructional challenge. A certain amount of stress and difficulty are involved in all learning. The important point which arises from his suggestion is this: when confronted with creative or frontier opportunities the learning mind – orchestrating its parts – has symbolic strategies for marking and holding on to these tensions and ambiguities until the time is ripe for their resolution. It has evolved in such a way that it usually copes with the contradictions and limited disharmonies which its parts create. Such exploitation of limited ambiguity is one of the main functions of symbols. As we have seen they sustain the inner dialectic and enable us to tolerate and often to transcend the ambiguities.

Many neuroscientists now accept a loosely hierarchical and holistic view of the brain, and would agree that its higher functions cannot be understood in a purely reductive way. Some, such as Sperry and Hofstadter (who is primarily an information theorist) are prepared to go further and to suggest that complex patterns of activity – symbols or ideas for instance – should be regarded as active fields of force in the brain which can be thought of as causal agents or growing points in the system.[2] This is how Roger Sperry expresses such a view in his essay, 'Mind, brain and humanist values' (Sperry 1983, 31–6). Notice how he uses 'representation' and 'idea' as if they were physiological terms.

In my own hypothetical brain model, conscious awareness does [involve] representation as a very real causal agent. . . . It comes down to the issue of who pushes whom around in the population of causal forces that occupy the cranium . . . [where there exists] a whole world of diverse causal forces, as in no other cubic half-foot of the universe that we know. To make a long story short, if one keeps climbing upward in the chain of command within the brain, one finds at the top those over-all organizational forces and dynamic properties of the large patterns of cerebral excitation that are correlated with mental states of psychic activity. . . . Near the apex of this command system in the brain . . . we find ideas. Man over the chimpanzee has ideas and ideals. In the brain model proposed here, the causal potency of an idea, or an ideal, becomes just as real as that of a molecule, a cell or a nerve impulse. Ideas cause ideas and help evolve new ideas. They interact with each other and with other mental forces in the same brain, in neighbouring brains, and, thanks to global communications, in far distant, foreign brains. And they also interact with the external surroundings to produce *in toto* a burstwise advance in evolution that is far beyond anything to hit the evolutionary scene yet, including the emergence of the living cell.[3]

Research and speculation such as Sperry's is posing many new problems, not only in the field of cognitive psychology, but philosophical and educational ones too. The aim of this chapter is to present, very briefly, some of the recent advances in one part of the neurological field and to follow some clues which lead towards a central educational problem: how is it that visualizing skills and verbalizing skills seem to be anatomically separated and yet can combine so well? First, however, we need to look more closely at the neurological arrangements which are the brain's basis for competence in these iconic and linguistic modes of culture. What sort of neuro-physiological foundation corresponds to the two top levels of our many-levelled educational model? What kind of brain circuitry relates them? In what other ways do the two sides of our brain communicate? And then – an educational question for chapter 9 – is there a systematic way, even perhaps a logical way, of understanding how visual aids facilitate the co-operative process?

Early experiments on split brains

A number of split brain operations were performed in the 1950s and 1960s on patients who had been suffering from intractable forms of epilepsy. There are several major structures or commissures linking the sub-units of the brain, and the largest of these is called the corpus callosum. It contains some 200 million neurons or nearly 20 per cent of the total number in the brain. This and the smaller anterior commissure link the two main cerebral hemispheres. It is these which have been studied most closely. Neuro-surgeons discovered that by cutting the corpus callosum, epileptic seizures which had originated in one half of the brain could be successfully prevented from spreading to the other half and thus causing generalized convulsions. For some time it was thought that after this operation there was no profound change in the patient's mental abilities. Only when Sperry and his colleagues developed precise techniques for testing left and right hemisphere functions in detail was the remarkable, independent capacity of the two brain hemispheres made apparent. It also became clear that patients whose commissures had been severed showed a remarkable capacity for hiding their loss and they would use many ingenious compensating strategies to do this. In other words each hemisphere has its characteristic way of making sense of the world, but also has a strongly co-operative attitude to the other hemisphere, even when inner communication lines have been disrupted.

We have noted the curious fact that in all vertebrates the main nerve channels entering or leaving the brain cross over from left to right and *vice versa*. There are, however, important exceptions: the nerves for the sense of smell, for example, and the nerves from the outer (temporal) areas of the eye's retina go directly to areas of the brain on the same side.[4] The general crossing over of the main nerve channels before they enter the brain has little to do with our present discussion, though it undoubtedly adds to the complexity of the situation. Figure 7 gives a simplified version of the lay-out of the visual fields in the two hemispheres. What is of special interest to us is that there are both internal and external exchanges between parts of the brain. The function of the commissures which link the hemispheres is to carry the internal messages. We are only beginning to understand how much communication between the brain's sub-systems happens *outside* the brain. It was these which the experimenters had to eliminate when they were studying what one brain hemisphere could do on its own.

In experiments, such as that described below, virtually all internal communications between the subject's two brain hemispheres is either permanently cut (by the operation) or interrupted by some local anaesthetic. In other respects the subject appears to be normal. He or she is able to talk, play and generally cope with life, partly because he had already learnt to do these things before the operation, and partly because most of the brain's other routines have not been interfered with.[5] It should also be emphasized that both halves of the brain are habituated to co-operating with each other and that this strong tendency continues even after neuronal communication has been cut or blocked. It is then that the outer means for communication will be brought into maximum use. For example, the right hemisphere listens to and understands a good deal of the speech generated by the left hemisphere even though it is incapable, itself, of generating such speech. This is a crucial point to which we shall return.

In a typical split brain experiment the subject is seated and is asked to look steadily at the middle of a screen on which informa-

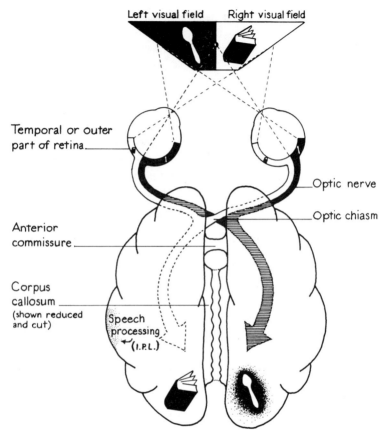

Figure 7 Schematic diagram of a split brain

The corpus callosum or large commissure is shown as having been cut. It has also been reduced in order to show the small anterior commissure. The latter is important for maintaining unity of feeling. The corpus callosum is the principal means, but not the only means, of interhemispheric communication. Each eye sends most of its visual information to the opposite hemisphere via the normal optic chiasm (cross-over) but it also sends a proportion (from the temporal part of the retina) to its own side. So a one-eyed person, even without commissures, who uses his eye actively, can keep both hemispheres fully informed by 'searching'. This is why experimental subjects have to keep their eyes fixed on a central dot. Then all the information from the left side of the screen transfers to the right hemisphere and vice versa. If the commissures are not functioning, either from having been cut or otherwise made inoperative, and if the eyes are fixed, then the two hemispheres will be visually isolated from each other.

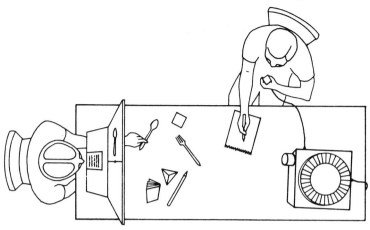

Figure 8   The layout of a split brain experiment (based on Gazzaniga and LeDoux 1978)

The subject is shown as having his main commissure severed. It is best to look at this diagram in conjunction with Figure 7.

tion is flashed for brief periods by a projector behind (Figure 8). One reason for fixing the patient's field of vision and for the brief flashes of information is that during normal perception people constantly search and scan their visual field, and each eye is then able to send back information to both hemispheres. Not only must the eyes be fixed, they must be fixed centrally, on the median line of sight. Why? This is because the outer, temporal, part of each retina is linked directly to the hemisphere on the same side and not to the other side. This is shown by the black and white parts of the retina in Figure 7. While the eyes are centred in this way the two components of the left visual field (the black bits of retina in each eye) are forced to communicate only with the right hemisphere and vice versa. Because the corpus callosum has been cut there can now be no duplicate information coming across from one hemisphere to the other. So there can, for the time being, be no searching and no overlap of visual fields. Only the pathways linking a given visual field to the appropriate, opposite hemisphere remain open. The experimental subject's visual fields are now hemispherically isolated, but his hands will usually be placed in such a way that he can reach under the screen to a table where he is able to feel, but not see, small, varied objects. In view of these complications it is not surprising that it took a long time for the experimental procedures to be refined sufficiently to unravel the various paths of left/right information flow.

A series of pictures (or words) is now flashed briefly onto one side or the other of the screen. If a picture (such as that of a spoon) is flashed on the left side of the screen it will be transmitted to the visual cortex at the back of the right or 'non-talking' hemisphere. If, then, the subject is asked what he has seen, he will *say* 'nothing'. But his right hemisphere *had* seen something; and if he is asked to feel with his left hand among a variety of objects under the screen he will be able to answer the question by silently indicating and grasping the spoon. If the experimenter were then to ask 'what have you got in your hand?' the subject would be likely to answer 'I do not know'. The tactile and pictorial equipment in his brain (right hemisphere) is linked up with the spoon in his left hand. *It understands the verbal question, but cannot produce a verbal answer.* The verbal and linguistic brain equipment of the left brain has been isolated from the right brain and does not know the answer to the question. If a normal person is placed in this blinkered situation the additional sensory information necessary for holistically and pictorially knowing in the right hemisphere and for analytically and verbally knowing in the left hemisphere would be transferred almost instantaneously by the commissures. Both kinds of knowing normally go in step and even after surgery both hemispheres continue to try to co-operate by whatever means are available.

I am indebted to the work of Michael Gazzaniga and Joseph LeDoux for a number of ideas in this chapter which come from their book *The Integrated Mind*. They summarize their own and other people's work on the traffic carried by the commissures and they make important suggestions about the way in which language and some fine skill-processing has become localized in the left hemisphere. They also offer strong grounds for accepting a more balanced understanding of the brain's working. This view goes against what Gazzaniga calls the 'pop' view of lateralization which has tended to regard the right hemisphere as the seat of mystical and intuitive faculties while the left is represented as coldly analytical.[6] The authors, while not denying that there are important innate and acquired differences on the two sides, see the hemispheres as essentially complementary. They suggest, further, that many of the most complex manifestations of mental activity are the result of both hemispheres being habituated to strategies of joint activity. Yet to investigate such suggestions in a normal (i.e. non-split) brain in action would be extremely difficult with present experimental techniques.

It is worth referring again to Gazzaniga and LeDoux's ingenious diagram (Figure 6) which suggests the sharing of basic information between the hemispheres more clearly than Figure 7 does. Each hemisphere is shown as having a complete picture of the visual field. This sharing of all sensory input comes, as we have seen, from three distinct sources: (i) there is the main input from the retina in the eye on the opposite side; (ii) there is the input from the outer, temporal, part of the retina on the same side which is available to a scanning eye; (iii) there is 'transferred' information, coming in across the commissures. This last is what the other hemisphere has just seen or sensed. If one thinks about the large number of vertebrates – horses for example – which have little or no binocular vision but strong sideways vision it is easy to imagine how the powerful commissural links developed in our pre-primate ancestors. Each side of the horse's brain had to know what the other side had seen and the different sensory inputs were shared to make a unified picture of the world. Our human memories, concepts and plans are, as we shall see, not so easily transferred from one side to the other as was the raw, incoming sensory information.

Two eyes for seeing in depth; two brains for thinking in depth

Richard Gregory speaks of 'the dark age' of perception theory when, from about 1900 to 1960, the active, questioning, inference-making nature of our sensory systems was overlooked. Eyes, ears, etc. came to be regarded as receptive openings to the world, analogous to sensitive (but inactive) photographic or phonographic systems.[7] How much of that still fashionable way of thinking about vision was due to the invention of the camera, both as a metaphor and as a begetter of increasingly passive recreational habits of viewing, would be hard to say. One result has been that a combination of the 'pop' and 'dark age' fashions has affected the way in which the brain is now popularly discussed. People who are aware of two hemisphere research often now refer to the brain/mind as if it contained two receptacles –

one for logic and reason, one for feeling and form. There is a more sophisticated version of the same interpretation which regards the two hemispheres as two kinds of computer – one digital and the other analog (resembling a slide rule). There is some value in this analogy (which I use below) but only if we remember that the active brain – unlike a computer – is constantly taking new initiatives, and that there is no 'little man' in there.

Sperry, in the quotation on p. 143, remarked that the joint activity of the two sides of the brain is by far the most advanced sense-making organization in our part of the universe. The sense which emerges, though always incomplete and open, needs to be understood as a unity which transcends its component parts. A commonplace example of the way in which the different brain hemispheres work together in a complex task is as follows. Have you ever noticed how, when you resume reading a book after an interruption, you can often remember precisely where on a page it was that you left off? Then, after your attention has been drawn to quite different activities, you can pick up your position on the page almost at once. Sometimes, though with less reliability, you can remember the whereabouts of a word or quotation on the page long after you have forgotten the other details. Here, it would seem, we have an example of right hemisphere 'mapping' skills making themselves available to complement mainly left hemisphere reading skills. Or consider face recognition. There is a very complex skill for this purpose, located mainly in the right hemisphere. Nevertheless the full use of the skill, in a social context, relies very much on a distinct, left hemisphere capacity for co-ordinated verbal recall. The ability to put a face to a name and a name to a face might seem to be a right hemisphere skill, but it also and essentially requires left hemisphere classifying and naming skills as well as pattern recognizing ones. Here again the capacity is synergistic: it depends on a co-operative dialogue between the two parts.

There is a parallel to this two-sided complementarity from an earlier evolutionary stage. The eyes of humans, of monkeys and their immediate 'ancestors' are forward looking (unlike those of horses) and so work together to give three-dimensional vision. The two eyes resemble each other more closely than do the two brain hemispheres, but because of their different positions in the head they undoubtedly send up differing sensory patterns for the brain to make sense of. This is the crux of the parallel. Many other sources of visual information are also brought in to the process of seeing (e.g. focus, apparent size of object, angle of each eye) and these are all integrated by the brain to form a clear, simple and, apparently, consistent mind's eye picture. One might put it this way: just as seeing in depth is a process which relies on 'seeing double' and on our capacity to resolve limited but informative visual contradictions, so knowing in depth is a continuous process of knowing double (or of multiple knowing) and of resolving many small discords and contrapuntal themes in the total creative work – of making, meaning and imagining.

The situation may be summarized as follows.

(1) The sensory input to the two hemispheres is practically identical.

(2) The way in which such input is *processed* appears to be the main functional difference between the hemispheres. The difference arises both from inherited characteristics (brain circuitry) and from acquired abilities.

(3) The principal evolutionary value of cerebral asymmetry appears to have been that it opened up new possibilities of tool use, of social action, of language and of new individual and collective ways of thinking about the future.

(4) Communication between the hemispheres is maintained, first and fundamentally, by the biologically ancient commissural system and, secondly, by another biologically very recent, cultural system. This communication is maintained largely *by external means* and it is done by each hemisphere 'observing' both what the other does and what it fails to do. I propose to call such interhemispheric communication the 'outside channel', in contrast to the inside, or commissural channels.

The inside and the outside channel

One of the characteristics of brain research in the 1970s was an increasing interest in the kind of information being sent across the commissures from one hemisphere to the other. Until the previous decade the commissures were regarded as probably having little importance. Hence, in part, the readiness of surgeons to cut these massive structures in certain emergencies.

Gradually, however, methods of studying the commissures have been refined. New techniques have been developed and a very different attitude now prevails. It is sometimes possible, for example, to give a short-term local anaesthetic which only affects one hemisphere and leaves the other active. Observations can then be made on people with commissures intact but with one hemisphere temporarily out of action. Gazzaniga and LeDoux have summarized the developing modern attitude with the words 'just as the split brain produces a split mind, interhemispheric communication maintains mental unity'.[8]

But how? How is such communication and unity maintained? It is clearly not just a matter for the commissures. Mental unity depends on other forms of interhemispheric exchange. When one of our sense organs passes a message to the brain that message will be received by both hemispheres. It goes, as we have seen, to one side directly and to the other, either indirectly via various scanning techniques (e.g. eye searching), or via the commissures – by what is sometimes called the commissural 'window'. This is relatively easy to envisage in terms of the old-fashioned model of the brain as a passive receiver – each hemisphere, as it were, with one large window open to the world and a side window (commissural) to the other hemisphere's view of the same world. If, however, we follow Gregory (and others) and regard our perceptions as being the *sense we actively make of* the raw information that comes in, some important conclusions follow. For one thing the incoming raw information will be automatically shared *but not the diverse patterns which different parts of the brain make from it*.

The basic bi-lateral symmetry of the brain, the commissural 'window' and the consequent sharing of incoming information are all very ancient evolutionary developments which go back to the earliest vertebrates and beyond. Binocular vision, as has been noted, is relatively recent, for it has evolved mainly with the primates. Even more recently, certain evolutionary processes in man and in his hominid ancestors have brought about the specialized asymmetry of the two hemispheres. Entirely new possibilities for complex information processing must then have begun to open up and these brought considerable individual and collective advantages to early man. Even contemporary man may still be adapting to the changes.[9]

Inevitably there has been much speculation on how all this affects our understanding of human evolution, of the emergence of culture, of tool use and the very early acquisition of language by human infants. Gazzaniga and LeDoux and other authorities point to the probable existence of different kinds of memory in different parts of the brain. This eases, though it does not solve, one of the continuing problems of brain science: where is the engram of memory? It has long been hoped that some kind of biochemical 'footprint' for memory would be found somewhere in the brain, but so far the search has been unsuccessful. At one time, because many people with severely damaged brains appeared to have remarkably good powers of memory, it was thought that memories might be spread out through the whole brain, like ripples on a pond or the diffuse information in a hologram. This view is now regarded as implausible but the problem remains. Memories certainly appear to have several seemingly redundant locations. Perhaps the concept of a memory *print*, with its suggestion of external impress, has been mislead-ing and we ought to have been thinking of memory as an internally coded *response* system. Gazzaniga and LeDoux make this very point. They emphasize that different parts of the brain are capable of processing different representations of the same perceived world and that this distinction is particularly marked in the complementariness of spatial and verbal memories. Their suggestion – and here they are referring to the example cited on p. 148 – is that the visual 'engram of memory of the spoon is encoded in neural language X and that speech, i.e. the word "spoon" in our example, is represented in neural language Y. *The two languages are insulated from each other and are not conversant with each other inside the brain.*'[10] Here the authors are using 'language' not to refer to natural language but metaphorically as in 'compu-ter language'. The momentous implications of this statement will now be examined.

Because each hemisphere has developed its own coding storage and retrieval systems, each must come to contain great arrays of knowledge whose raw elements it once shared with the other hemisphere; yet many of the constructed response patterns built up from these common elements, cannot be transferred through the commissures. What follows? Such high level pat-terns of information – a critical question enunciated by my left hemisphere, for example, or a map envisaged by my right – *can only be shared by the brain as a whole by action in the world outside, with 'me' (all my faculties) watching*. In other words: *by the 'outside channel'*.

At this stage in the argument I am going a little beyond the inferences and suggestions made by Gazzaniga and LeDoux. Nevertheless they have reached an extremely interesting conclusion in *The Integrated Mind*, one which is of such importance for education that it deserves to be brought out clearly, even if only to invite subsequent checking and qualification. It concerns the manner in which the hemispheres help each other. There is almost certainly great scope for educational experiment in this field, especially in regard to *the varieties of active learning*. In the next chapter we shall consider some of the different meanings of this phrase – 'active learning' – especially in regard to the educational use of pictures.

It seems clear that the right hemisphere cannot receive linguistically coded memories or language-like instructions from the left hemisphere by way of the commissures. The two halves 'are not directly conversant with each other' in language or by any complex representational system. But how much meaning from speech and writing can a normal right hemisphere receive from outside? This is a vexed question. There is no doubt that, under special circumstances, a right hemisphere can *learn* both to receive and to generate speech. This happens if the language centres of the left hemisphere have been damaged. Children and women make such readjustments more readily than men. Work by E. Zaidel, using new techniques for lateralizing vision, suggests that right hemispheres have considerably more capacity for understanding language than had been thought.

> On the vocabulary tests, the right hemisphere did at least as well as a normal ten-year-old, although with the [Matching] Token Test . . . it experienced difficulty characteristic of aphasic [language loss] impairments. . . . When the right hemisphere has adequate time to process a verb . . . it appears to do as well as the left hemisphere. (Springer and Deutsch, 1981, 40).

There are also many examples of isolated right hemispheres being able to respond to questions such as 'what have you in your left hand?', provided that there is scope for a reply to be made by pointing or choosing.

This whole question of how, and how much, the right hemisphere can acquire limited language skills is currently being debated (Gazzaniga, 1984). The following probabilities and possibilities are worth bearing in mind:

(i) The right hemisphere's capacity to learn language can be triggered by early injury to the left brain. There are even a few examples of active language developing in both hemispheres. Is it possible that right brain linguistic sensitivity could be brought about by a person's having to undergo other forms of untraumatic pressure – sustained curiosity, for example?

(ii) The typical right hemisphere not only deals best with manipulo-spatial actions and relationships, it also seems to have a gift, which contrasts with the left hemisphere's analytic powers, for offering holistic and synthetic solutions to problems. These can be made available, externally, to the language side as, for example, when we draw a diagram of some puzzling phenomenon and then derive a verbal explanation from the diagram.

(iii) When confronted with difficulties or problems, each hemisphere shows a capacity for helping the other. They are not competitive (MacKay, 1982). It would seem probable that this readiness to co-operate with, and to defer to, the other side may be an important variable – one which could be greatly affected by culture and education. It might explain what is commonly referred to as the difference between convergent and divergent thinking (Hudson, 1966; Kuhn, 1974).

For education the crux of the matter seems to be this. *The co-operative sharing, between one hemisphere and the other, of relatively complex information patterns happens largely by the outside channel.* Such sharing may occur subliminally, as when small muscular and physiological reactions provide a cue. There is the famous example of a woman whose surgically isolated left hemisphere had to think up an explanation for the cause of blushing and a feeling of embarrassment. Only her right hemisphere had seen the nude photograph in the experiment, but the left hemisphere was well aware of the mood and of the blushing and so tried to make sense of it. This is an instance of what is called cross cueing.

In normal situations of active learning, as in autonomous research or in education, the sharing of two cerebral viewpoints will produce a constant, largely unconscious dialectic. Something keeps happening or being done on the desk or in the lab which demands, first an inner comment, then a mental picture and then, again, a comment. The left (linguistically apt) hemisphere sees a diagram or a model and analyses some of its principles or possibilities. The right (spatially apt) hemisphere, seeing the problem more as a whole, may nevertheless become aware of crucial bits of spoken language for, because it can often *understand* speech to some degree, it is capable of responding in the iconic or enactive mode to the left hemisphere's comments and questions relating to what confronts them both. For example, try naming a scientific problem which worries you – say it out loud – then build up in your right hemisphere the picture which corresponds to it. In any such work the right hemisphere seems to prefer not being hurried. Problems need to be given time in order that concrete operations and manipulospatial processing may proceed at leisure. A difficult matter can be 'slept on' or may go fallow for months. There is a sense, however, in which language is especially good at triggering activity in the right hemisphere, at handing it new problems, or even creating them. Bruner, in a characteristic phrase, reminds us of language's incredible agility, how, with systems of sign and syntax it can 'turn reality over on its beam ends beyond what is possible through actions and images' (1967, 11).

There is evidence that each hemisphere is aware of its own strengths as well as of the limitations of the other. Each will, therefore, often know when to take the lead (Blakeslee 1981, 15–16). In cases of commissurotomy, one half brain, when short of information, may attempt to get more by interpreting whatever inconspicuous evidence happens to be available. We have noted instances of this in examples of cross-cueing. Sometimes the lack of information or comprehension on one side may lead to more than the guesswork about a blush or a tremor. In an extreme case, similar to that quoted on p. 142, the split brain patient 'was angry and forcibly reached for his wife with his left hand while his right hand grabbed the left hand in an attempt to stop it' (Springer and Deutsch 1981, 35). Such examples are rare. The mind (by which I mean all the parts working in concert), even after injury, generally acts as a totality which is committed, at conscious and unconscious levels, to making sense of what is going on. Its need for extra cues and for alternative interpretations of events (sometimes called curiosity) is likely to be especially strong whenever new and difficult, i.e. 'frontier', tasks are under way.

We now begin to see why learning by doing can justify its claim to be at the very heart of genuine education. Such 'doing' may be unspectacular and invisible to an observer but it is the essential condition for full interhemispheric consultation. The occasional importance of doodling or of words spoken under the breath also begins to be apparent. A teacher's presentation of a verbal cue or a diagram is often of great importance, but it is the learner acting on it which brings about the acquisition of a new concept. Whenever he or she is at an intellectual frontier it would seem to be especially important for one hemisphere to let the other know that there are new, challenging problems or patterns in the offing. There are occasions when such dialectical responding action can happen secretly, as it does in many meditative practices. The silent worshipper, for example, will activate fairly repetitive inner speech (*mantras*) in order to free the right hemisphere so that its work of imagery may be more spontaneous. In teaching, such acts may be no more than a scribble on paper, the humming of a tune or the trying out of an experiment, but they may still be growing points. The teacher's intervention at such early stages must be gentle: a clue is proffered, the learner's doubting gaze is honoured, questions are left open.

It may be helpful to represent the idea of identical data being stored and processed differently by an analogy. The situation is rather as if there were two blocks of government offices, both concerned with studying and, partly, with controlling one or two spheres of activity in a state. Let us assume that both buildings handle information relating to population and economic trends. We do not quite know what goes on in each building except that there is a lot of data being circulated. Some of this, if we could eavesdrop, would seem to be about simple matters easily understandable in both office blocks. Some of it, however, is in highly technical codes and jargon, only properly understood by those who work on one of the two sides. The general arrangements, such as plumbing and electrical supplies, are similar in both buildings. There are also several extremely busy telephone cables (the commissures) connecting both blocks, but these are not used for discussion of policy or other complex matters. Almost all the basic data that is recorded about the state goes into both blocks either directly or by being shared through the telephone link. It is then recorded. The main differences are in the manner of the recording and processing systems. Consequently, when you come to examine the ground floors, where the final processing goes on, you find that the output of the two blocks appears to be quite different. This is because one block has recently acquired, and found room for, a high-powered digital computer and storage system which can handle small bits of information at great speed, while the other block continues to rely on well tried and flexible graphic display systems. One block turns out lists of names, statistics and logical relation; the other prints analog material – maps, charts and graphs. A naive observer might see little connection, but he would, of course, be wrong. We, the 'senior civil servants' – even though our knowledge of how the recording systems work is sketchy – are able to make use of such maps and of statistics and to apply them to practical problems outside. We can, therefore, get a far better understanding of the state by combining the two modes of representation.

At this point the familiar philosophical problem appears: who *are* 'we' or the 'civil servants'? It is always wise to avoid seriously postulating a 'little man' inside the real brain or, for that matter, locating a soul or even a 'seat of consciousness' there. This is the limitation of all such models. Rather than a 'little man' it would be nearer the truth to speak of a pervasive 'consciousness' or a variously focused information flow, moving to and fro in order to integrate the output of both. In this way we can represent the outside channel and the two, internally connected towers as resembling one meaning-making system or 'mind', with both inner and outer communication systems hard at work.[11]

If the scientific study of the brain can give strength to our intuitive suspicion that passive learning, the merely verbal or the merely photographic memory, is not of great value, so much the better. It should now be possible for teachers to approach many old problems with less guesswork and more systematic understanding. A beginning is made along these lines in the next chapter. There are, however, one or two further important ideas deriving from Gazzaniga and LeDoux's work which should be considered first. They do not belittle the importance of right hemisphere abilities nor the crucial, still often mysterious, functions of other parts of the brain, but they do suggest that there is an important sense in which language-like systems of representation take priority over other information processing systems (Gazzaniga 1984, 56).

Fine skills and language

Gazzaniga's theoretical understanding of language, on which the above analogy is based, focuses on one particular small bulge which exists in both hemispheres and is called the *inferior parietal lobule*. Its approximate position is shown in Figure 7. In non-human primates this – the IPL – is concerned with fine manual control and manipulation of things in space – leaping, grasping, handling food, etc. In normal humans the IPL in the left hemisphere is especially adapted to the linear processing of language, whereas the right IPL continues to control many of the large scale manipulospatial activities.[12] Other parts of the brain are also concerned with aspects of language, such as its comprehension, its storage, etc. Gazzaniga and LeDoux suggest that language *emerged both with and out of tool using*. Both activities require an ability to identify and to classify quickly; and they require the flexibility to enlarge or modify classification systems when necessary. When someone reclassifies an unusual object to serve as a tool, say, in place of a more customary one, the choice is not random; certain abstract criteria (not necessarily verbal) will be used. (Has this stone the *sharpness* and *strength* to be a knife?) Gazzaniga and LeDoux put it thus: 'Tool-using precipitated a focus on objects, and object naming was the result'.[13] But there was, surely, more to it than classifying. The most striking feature shared by language and fine manual skills is the degree to which they both depend on precise linear planning in their expression – that is in getting the right sub-units of action quickly in the right order without too many errors and without excessive spacing and retracing (Springer and Deutsch 1981, 200, citing Kimura).

This matter of linear planning relates to the aspect of early language which Marshack calls the 'storied' part (1972, 36–7). Marshack accepts the further idea, also suggested by Susanne

Langer (1957), that many forms of non-verbal communication, such as the gestures and rituals which symbolized seasonal or territorial boundaries, were all woven into the ancient web of early human communications. Symbols were, in essence, powerfully charged and often ritualized markers for momentous happenings which patterned and punctuated time, territory and organization. If this supposition is correct, it would appear that two main kinds of sign system for holding and dealing with complex information began to evolve together – stories *and* symbols. The former are essentially sequential and language-like. The latter can be made (represented) at many levels of psycho-motor action. They seem to be connected, very often but not exclusively, with the right hemisphere and with its need to be in communication with the left hemisphere. There must always have been overlap and complementarity in their use. It is hard to conceive of the left hemisphere of early *homo sapiens* evolving unilaterally, with language forging ahead and picture-making lagging. So the suggestion which I am putting forward is that man's picture-making propensities (both internal and external) played an important part (as they still should in education) in enlarging culture and in feeding the left hemisphere with new, subtle and challenging problems.[14]

In a passage of particular interest to developmental psychologists and teachers Gazzaniga and LeDoux make two suggestions about how the fine skills of language became localized in the left IPL. They note that in cases of early injury either IPL *can* make 'space' in its nerve circuitry for language; but because human infants are adapted to complete dependence on an adult and because they attain extensive manual and bodily skills belatedly, the left IPL which has evolved as the most 'skilful' part of the brain is available for language learning. Under the heading 'Competition for synaptic space' Gazzaniga and LeDoux (1978, 60) write as follows of a human infant:

> The burden is on language to acquire space. One way this could happen is for language to be programmed to emerge in development prior to manipulospatiality. As it turns out language does emerge early. . . . In contrast manipulospatial functions come in much later. As Inhelder and Piaget have shown, the ability to draw and copy geometric designs and

manually appreciate spatial forms is a late-developing skill (sixth or seventh year). This later development correlates well with the timetable by which language, which starts out bilaterally in development, becomes largely left-lateralized in most right-handers. . . . This places the burden of [developing] the body-space map entirely on the right IPL.

It seems not unreasonable to suggest that primitive tool use, primitive word-stringing, primitive symbolizing, all combined to lay down rule-governed social interactions and shared cultural experiences from which grammar, speech (dominating one hemisphere) and art (dominating the other) gradually developed. Each development would help the other. We can paraphrase Hamlyn (1978, 76) and say that the most highly skilled acts resemble language in being 'propositionally styled'. There are inescapable logical elements in lighting a fire, for example, or in building a hut. It might then be asked, where were the finest rule-governed, proto-linguistic procedures 'laid down'? Presumably, as has been suggested (chapter 6), this happened first in the culture of a group, and the process would sometimes be activated and focused by pictures, dances or rituals. Secondly, at a much slower, more selective, phylogenetic pace, the patterns were laid down in the evolution of the brain; but especially – it would now appear – in the 'fine wiring' of one particular lobe – the left IPL.

Two further considerations mesh nicely here. Gazzaniga and LeDoux produce some evidence to suggest that language took over some of the spare (i.e. duplicated) brain tissue that had been available for manipulospatial purposes such as jumping and handling. But why was it 'spare'? They do not suggest this but it is hard to resist the idea that it may have been spare just because those hominid ancestors had 'come down from the trees' a few million years before. You can afford to make manipulospatial mistakes on the ground which would cost you dear up aloft; and you can also make manipulospatial experiments with loose sticks and stones. This links with the increasing richness of social life and with the 'educational' problem mentioned above, that not only was it necessary to find synaptic space – spare circuitry in the brain – which could be made over for innovations in very fine skills and language, but that the problem of finding time and space for learning must also have become increasingly acute: how were those hominid young to find time, in a crowded and dangerous developmental programme, for all their language learning to be achieved? Gazzaniga and LeDoux suggest that the evolutionary answer was to get language learning over very early, before most of the manipulospatial skills have to be learnt. Hence the gradual extension of the mother-dependent babyhood of humans and the laying down of patterns of interpersonal skills and – small price with parents taking an interest – the delay in acquiring survival skills.

One obvious objection to the main idea may occur to readers. How has it come about that a person's right, more skilful hand remains, apparently, under the control of the left, language-based hemisphere? If the linguistic 'circuitry' of the left IPL has crowded out some of the left hemisphere's synaptic space formerly specializing in manipulospatial control, we would expect the right hand to be less skilful. Gazzaniga and LeDoux have experimental data, based on brain damage studies, which suggest an answer (1978, 59–62). There is, in the region of the left IPL a group of nerve cells which still retain control over the right hand's most precise skills, and yet these appear to be controlled by a combination of both hemispheres. The right hemisphere seems, in some way, to map out the general strategy of skilled manipulospatial acts and then to send signals, probably across the corpus callosum, to the left IPL as to how these plans may be given detailed, linear programming and transmitted to the right hand. It seems, therefore, as though language evolved as a super-skill out of, and to some extent replacing, high level manipulospatial abilities. The highest manual skills of all (writing or manipulating fine tools, for example) draw both on the mapping powers of the right hemisphere and on the very fine, language-favouring circuitry of the left IPL. This is not, I think, running too far ahead of Gazzaniga's suggestions. It is just one more example of a general principle that difficult mental tasks (difficult usually meaning in some sense *novel*) require a co-operative, integrated endeavour from the various 'component' brains which, as a system, constitute the mind.

Education of the whole

There is a danger, when we think about learning and education and about the physiological structures on which they depend, that we reify the process; we make a thing or a machine out of a learner, or we lapse, inadvertently, into what Karl Popper calls the 'bucket theory' of learning (1972, 60–3). 'Inculcate values; pour them in!' people say, and we easily go along with innumerable variations on that sterile, instrumental way of thinking. A number of writers, reacting against this trend, have seen some of the revolutionary implications of twin hemisphere research for education. Yet we are only just beginning to come to grips with these (Bogen 1975). If any normally educated readers (i.e. not artists or musicians) have doubts about the potentialities of their right hemispheres they might find it worthwhile to spend a few hours working through Betty Edwards' *Drawing on the Right Side of the Brain*. To follow her exercises carefully can be a remarkably revealing and therapeutic experience. Nevertheless, for anyone who thinks about this subject, there is a danger of becoming trapped in yet another version of the bucket theory. 'Unleash the hidden genius in your right hemisphere!' the advertisers will say, as though the hidden genie were *in* there. Whereas the truth seems to be that your or my 'hidden powers' will only be adequately tapped by an education concerned with our active wholeness, with word and image and feelings and physique and community – with the whole 'orchestra' creating the music – *out there*. So when we, as teachers, think about brains or parts of brains as learning and growing systems, it is generally important that we do so within this kind of overriding concept: that the whole orchestra is understood as being an exploring, hypothesis-making, hypothesis-testing, ambiguity-sustaining, meaning-seeking *person*. And not only this, personal knowing all goes on within a patterned flow of language and art, of shifting human feeling and intention, a flow which has a very ancient, influential history and a future too, patterned with antiquity.

It is inevitable that we sometimes project mechanical and partial explanations onto living systems; as we might if we were surgeons and were trying to mend the systems. We tend to remain at that level and this comes largely from our unwillingness, especially when we try to speak with the authority of science, to acknowledge that higher orders and emergent systems *do* exist; and that they exist most obviously in the living world and in that growing boundary of life which we sometimes call mind and spirit.[15]

In the educational model which we have been considering it has been an active person who, as teacher, mediates structure to a corresponding learner who assimilates and integrates what is offered. Active learners unconsciously use the whole of their brain-body system, without much thought about which subsystem is leading and which is following. It generally depends on what kind of problem is being faced; but also on prevailing beliefs and fashions. In the contemporary reductionist climate the individual person is far too readily seen as a victim of his or her environment or of hormones or even of 'nerves'. Yet our whole nervous system is in the business of meaning-making and meaning-seeking. Bits of it (the retina of the eye for example) build up their own minor patterns of sense in advance but the major patterns or representations of our world – those on which our life depends for its coherence and success – can only be apprehended, and perhaps enlarged, by the brain-body as a whole, with all its parts working in reasonable harmony – exploring, creating, minding.

We have considered a combined neurological and psychological account of the way in which the two hemispheres probably work together. The scientific evidence for this is accumulating. There is corroboration too from general educational experience and from those not very reliable sources, introspection and intuition, that the highest forms of creative action and discovery depend on complementary functioning of the two hemispheres, acting as one whole. Roger Sperry warns his colleagues not to lose sight of the reality of this conscious, high level unity and of what he calls the 'emergent property of cerebral activity as an integral component of the brain process . . . which exerts a directive holistic form of control over the flow pattern of cerebral excitation'.[16]

Much unexplored terrain stretches ahead here, with many blanks and daunting puzzles; and neuropsychologists will be right to warn us, teachers and generalists, not to jump too far. Nevertheless I think we are justified in feeling greater confidence in many of our hunches about the need for breadth and for dynamic balance in education. Not only is there a constant *Tao* or creative middle way to be sought between the two main kinds of cerebral process, but we must also assume that similar integration goes on between these and the other brain systems, and between all these and neuromuscular and endocrine activities which underly them. They all affect our moods, our health, our energy and our direction.

Gazzaniga remarks, in a phrase reverberating with philosophical and educational import, 'one's system of beliefs about the world arises *as a consequence of considering what one does*' (p. 150, my italics). The commissures are certainly of great importance. They share out all the basic data, transmit vital, staccato instructions and, doubtless, do much more. They are necessary for unified mental development but they are only one means among many, to this end. *The most sophisticated communication between right and left hemispheres, the facing and sharing of difficult problems, much of the emotionally charged frontier work, goes on right in front of our noses and it depends on what we actually make and draw, play and say.* This, in my opinion, is an educational bomb-shell which the neuropsychologists have detonated, the implications of which teachers and educational innovators must now begin to explore.

Notes

1 Quoted at the head of chapter viii in *Kim*.
2 'My belief' writes Hofstadter 'is that the explanations of "emergent" phenomena in our brains – for instance, ideas, hopes, images, analogies and finally consciousness and free will – are based on . . . an interaction between levels in which the top level reaches back down towards the bottom level and influences it, while at the same time being itself determined by the bottom level' (1979, 709). He is, apparently, both a determinist and its opposite. When hard-pressed, original thinkers often find themselves playing with contradictions.
3 In *Science and Moral Priority* (1983) Sperry is much more convincing about 'who pushes whom around' in the brain than he is when he tells us how scientists and others might create a value system for the world. (The quotation is from pp. 31, 32, 33 and 36.)
4 For an ingenious suggestion as to why the main nerves of the (primitive) sense of smell are not crossed over and how it came about that, at an early, pre-vertebrate stage of evolution, all the

other main nerve channels were crossed over, see Kingsbourne (1978, 553–6).

5 It is rare for the anterior commissure to be severed because of its involvement in maintaining a person's emotional sense of unity. But it is still possible to arrange experiments so that crucial information does not leak across. For a full account see Springer and Deutsch (1981, ch. 2).

6 Ornstein's *The Psychology of Consciousness* (1975) is wide-ranging and interesting but exemplifies the 'pop' view.

7 Richard Gregory's account in R. L. Gregory and E. H. Gombrich (eds), *Illusion in Nature and Art* (1973), is useful and his appreciation of and criticism of *gestalt* psychology is particularly interesting.

8 Op. cit., 18.

9 I rely more on the social and co-operative picture of hominid evolution, as outlined by Richard Leakey and Roger Lewin in *Origins* (1977), than on the, perhaps, over-aggressive picture which has been popularized by Lorenz, Ardrey and others. But see Midgley (1984, 65, 210).

10 Op. cit., 132 (my italics).

11 For a survey of some of the philosophical problems raised by the question of a homunculus in the mind see Rorty's *Philosophy and the Mirror of Nature* (1980), ch. 2, 'The invention of the mind'. See also Fergus Kerr's 'Demythologising the soul' in *New Blackfriars* (April 1983). The emphasis of both is that inner meanings and inner entities – 'mentalism' – should not be taken too seriously. The more fundamental meanings are those that people share in social and cultural action; and most inner words, pictures and 'operations' derive from these. 'Those who want to find inner essences are just as bewitched as those who find entities in the mind' (Kerr 1983, 191). See also my note on p. 136.

12 Ch. 3, op. cit. There have been a number of cases where a brain tumour affecting the whole of one hemisphere has been successfully removed. A minority of such cases have involved excising the left hemisphere and even here, after a period of re-learning, a measure of language ability has been regained by the remaining (right) hemisphere. This shows how similar the potentialities of the two hemispheres are and how linguistic and other memories are retained in each. It might also be adduced as an argument against the kind of innate specialization in the left IPL which Gazzaniga and LeDoux propose. However the question is not likely to be resolved by studies of adult cases, for there is no doubt that some early memories are stored in both hemispheres. It is possible to imagine a right IPL, forced to function on its own, developing the ability to

convert its largely non-linguistically coded memories to serve as a basis for language, thus gradually coming to resemble its innately more flexible 'twin' – now removed.

13 It will be clear from the next paragraph that I do not regard the 'object naming' suggestion about the possible origin of language as being sufficient. The more extensive view derives from Susanne Langer and others. For a summary of the wider view, which is in opposition to E. O. Wilson's sociobiology, see Marshall Sahlins (1976) quoted in Michael Gregory *et al.* (eds) *Sociobiology and Human Nature* (1978), 222.

14 One of the difficulties about accepting Julian Jaynes' ideas in *The Origin of Consciousness in the Breakdown of Bicameral Mind* (1982) is that he compresses the alleged happenings into such a short time span.

15 T. F. Torrance, in a number of his writings, has developed the theological implications of this view, of the many layered cosmos 'as an open textured system in which novel forms of order constantly emerge'. See, for example, his *Divine and Contingent Order* (1981), ch. 3, 'Theological and scientific world views'.

16 Quoted by Gazzaniga, op. cit., 141. In *Science and Moral Priority*, where Sperry develops these ideas, he also makes a series of political suggestions about how an élite group of thinkers could establish a world-wide code of ethics. He quite rightly removes a 'little man' or 'seat of consciousness' from the brain, but then postulates a 'little committee' for the world as a whole, but see note 2 above.

9 Words and images

I do not think we have begun to scratch the surface of training in visualization – whether related to the arts, to science, or simply to the pleasure of viewing our environment more richly. (Bruner 1968, 34)

It is better to speak of imagin*ing* structures and formulat*ing* propositions, of Picturing and Sentencing. . . . The vehicles for scientific thought are not only propositions but pictures, models and diagrams as well, because these latter control, to a large extent, what propositions appear in the heart of a theory. (Harré 1970, 13, 15)

Gazzaniga and LeDoux were not the first people to suggest that some of the most characteristic and creative mental activities do not occur *in* a certain part of the brain but happen, rather, *outside* – between people and between the different parts of the brain. Their precise way of formulating this, in terms of the need of each hemisphere to draw on the experience of the other by watching what it does, is arresting, and it bears on a central problem of visual learning. Gazzaniga emphasizes that it is our *belief system* about the world which is crucial – all those hypotheses and constructs and sense-making patterns which we hold in readiness, and even the contradictions which these may involve. Consciously and unconsciously we assemble and extend this system of beliefs by attending to – often unconsciously watching – our own and others' acts. Our main mental sub-systems are therefore open to feedback, not only from their own performances but from those of adjacent sub-systems too: hence my analogy of the small, conductorless, orchestra for the active, learning mind.

It is useful to remember Polanyi's teaching at this stage: that such learning-from-what-we-do does not in general mean stopping action and thinking about it, though that may sometimes be helpful; nor, certainly, does it mean introspection and self-concern. Gazzaniga is referring to something like Polanyi's integration of sub-skills along with focal awareness – a movement from subsidiaries towards competent integrative action and knowledge. What results from such integrative action is both an external achievement *and* the enrichment of our tacit knowledge which itself is the ground from which competences and belief systems arise. It is the quality of all such action or potentiality for action which counts; and quality – as in an orchestra – is not only located in one mental faculty or part but also in the synergy of all.[1]

Once this shift of viewpoint is made – that we really do learn more by what we do than by what we passively receive through our senses and why this should be so – a number of new educational problems and possibilities begin to appear. They are particularly interesting because formerly some were not much more than teachers' hunches, but they now take their starting point from a promising neuropsychological base. They also open up towards sociological, theological and even political issues. What sort of learning action, for example, is involved in a handshake? Or where does prayer fit in? Or school ritual? Or examinations? Or pornography? Or television viewing?

I propose after a brief discussion of television, to follow up a selection of these issues and to group them round three focuses of current educational importance.

(i) What *is* a visual aid and under what circumstances do pictures bring learning to life? If we can make sense of the great variety of iconic representations which are involved in education can we also get clues as to how they might be used more effectively?

(ii) What would happen if all children were to perceive themselves as generally competent and successful? And what might be the consequences of putting into practice a curriculum based firmly on the main modes of human competence for culture which have been outlined in this book?

(iii) And then, how can we create or recreate an educational system in which all young adults would see reflected something of their own great potential? This would require a far more open secondary and tertiary system, in which frontiers would be seen as real and challenging. How, in short, might rising generations come to perceive themselves not only as members one of another but also –

fleetingly perhaps – as part of One much greater? This is the question which chapter 10 will address.

Visual dope

Television and its derivatives provide the main pictorial experience for the majority of people in affluent countries. That experience is very largely passive and that is why, in large doses, it has harmful effects. 'Prove it', say all the media apologists, and if the case against them makes any headway they mention the fact, as though it were a trump card, that there is, after all, a 'switch-off button'. Popular concern about this tends to focus on violence and crude sex. It will always be difficult to demonstrate a clear causal chain between suggestive material on the screen and selfish behaviour off it. Such causation may be powerful and may work in diffuse and roundabout ways. The evil is not just a question of excessive violence and carnality. Even if these were the heart of the matter it would always be difficult to demonstrate either a sufficiently precise and significant statistical trend in youthful behaviour or a clear causal chain between, say, a violent video and a violent crime. There probably are such causal connections but they almost certainly operate through networks of synchronic causes and not through identifiable chains. It is clear, at all events, that the problem is complex and deeply rooted.

Despite the difficulties of proof in such a controversy, it is interesting to bring to bear on the question of television viewing some of the ideas which were touched on in the last chapter. First there arises the question of a person's 'belief system' and the degree to which such systems may be impoverished or enriched. Then, secondly, I shall suggest that just because television and similar forms of viewing inhibit active responses, and in particular active interhemispheric dialogue, the medium should not normally be regarded as educational at all. Some exceptions to this will also be noted.

We have been thinking of a person's belief system – all his or her emotional and cognitive readiness for making sense of the world – as having its leading edge 'out there' in a person's external action and in the corresponding external dialogue of an active person's two hemispheres. True, the total system's conclusions, tested schemas, maxims and memories are filed away in various memory stores, but these remain significant because they – the stored word and image patterns for example – might get together in the future and be active again outside. Such *potentiality* is extremely difficult, if not impossible, to measure empirically but its importance is obvious.

The possible dangers to mental systems can now be seen in two guises: first as the impoverishment or undernourishment of these word-and-image potentialities and secondly from their possible 'pollution'. Any discussion of this kind of problem is likely to be put out of court by the common prejudice of intellectuals against the use of any negative, strongly evaluative words such as 'evil', 'corruption' or 'pollution', when cultural matters are under discussion. It is easier if you coin a technical term, as Bruner did when he described the focus of fear and panic in a child's mind as a 'pre-emptive metaphor' (see p. 44). However, the intellectual climate in this respect is changing and we may come to understand better how to diagnose our problems in intellectually respectable terms. Practical solutions, it must be admitted, might involve some censorship but far more important will be the development of more adequate immune systems in the minds of both adults and children. It is no more possible to measure the quality of a cultural milieu then the belief systems which it nourishes, but a useful touchstone is to ask: what kinds of human action and interaction characterize the period after the off switch has been turned?

The strongest – and rarely emphasized – case against television arises from the passivity of those who watch, and this is given additional weight by the ideas of the preceding chapter. There is a passionate and confused indictment of television (also some shrill polemic) in Jerry Mander's book *Four Arguments for the Elimination of Television*. Two chapters – 'How television dims your mind' and 'How we turn into our images' – bear closely on the present theme. The most crucial point, however, is only made obliquely in a quotation from Merrelyn and Fred Emery's study of Australian television:

> The evidence is that television not only destroys the capacity of the viewer to attend; it also, by taking over a complex of *direct and indirect neural pathways*, decreases vigilance – the general state of arousal which prepares the organism for action. . . .

The continuous trance-like fixation of the TV viewer is then not attention but distraction – a form akin to daydreaming. (1978, 205–6, my italics)

The concept of 'attention' here is the same kind of active interest in the outside world which true education always involves. The Emerys do not amplify their reference to 'direct and indirect neural pathways' but the phrase seems to imply something very like the idea of inner (commissural) channels and an external channel between the hemispheres which we have been discussing.

Just how might interhemispheric co-operation suffer when one is watching television? The answer is suggested by the story of the school inspector who once asked a child why she preferred stories on radio to stories on television and received the reply: 'the scenery is so much better on radio'. The anecdote may be apocryphal but its truth will be evident to readers who have seen the television version of a novel which they know well. Sometimes the television scenery is authentic and colourful but it rarely seems right. Your own visual version, even though it may fade and change over the years, does feel right because it is part of your own response to the book. The process works the other way too. If you have been in the habit of looking at natural scenes or at still pictures attentively you probably scan and search and ask questions of them in considerable detail. As you move along the following spectrum – natural scenes, detailed paintings, theatre, cinema film, television – your eye movements and your opportunity to pause and reflect become less and less, and the stories you tell and the questions you ask in response to the pictures become fewer and fewer. At the limit you find yourself neither putting your words to those pictures, nor your pictures to those words. It is all done for you. A similar critique can be developed in regard to students' activity or passivity in their use of computers.

On the other hand there is evidence to suggest that children around the age of 6 or 7 often operate differently. They can, it seems, use television as a kind of 'image bank' to enrich their own repertoire for concrete operations thinking.[2] At a more advanced level too there can be value in the way in which illustrations of unusual phenomena or of complex scientific concepts can be shown on short bursts of video. Here, as in the earlier example, the educational gain will be substantial if the viewing is done against a background of discussion and of parental or teacher involvement.

The harmful effects of heavy television viewing are probably greatest in early adolescence. My evidence for this is anecdotal but it does appear that young adults are particularly prone to becoming hooked on television. This stage – round about the age of 12 to 15 – is when a person's cognitive abilities are moving towards abstract thinking and this development should take place quite rapidly. Piaget called it the period when 'formal operations thinking' is rapidly acquired and consolidated. By this he means the confident handling of abstract ideas in addition to those 'concrete' operations (mainly inner picturing) which have been the mental stock in trade of, for example, a 9- or 10-year-old. In order to make this move towards formal operations thinking an adolescent needs to be adventurous and to have plenty of practice in using his existing inner kit of diagrams at a demanding level (i.e. at the 'frontier') and in relating these to abstract verbal statements.

Seymour Papert gives an example of how the foundations for a move from concrete to formal images are laid down. From an early age he was haunted and inspired by inner images of gears and gear boxes. They were an essential component in his inner tool kit of models and images. 'Anything is easy' he writes, as he looks back 'if you can assimilate it to your collection of models.' He even claims that these gears became his 'transitional objects'; he fell in love with them. The point is not that the young learner abandons the use of concrete, inner images but that he or she acquires sufficient experience and confidence in their use to make mental images and mental sentences co-operate whenever the problems faced are of sufficient complexity to require this.[3]

To argue for the 'elimination of television' is certainly far fetched. If a child is watching television for an hour or so each day and is discussing it with others, and if that child is also engaged in playing, discussing and reading, in making things and helping, that might be regarded as a balanced diet. But the difficulty arises because so many parents work under heavy pressure of time and space and they give up the struggle to keep lively interactions and activities going. The current towards passive entertainment easily builds up to the point where it is irresistible.

We need to cut through the common cant which defers to TV as essentially an ally, as a 'most promising educational aid', etc., and to recognize it for what it generally is – a kind of technological valium with addictive tendencies. The real life alternatives are infinitely more interesting; but they are hard to get at. You need some basic competence to explore real mountains or real forests and you need trained senses and trained bodies to respond actively to them. Even more, you need social and linguistic competence to cope with crowded streets and busy homes.

Pictures for telling stories from

One of the most urgent long-term needs of education, and especially in the education of young adolescents, is a great enrichment of 'right hemisphere' competence – competence in visualizing, in making music, in bodily movement and in social feeling. Yet such gifts should not be thought of as being *in* the right hemisphere: rather, they involve it. Just as language itself needs to be woven in and out of the whole curriculum, and mathematics throughout much of it, so do these predominantly right hemisphere competences.[4]

In the 1970s David Warr and I were making some research enquiries in this direction. We were trying to understand *what visual aids were*.[5] Both of us had worked in poor countries, as well as in rich ones, so we shared a view – perhaps a prejudice – that simple visual aids might turn out to be educationally better than some of the high technology gadgets that were finding their way into our relatively affluent schools. If simple visuals, such as those used by Paulo Freire (see pp. 176–7), *were* better we wanted to know how this potential might be more fully realized.

Our enquiries eventually led us to the work of the neuro-psychologists which has been discussed in the last chapter, and so to the idea that visual aids were primarily to do with one part of a person learning from another part (as the left does from the right hemisphere and *vice versa*) and only in a secondary sense were they to be understood as being the information which comes from you, my teacher, or from you, my television screen. In our terms a visual aid would be described as *any iconic representation of the world (map, diagram, etc.) which enables an active*

learner to enlarge his understanding. Such a definition covers both
'inner', self-generated representations (Papert's mental gear
wheels for example) as well as teacher-provided or culturally
provided pictures; by stressing the active enlargement of understanding this definition effectively excludes the more extreme
forms of passive entertainment.[6]

We started with teachers and children in the classroom –
mainly 12- and 13-year-olds in Oxfordshire middle schools and in
one private school. Almost all the teachers in our survey believed
that visual aids were important and they frequently used them,
but there was an extremely wide divergence of view as to how
this should be done. Nor was there evidence of a coherent
theory to guide such use. We tried to discern a pattern or taxonomy for visual aids and it became clear that we would not
find any satisfactory classification of pictures *per se*. On the other
hand a classification of *picture use* in learning did seem to be
emerging.

One hypothesis had to be discarded early on. We had assumed
that the use of pictures would, almost automatically, be accompanied by more questioning and more 'openness' among the
children than in mainly verbal teaching. This was far from being
the case. One history teacher, whom Warr studied in considerable detail, used pictures constantly, but it was almost always the
teacher's story which had to be told by the children, from any
given picture, and it was his interpretation – generally a clear-cut
story of goodies and baddies – which predominated. The main
reason for this was that a selective examination was not far away
and even though the children enjoyed learning, they did so in an
atmosphere in which testable facts seemed more important than
imagined feelings or interesting problems. In contrast to this
there were other teachers of history and of English who used
pictures to generate stories in a much more flexible way. One
such teacher would ask children to think about a picture in terms
of the emotional experience of the gaolers as well as of the
prisoners. And she would then look for alternative and even
contradictory explanations about what was going on in the world
beyond the picture and would sometimes leave these alternatives
in the children's minds, with a question mark hanging between.
Children certainly need a framework of fact and firm data but
they also need to hold on to, and to feel at home with, big

Figure 9　Freire's 'cultural action' – an example of the use of generative words and pictures

Paulo Freire's writings have sometimes been underestimated in Britain and the USA. This is partly because his meaning is frequently obscured by his translators; also because Freire is seen as politically subversive. Perhaps any education which questions current 'realities' will have some subversive effect and the tension becomes acute when rulers or owners of machines or land are oppressive. Another aspect of Freire's work which has not been fully appreciated is the way in which he sets up an interaction between the adult learner's rich mass of visual

experience and his limited but potent verbal powers. Freire builds on key words such as: Slum, Rain, Plough, Land, Food, Dancing and Well. These are the first seven of his seventeen chosen words. They are already charged with feeling and are capable of being simply illustrated with home-made pictures. Freire's is one of the best thought-out instances of a low-cost 'appropriate technology' of education. It fits neatly with our analysis of picture use and this could very well be used as a guide for further exploration of the method.

FIRST SITUATION
Man in the World and with
The World, Nature and Culture

Through the discussion of this situation – man as a being of relationships – the participants arrive at the distinction between two worlds: that of nature and that of culture. They perceive the normal situation of man as a being in the world and with the world, as a creative and re-creative being who, through work, constantly alters reality. By means of simple questions, such as, 'Who made the well? Why did he do it? How did he do it? When?' which are repeated with regard to the other 'elements' of the situation, two basic concepts emerge: that of *necessity* and that of *work*; and culture becomes explicit on a primary level, that of subsistence. The man made the well because he needed water. And he did it because, relating to the world, he made the latter the object of his knowledge. By work, he submitted the world to a process of transformation. Thus, he made the house, his clothes, his work tools. From that point, one discusses with the group, in obviously simple but critically objective terms, the relations among men, which unlike those discussed previously cannot be either of domination or transformation, because they are relations among Subjects. (Freire 1972)

questions which don't have easy answers. Pictures, well used, offer fact, feeling and fertile ambiguity.

As we considered a great variety of visual material in actual use we found ourselves concentrating on one large category – the one we called 'pictures for telling stories from'. At one end of this were simple scientific and technical diagrams, from which only one main story was intended to be told. As we moved along the scale of complexity in this continuum, pictures seemed to become increasingly rich and fruitful and were yielding not only a diversity of stories and speculations but also that kind of enigmatic, limited contradictoriness between stories which, elsewhere in this book, we have been associating with symbolism.

The history of art constantly offers examples of pictures from this rich, enigmatic end of the spectrum. One of the main functions of popular and religious art – especially before widespread literacy – was to evoke in the minds of the beholders, their own story-telling responses. To this end, explicitness *and* ambiguity would be used together. A famous example which goes some way towards explaining how such evocation is brought about is Gombrich's analysis of the Mona Lisa (1950, 219). In this portrait (and elsewhere) Leonardo da Vinci uses two kinds of ambiguity which trick us into uncertainty. The skyline behind the figure is at two levels and this has the effect of making anyone who looks at the picture slightly uncertain as to whether they are looking at the face on a level, or looking up at it. There is just a doubt as to whether loving intimacy or loving awe should be in the ascendant as we approach. Then there is the Mona Lisa's famous smile. The enigmatic expression with which she gazes at us is achieved by a technique known as *sfumato*; there is a smudging at the corners of the mouth which leaves to us, the viewers, the decision as to just where the lines of the mouth and lips are supposed to be. First of all, therefore, we are involved to a small degree, in having to create the smile that we see – what Gombrich elsewhere calls 'the beholder's share' (1960, 181–287). Then, it is of the nature of smiles to be evanescent and changing, and this too is achieved by controlled lack of definition. And finally, no matter how long we look, the same kind of fundamental doubt is left in our minds as to what kind of smile it is. This example, though well known and relatively simple, offers a paradigm case for an infinite class of powerful, intentionally unresolved ambiguities in art, literature and religion.

It should not, perhaps, have come as a surprise to find that this 'pictures for stories' category was so extensive. When one considers how the language which we utter and comprehend ranges in complexity from simple commands and statements to the extreme allusiveness and symbolism of poetry, it should be obvious that the visual experiences which often trigger such linguistic activity will be similarly diverse. We were also beginning to realize that there were other, less obvious but no less important, ways in which pictures facilitate learning and discovery and that they all fall into a pattern. The reason why we tended to start with 'pictures for telling stories from' may have been that teachers almost inevitably do start with the assumption that their role is to know answers and verbal explanations, as did the young man teaching those history lessons; but there are other kinds of teaching and other kinds of visual learning.

Other kinds of iconic learning

Some of the alternative ways of using pictures in learning have already been suggested. There is the 'art for art's sake' category when we practise a skill of looking or drawing or painting in order to do it better and so explore the iconic mode further. This category and the one we have just discussed was suggested by the boat-hook arrow in Figure 5 (p. 118): you can either go on picturing or you can tell a story or a theory from it. We touched on yet another kind of visual activity in reference to those mental pictures which people make 'in their heads' when they listen to a story – on radio for example. This too – 'pictures from language' – like its reverse which we started with – 'pictures for telling stories from' – is a huge category, and yet it is one which easily gets neglected.

When we run into any intellectual problem, a common and often productive move is to make a diagram of it. We are then like the child mentioned earlier who, finding the algebra difficult, solves the problem with 'geometry'. In making such a move we are in good company. The history of science is full of examples of thought experiments in which some intransigent verbal conundrum was actively visualized and then inwardly manipulated by a persistent and original thinker. Perhaps the greatest mental voyage of all time was when Einstein launched himself from an imaginary exploding star at the speed of light and then pictured where he and his contemporaneous energy would be a few 'years' later. It is important to remember that he could not possibly have made this mental trip without a firm, yet flexible grasp of highly abstract concepts such as speed of light. He needed the ability to make bold surmises about space and time, and even about the possible equivalence of concepts which language conventionally separates such as light, energy and matter. He was probably the only person in the world at that time capable of grasping these *and* of playing constructively with them. Thought experiments are the complement of conventional scientific diagrams, a particularly disciplined form of fantasy, moving from language to a less abstract mode.

If a scientist – old or young – takes his scribbled diagram or his thought experiment and then starts to make a working model of it he is then making a move which is in yet another class of visual activity. He is using a picture to guide his sensori-motor skills to make something or to measure something out in the world, or in that part of the world which is called a laboratory. This is a further move away from the abstraction of language.

We can summarize all this diagramatically by isolating and enlarging the rectangle which we termed the 'iconic mode' in Figure 5 (p. 118) and then thinking about the way in which iconic representations relate to other representational systems (Figure 9). In culture this 'space' lies between all our abstract language-like activities, on the one hand, and all our bodily, sensori-motor involvement with our environment and with people, on the other. The main types of iconic activity which assist learning can now be set out diagrammatically as movements out of or into or within this space.

So far we have mentioned the following: pictures for telling stories from (no. 1); pictures derived from language activity (no. 2); pictures for guiding sensori-motor activity, i.e. our skilled map-guided acts of exploration (no. 3); and we also touched on the 'art for art's sake' activity (no. 5). The remaining type of learning activity which involves pictures – no. 4 – will now be quite obvious. It is simply the making of pictures from nature or from culture. The learner draws what is observed under a microscope or makes his or her own map or picture of some journey.

The taxonomy is highly artificial. In reality one type of activity

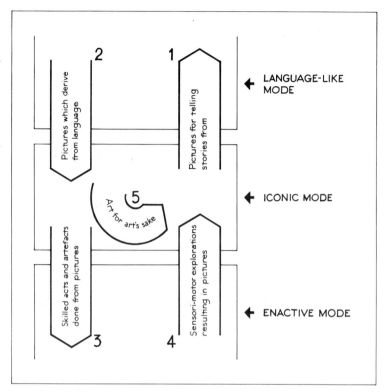

Figure 10   Pictures for learning with

This shows the main kinds of active learning which relate the iconic mode – diagrams and pictures – with other modes of action.

flows into another. We observe and draw and then we look at our picture and try to extract an explanatory story from it – so no. 4 runs into no. 1. Or we enunciate a problem and then we go back to diagrams or to nature in order to check where the problem fits in (no. 2 running into no. 3). Or we actively look at a picture, searching it more closely, and we practise our own skills by copying someone else's – no. 5. Then when we check our explorations of pure form by referring back to 'nature', and so no. 5 merges into no. 4.

We have been focusing, perhaps too exclusively, on the way in which learning and teaching strategies often flow, as it were, through the iconic mode or, which appears to be the neurological foundation for all this, through the right hemisphere. We should not overlook the fact that there are many other kinds of human action, and certainly some kinds of instruction, which appear to be carried out satisfactorily without the intervention of any pictures, either external or internal. A mother interacts with her baby with little or no recourse to language or pictures. A soldier, jumping to attention or rapidly initiating some gun drill, has been trained not to reflect unnecessarily. He links words and action directly and almost unconsciously when certain signals are given. An apprentice, at least in the early stages of his training, may similarly need to be equipped with habitual motor responses to verbal or enactive signals.

In contrast to the obedient and, supposedly, unreflective trooper, consider the High Command. Does there not immediately come to your mind the picture of a large room with maps on huge tables, computer simulations on the big screen and innumerable little flags and toy tanks or ships? This is a special, rather sinister kind of play space. Wherever carefully planned, reflective and flexible action is likely to be required, men have learnt, over the millenia, to take extra time for the serious mental exploration of possibilities, and to maximize, for this purpose, the interplay of pictures and words, of maps and mathematics. The high command creates, for its members, some shared iconic space and, closely linked to it, some verbal freedom or language space in which the planners can explore the realities of the present and the many alternative future stories – the option trees – which open from it. In developing this military analogy I am not suggesting that visual space is the only mediator for reflective action. We have said little of music, or touch or taste. (Do not lovers learn to create tactile and kinaesthetic space? And has it not been frequently observed that poetry can trigger, and be triggered directly by, our sense of smell?) Nevertheless, if you go into a lively school and enjoy the rich array of pictorial life on the walls or attend to the flow of talk and gesture that happens whenever the pressure is off, or if you examine what is being done on paper or on the bench when the pressure is optimally on, it will be obvious that manipulospatial action *is* constantly being guided by iconic images and these in turn are being scrutinized and developed by the problem-spotting, story-telling, theory-generating activity of children's language.

Even when we prepare lectures or speeches and certainly when preparing for examinations, most of us can improve our performance by a judicious enlistment of right hemisphere skills.[7] It is our own home-made diagrams that do this best. Any reader – parent, teacher or student – who feels inclined to attempt to get the better of some external examination might try experimenting with the systems of concentrated note-taking – skeleton notes, etc. – advocated by Tony Buzan (1974). Such map-like schemas are far more easy to retain and to draw on from memory than equivalent wads of notes (see p. 184).

There is much more experiment to be done in this field. We have, indeed, only begun to scratch the surface. I conclude this section by asking whether some current and intractable curricular problems might not be eased or solved if a lack of balance in their visual content could be identified in terms of the proposed classification.

(1) Is most college level art education too much focused on no. 5 – the 'art for art's sake' type of activity? Why should it not involve more of no. 4 (seeing and recording natural form) or no. 2 and no. 3 (inventive and technical drawing). These last two would tie art education more closely to skills and the practicalities of making things that work well.

(2) The well-worn trail in conventional science teaching uses no. 4 and no. 1 – the student observes, measures, draws and explains. One might ask, however, if much of our science teaching may not be short of no. 2 and no. 3 activities – the ability to spot problems, to generate thought experiments and make models of them?[8]

(3) Technical drawing used to seem so attractive and then, for many, it would become so boring. Is CDT (craft, design, technology) in the same kind of doldrums? May it not be short of no. 4 – the bold exploration of natural form? And may it not also be starved of no. 1 and no. 2 – the disciplines of scientific explanation and the complementary agility and 'problem-sensitivity' which confident exploratory discourse makes possible?

If, as I believe, the answer to most of these questions is 'yes', there is some scope for rectifying the situation by broadening the existing secondary curricula. But the roots of the trouble lie back, much earlier in the school system, where non-language-like

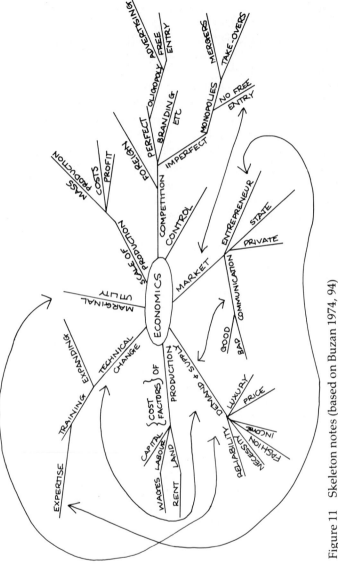

Figure 11   Skeleton notes (based on Buzan 1974, 94)

These were made on the system advocated by Tony Buzan in *Use Your Head*. This was the work of a boy who twice failed O level Economics and who was described by his teachers as having enormous thinking and learning problems.

competences are so often, in subtle ways, devalued or isolated from the astringent influence of speech.

Notes

1 In *The Modularity of Mind* (1983) Jerry Fodor suggests that the time has come to consider an updated version of the old faculty psychology. He argues that the main input systems to the brain not only are, but must be, largely 'encapsulated' from each other. This leads him to conclude that the search for a central control system which would imply extensive high level links between the sub-systems may be unfruitful. My 'chamber music' analogy is consonant with Fodor's modular idea but his argument is, as would be expected, much more theoretically dense. He cites language as his main example and face recognition as another. He also offers a caution about making too much of hemispheric specialization (p. 104).

2 David Anderson, *Child Development* 50, 722–7.

3 In her *Cognitive Development and Education* (1984) Johanna Turner sums up the situation as follows: 'While concrete operations are "first degree" operations that apply to real objects and events, formal operations are *"second degree" operations that relate to statements made about the concrete operations* and their real-life objects and events' (p. 122, my italics). In surveying the experimental evidence relating to concrete and formal operations thinking Turner does not offer much to support my claim that rich and active concrete operations are a necessary springboard. There is plenty of indirect and anecdotal evidence, however: Seymour Papert's is only one example. I have not come across much discussion of the importance of *feelings* in regard to favoured mental images. Papert's reference to his passion for gear wheels is a good pointer. Though gear wheels and sheath knives are not exactly furry, they can be both comforters and powerful symbols pointing forward to future action in concrete and in abstract fields.

4 In the past two decades British geographers have made an effort to get *graphicity*, i.e. mapping and pictorial skills, acknowledged as having a fundamental importance similar to that of literacy. They have not made much impact on the curriculum so far, partly, in my opinion, because the theoretical underpinnings of their case have been weak (Balchin and Coleman 1972).

5 Warr (1982) gives a full account of this enquiry and outlines the work of others who have tried to make sense of visual aids. Knowlton's ideas (see bibliography) were, in part, similar to ours. See also Sless (1981).

6 There is much to be said about these matters in terms of information

theory. For a clear statement of the issues relating to similar aesthetic problems see E. H. Gombrich, *The Sense of Order* (1979), 103–5.

7 For the importance of the right hemisphere in memory training and in educating people for rhetoric – in the ancient meaning of the word – see Frances Yates, *The Art of Memory*.

8 This suggestion was made by Terry Allsop of the Oxford Department of Educational Studies. One of his research interests is why academic science does not flow more readily into the direction of technical inventiveness.

10 Success for all children

Neither in the theoretic nor the practical sphere do we care for, or go for help to, those who have no head for risks, or sense of living on the perilous edge. Our religious life lies more, our practical life lies less, than it used to, on the perilous edge. (James 1917)[1]

Some success in all the main forms of human competence should be the experience of every child; and a sense of achievement in some of them should be the experience of every adult. A school, or a regional authority, or a government, *could* make the success and competence of all children their over-riding educational aim. Whether or not a Mozart or a Mother Theresa would emerge from the system is (almost) another question. Teachers must be deeply concerned with the genesis of such creative individuals and the groups which nourish them; but we can only *hope* for a harvest.

The themes of this book all converge on the concept of a human being as an explorer who, though sometimes solitary, works imaginatively within the culture of a group. But to what sort of practical outcome do these, our main themes, point?

- The infant explorer and his or her need for space to play.
- The requirement that parents and teachers should both safeguard such learning space and enrich it with appropriate structure; hence 'instruction'.
- The perception of the learner that such space opens onto what appears to them as various kinds of danger and mystery; that is, to a problematic, existential frontier.
- Within such space the creative cycle (play → exploration → play → practice →) operates, and this happens at every level of culture.
- These levels of culture, of which five or six main ones can be identified (language being the most conspicuous and abstract), are characterized by modes of representation which come to life in a community, yet are grounded in an individual's varied neurophysiological make-up.

- Competence in all these modes is open to all people, and such competence, when acquired, tends to be self-motivating.
- When young humans approach maturity their need for a sense of the frontier and for vistas in which competence can be stretched outweighs their need for certainty and safety. Yet there is always a great diversity among individual learners as to which particular competence is most ready to be stretched at any particular stage in that person's development.
- The human mind should not be thought of as being located only in the brain. Mental activity is a co-working – a synergy – of several extremely complex systems, including some, such as the endocrine system, which are in the body but outside the brain; while most of the crucially formative mental acts – such as speech and gesture – are not within, but *between* people.

Our thinking about education and the innovations and experiments which will shape it during the next century will, I believe, be guided by some such principles as these. And we need to work out more of their implications, especially as these bear on the idea of life-long education. This list does not claim to be exhaustive. It is preparatory, opening the way to education in the imagination and dreaming, and to new forms of celebration, adventure and worship.

What kind of primary education is likely to be most appropriate to the new conditions of the twenty-first century? And for young adults, what kind of learning experiences will lay down good foundations for communities in which intelligent, co-operative and skilful action will be widely diffused?

In the 1970s I often found myself trying to find answers to questions such as these about the direction in which our education should be going. This was partly stimulated by discussions with Commonwealth students who thought that we, in England, had found the answers. And we hadn't. In a sense the present book has been an attempt to identify and clarify the basic problems. And the thing about interesting questions is that they can sometimes be joined together to form an incomplete but serviceable theory. One often travels thus, half knowing one's destination, half wanting to go and less than half knowing why. In some such back-to-front way as this, the final, least theoretical chapter was written before the others.[2]

It may be that some of the developments suggested below are

unrealistic; but they do illustrate a possible trend. Some of these will certainly have to evolve over a greater time span than is implied. Nevertheless, we must adapt, and some such way as this is where education should go if our human desire to learn and our human capacity to teach are to gain in scope and freedom.

Education 2000

The remarkable thing about the so-called Great Debate on education was its smallness.[3] How confined and backward-looking many of the issues seem! We argue about heredity and environment, freedom and discipline, progressive and traditional, as though these were alternatives on one of those questionnaires which only allow 'yes' or 'no' answers. Yet the obvious, right answer – '*both*, and get on with it' – is rarely heard loud and clear. And in any case that is only half the answer because great changes are upon us whether we like it or not.

It is unfashionable at the moment to raise questions about the good life or the great society or to wonder whether, perhaps, we have got the whole thing seriously wrong. There was something to be said for the optimism of the early 1960s or even for the euphoria of Paris in 1968. At least many people were thinking in radical terms. There was wisdom too in what Freire was saying about thought going along with action – wisdom which might help us to understand why young people are not attracted to work in industry; and even that wild man Illich had powerful, negative things to say about parasitic professionalism and the folly of exams. And he questioned the idol of 'schooling'.

The sketch which follows is not meant to be Utopian in the sense of being a remote and unattainable *jeu d'ésprit*. Nor is it meant to be a blue-print for immediate action. But massive changes are already looming ahead and we are going to have to wrestle with these in education, as in every other part of society, and wring from them something good; or sink and suffer. The current debate ought, therefore, to be concerned, at least in part, with the question of what kind of better society we might be trying to create in the year 2000. Is there not a path of humane freedom to be worked out between the centralism of Eastern Europe, on the one hand, and old-fashioned Friedmania on the other? And what sort of education might be appropriate to such an 'Open Way'?

The disease

There is one particular respect in which we are all hell-bent down a wrong educational track. It is connected with the 'Diploma Disease' which Ronald Dore (1976) so ably diagnosed in his book of that name. But he did not make it sufficiently clear that universal secondary schooling has become the hot-bed of that disease. We all know that schooling does not equal education. Yet we go on making the old-fashioned assumption, appropriate only to narrowly élitist societies, that all proper secondary education should take place *in schools and between the ages of 12 and 18* and that part of the process must involve almost irreversible, life-chance-allocating examinations. No wonder that it requires organizational and teaching gifts of a rarity approaching genius to make a success of comprehensive education. But why do we go on with the almost impossible task? The main reason is that it used to work well for the small minority when limited, prestige-laden universities and more or less limited professional and white-collar openings gave point to it all. But now the point is blunted and bent; the Empire has popped and the economy is a wrinkled balloon. Yet we go on shutting up young adults in order to sort them out, accepting the absurdity of a fixed school leaving age and the invidious task of discriminating and conspicuously labelling the 'good, promising' minority from the 'bad, unpromising' majority. And banding or destreaming, setting or zoning, team teaching or new kinds of external examinations only tinker with the problem. In our impatience with the system, however, we would be foolish to decry all élites, all specialization and the pursuit of excellence. It is the road of the diplomated mandarin, not that of the achiever, which should be decried. Whatever our politics, whether we favour rapid or slow change, we ought to be increasingly concerned about how people attain and make excellent things; and how millions get – and feel – shut out.

Secondary schooling is not the only cause of vandalism, alienation, drug, alcohol- and pool-dependence, rejection of parents and tradition, of boredom and passive sport; but for many adolescents the confined experience of school gives them a shove that way. In Britain, thanks to deeply rooted values, thanks to our admirably untidy arrangements and to many heroic, individual teachers, the system has had less disastrous effects than in many developing countries which have copied the western model. In some of these the Diploma Disease and 'Secondary School Sclerosis' have taken almost fatal hold.

There are, I believe, two hopeful roads towards recovery: first there is still scope for vast improvement in primary education, not going back to passive parrot learning, but moving ahead – way beyond Plowden. The second road, which Conservative spokesmen sometimes touch on, only to ignore its revolutionary implications, is to reduce the compulsory school leaving age (the easy part) and then to set about creating a universal but enormously diversified system of secondary and tertiary training and service options – exploded secondary education followed, rather later than at present, by university courses for those who want and can attain them after a period of work and service and suitable academic preparation. Everyone would have a right to coupons for a minimum of, say, five years of secondary and tertiary education some time during their lives. A right to more could be earned in various ways.

But meanwhile how are you going to keep all those youngsters 'off the streets'? This is not really an educational but a political problem. Usually the youngsters are on the streets because their energies and talents are not wanted by *you* who ask the question. You demand mass-made products and passive pleasures. But in so far as there is an educational question it would be enormously reduced if the young had all succeeded in their primary and middle schools. We shall return to the problems raised by our secondary/tertiary revolution later; but now the first main question is – why *not* success for everyone by about 13 or 14?

Success at 13

The overriding objective in a developed, national educational system should be success for all in a number of basic competences: literacy, numeracy, music, graphic and craft skills and simple athletic-gymnastic attainments. Up to this stage the notion of a core curriculum makes sense; but not after. Skills such as basic musical or linguistic competence can be assessed quite easily, with fair objectivity and without norm-based 'failures'. Indeed assessment can be a challenge for the children, and should be a valuable source of self-diagnosis for the institution, provided that the process is not contaminated by 'selection'. There would have to be special provision, perhaps in superlatively staffed boarding schools, for the few who, because of accident or ill-health, failed to make the grade. This might be a future role to which some of our preparatory schools could adapt, as many, though not necessarily all, would lose their *raison d'être* once 'selective' exams are made illegal and this, as we shall see, is what should happen.

It is important to remember that the nature of the educational process changes quite markedly around the age of 12–13. Up to that age an educational system can be strongly normative, working, that is, like medicine or law, towards widely accepted standards of what is the appropriate behaviour or level of competence agreed on by common consent. When adolescence has begun, however, an individual's need for the experience of autonomy soon outweighs his or her need for conformity and protection. At this stage the educational process should tend, like any lively culture, to develop that life, to present the past in new lights, to generate new undertakings and to encourage unusual, questioning individuals. This tendency towards individual and group action is always present, even in rigid or totalitarian societies; but in open, pluralistic societies such as that of North America or western Europe, the urge towards experiencing diverse excellence and creativity needs to be given rein, and the secondary and tertiary stages of education should be opened up to that end.

The value, in social and psychological terms, of success around 13 for all children would be enormous. Contrary to what is widely believed the main ingredient of all motivation is the individual's sense of competence. External prods and carrots have short-term value; but if you can do something well you will probably *want* to, and very many of the failures and frustrations of teenagers stem from an inner sense of incompetence, reinforced by the later stages of school experience – the fact, in brief, that they have had so much done to them and have done so relatively little. A revolution of this kind in primary and middle schools with the emphasis on autonomy after 14 will not solve all the problems of adolescence, many of which run far beyond school. But it could greatly ease them and thus lay the foundation of confidence and responsibility which would be essential for the new, open secondary system.

The primary and secondary revolutions which I am proposing interlock in other ways too, and they make better economic sense than might at first appear. Any learning situation in which there is strong 'motivation' is efficient because it can be self-energizing. Or consider an obvious manpower difficulty: you could not reform the primary sector on the lines proposed without greatly increasing and improving the teaching strength in the schools, and you could not open the secondary system and turn it towards work and service without creating a very large number of short-term job opportunities. Primary education should therefore be redesigned so that there would be three young adult *school helpers* working with every fully trained teacher. And the latter could be more highly trained than at present in one or two specialist areas, as well as in general pedagogy. It was the American educator Bereiter who clarified the logic of this (1972). All education, he pointed out, falls roughly into two phases – the caretaking, playful aspect and the 'instructional' aspect which is to do with the presenting of new structures of knowledge, skills, concepts, etc. at the right stage and in the best context so that these can be actively assimilated with the optimum balance of challenge, play, practice, uncertainty and reward. The second instructional phase needs great expertise and there is evidence from many developments in education today, such as the remarkable success of Suzuki music teaching, that great possibilities of progress lie ahead if we could develop such expertise. Yet at present we demand far too much from our primary teachers, expecting them to be expert instructors, therapists, temporary mums, administrators and equipment makers – all more or less at the same time. If they could be freed from some of the simpler, but still very important, tasks to allow more time for seeing that good methods actually work, for helping those with special gifts or special difficulties, and if school children could have more opportunity for playing and practising with partly trained but responsible young helpers, working and learning within the system, then why should not all, or almost all our children, know their tables, sing in tune, read well – and *want* to?

There would of course be overlap between fully trained teachers and their helpers. Indeed one of the many advantages of this type of teaching apprenticeship would be that the school helpers would be ideally placed to acquire the informal experience and the intuitive qualities needed as a foundation for subsequent periods of training; qualities which it is notoriously difficult to impart in formal teacher training and in similar professional courses.

Exploding the secondary schools

Education is always a mixture of doing things to learners and letting learners do things – largely, of course, what are regarded as 'good' things. As we have seen there is a shift in adolescence towards the second part of the equation – towards autonomous and group action. For young adults (sometimes called teenagers) school is only acceptable when it is perceived as a spring-board for various kinds of action. Fifty years ago secondary schools could be seen, despite the cast-iron desks and the brown paint, as leading on to vistas of achievement, service and esteem. For a dwindling number of the young this is still true; but for most of those undergoing secondary education the prospects ahead are not powerfully alluring: a polytechnic or university course at the end of the escalator for those who have the 'able' label, the civil and less civil services, selling, factory apprenticeships, agricultural labour and the Job Centre. It is the lack of challenge and interest which, rightly or wrongly, makes many of these openings seem dim. This is a problem which has been seriously over-simplified in recent educational debates. Worried industrialists and politicians won't get far by advocating curricular changes or by giving the world of work a better image. Part of the problem lies in the huge scale and alienating nature of much of industry; but part of it lies in the schools, which seem to say 'this is your lot, the die is cast'.[4]

What kind of post-industrial world do we wish our children and grandchildren to face? One does not need to have worked long with mildly disturbed or backward children to know that unsuspected riches often lie below the surface. So I suppose we must work for a society, planned just enough, yet open enough to everyone's talents, to all their knowledge, skill and goodwill.

THE FIRST EIGHT YEARS OF EDUCATION

Main modes of representation	*Basic educational ingredients* for the curriculum of a prosperous, civilized society, Western or Eastern, industrial or rural, communist or capitalist
Language-like	Speech Elements of another language Reading and writing; logic Number and elements of algebra Musical notation
Musical	Singing in tune ⎤ Individual and Instrumental ⎦ group work
Iconic	Graphicacy (geometry, graphs, diagrams and mapping skills) Imaginative drawing and painting
Enactive	Crafts Dance and games Athletics, gymnastics and swimming
Interpersonal	Social skills, empathy, duties and valuing

Education for competence

This suggests a universal way of thinking about primary education and its curriculum. The five main types of 'representation' and the five corresponding blocks of skill, or competence, are the main paths by which children grow into human culture. The nature and selection of activities which children would *do* in order to acquire acceptable levels of competence will always be culture dependent. Provided that even more fundamental needs – for security, food, shelter – are met, it can be argued that children have a *right* to acquire these competences. A corresponding argument does not apply in secondary and higher education where young adults should be regarded, as far as possible, as free and competent agents with, increasingly, responsibility for their own further learning.

Certainly this will mean further moves towards 'equal opportunity', but opportunity not so much for having and owning as for *doing good things* and that means doing one's share of 'good' work. An unattainable ideal! Certainly; but much more in keeping with human nature and human values than the boring alternatives, popular with some futurists and even with some socialists, of maximizing or equalizing everyone's chances for money and idleness.

An open society must be concerned both with a certain basic freedom and with freedom of a higher order. Michael Polanyi expressed the distinction neatly when he spoke of 'the freedom of the subjective person to do as he likes' – within the law – 'and the freedom of the responsible person to do as he must' – according to the principle which he perceives (1958, p. 309). Education needs to be understood similarly at two levels: at the normative level which we have discussed, of bringing all children up to the basic threshold of skills which they need in order to cope with their society; but also at a higher level which merges gradually into an active and responsible commitment to culture. At this level notions such as responsibility, service, adventure, creativity and the holding of ideals become central. Such allegiancies increasingly demand personal judgements, adventures and evaluative acts; and there is always corresponding risk of error; fanaticism, folly or disaster. Such 'goods' and such sharp lessons cannot be shared out by edict, for they must constantly be sought for (or mitigated), discovered and earned by people.

Up the age of about 13 or 14, therefore, education *can* be seen as a right – provided society is rich enough to afford it. But beyond adolescence it is nothing of the kind. Education becomes increasingly something people do and make. It must be diversified, related to work, to cultural activities and to excellence in many directions so that as many people as possible can see far horizons and wish to move toward them. The basic skills will go on being used and perfected but the essentially qualitative process should not be quantified or interrupted in order to give selective rewards and privileges. When people are to be chosen for any particular responsibility which carries with it desirable prestige or power they should be chosen mainly on grounds of what they have actually achieved.

What then might the young be doing in the 4 or 5 years before they reach 18? This is where another debate might start, but here are some suggestions. There could be four linked and inter-dependent elements in the new secondary education: *initiation, earning, service* and *learning*.

Initiation (or orientation)

At some time during the two years after leaving school all children would have the chance to go on a six-month residential course in a Junior College in some part of Britain or of Europe, preferably in an area contrasting with their own home back-ground. There would be wide choice, but successful passage through one of these courses might be made a condition for various minor privileges, such as cheap student travel or early training for motor cycling and driving. The common theme of the course would be the problems, opportunities and complexities facing men and women in the modern world. Students would choose at least one verbal, predominantly 'left hemisphere' sub-ject and one non-verbal 'right hemisphere' subject for intensive study. Drama, the arts and elements of Outward Bound would play a considerable but varying part in the curriculum. Some of these courses would be secular and run by local authorities, others would be the responsibility of independent religious and educational foundations. There would be close links too with a national network of counselling officers whose task it would be to advise young people about all the opportunities for work, service and education which would face them on leaving the college.[5]

Earning

From the age of 13+ everyone would be expected to earn, if not their livelihood, at least a significant part of it. Something like 2 million junior jobs would have to be created, assuming that at any one time about half the 'secondary' population were working. It would be one of the essential tasks of industry (an alternative to taxation perhaps?), of commerce, agriculture and local govern-ment to rediscover and sustain apprenticeship roles. Small businesses and small craft enterprises would be particularly suitable in this respect and special incentives could be given to encourage the use of young learner-workers. Many unpopular but socially necessary jobs could be done by young men and girls in their later teens, and higher levels of pay and additional educational coupons would be an obvious reward. It is interesting to think of the number of useful jobs which are currently being 'rationalized' out of existence but which could usefully be done by learner workers: extra postal services, more adequate care of domestic animals on farms, and even – dare one say it? – domestic service, especially in hotels and in residential institutions. And there are many tougher jobs too – coal mining, deep sea fishing, street cleaning, farming, where the young could work and enjoy doing so. Whenever state encouragement is given to the Arts it should be in fields where the young are actively involved. In opera, ballet and theatre 'cheap' learner-workers could contribute to the welfare of all. This is an area where management and labour organizations will need to undergo radical changes in both their perceptions and practices.

Service

The line between productive and 'helping' work is often arbitrary but the rough criterion is clear: wherever people are below the level where they can cope – young children, old and handicapped people, or wherever some disaster or danger threatens – these are the main areas of service. For work in all such fields there would be a period of intensive (and free) training, periods of active service and longer periods of stand-by duty. Two years, including training, would be the minimum contribution. The armed forces might once again be manned to about half their number by national service men and women. Something like half a million school helpers would do their service in nursery schools and in the 6–13 primary-to-middle schools. Sea rescue, mountain rescue, the fire services, conservation tasks, traffic control, work with old people and many ancillary health tasks would be opened up for service. Discipline and training would have to be effective. Voluntary international service is also a field whose two-way value is still not fully appreciated. It is possible, so strange is the pendulum of fashion, that the ancient sentiment of patriotism might help to sustain people who serve their country and community, and face, thereby, periods of danger and monotony.

Learning

A great range of study opportunities would have to be made available: day release, evening classes, Open University type mixed-media courses and periods of concentrated residential study. Car driving and maintenance courses, basic electronics, project technology and a wide choice of craft and design courses would be offered. It would be important, in all these, that sufficient weight be given to the theoretical content. One of the greatest dangers facing the post-industrial society is the 'black box' mentality, by which even highly educated people have a totally passive attitude to the tools and techniques of our culture (Stanley 1978, and see pp. 130–1). Except in the case of strictly remedial courses, some payment – either by cash or coupon – would be required for all secondary and tertiary education. This would only cover a small proportion of the true cost – perhaps a quarter – but the proportion should remain fairly constant in all fields so that there would be an understanding of the value of what can be acquired.

Many courses would have to fit into a series of modules – introductory, middle, advanced; and successful completion of one would be a condition for entry to the next. Admission to higher, university courses would be partly dependent on skill and knowledge qualifications. But as, for most people, tertiary education would not start till they were in their twenties, an applicant's record of work and service would carry as much weight as the qualifying courses he had covered. Even so, however, it is likely that university lecturers might have to learn to teach more effectively than at present and, though they would not receive the particular brand of academic 'cream' to which they have become accustomed (and which they often complain about), they *would* have a higher proportion of highly motivated students whose first interest would be learning.

The risks

Of course there would be muddles and risks in such a system. Some young people would play more than others; some would turn to crime – old varieties and new, such as forging educational coupons; but whatever we do now we are likely to face colossal

---

What independent schools might do

In a paper given in 1983 to heads and governors of Quaker Schools I criticized the Society of Friends (of which I am a member) for our apparent inability to face the present crisis in secondary education. Traumatic social and cultural problems have been emerging since the Second World War and these bear particularly heavily on young people. Yet all our nine Quaker boarding schools have continued, relatively unchanged, to offer exam-oriented schooling to a largely privileged clientele. Other groups of schools run by religious organizations are in a similar trap. Where is the prophetic action? I suggested some ways in which we might break out and, in a fantasy, indicated the kind of experimental diversity which we ought to be trying to develop by the year 2000.

What might have happened to our nine schools as we approach the year 2000?
School A has become an international one-year college with a great reputation for preparing students, between school and university, for advanced study. This success grew out of some enterprising courses for overseas students which combined 'teaching English as a foreign language' courses with study method crash courses. One third of the students are now funded by Local Education Authorities. One third are subsidized by the churches and are mainly from overseas. The rest pay full fees. The Quaker influence still shows in a strong peace studies course.
Schools B, C and D have not changed drastically. They all

---

problems of deviance, of boredom, of youthful unemployment and crime by the year 2000, and this prospect increases the need for us to explore less pathogenic systems of adolescent 'containment' than those we now have.

What would be lost? First of all the examination boards would close down. Indeed it should be an offence to set up any external examination system or ability-testing bureau which claims to evaluate human potential. It cannot be done. The truths which well-meaning boards manage to tell us from time to time are insignificant compared to the falsehoods which the system as a whole constantly suggest. If only the universities could start in this direction now, following the example of the Open Univer-

recruit children mainly at 11+ from primary schools. One school has a very strong musical bias. School C has a world-famous centre for the study of intermediate technology in the campus, closely linked with the nearby university. The proportion of Quaker staff in all three has gone up to over a half. Approximately one third of the children are now Quaker.

School E sold its premises and opened up in a big city centre as an adult education college with close links to the Open University and Trade Unions.

School F, on the edge of some northern hills, is a highly efficient intermediate treatment centre, though by another name. It runs six month courses which combine outward bound elements with computer studies, design technology and drama. An interesting development is that it contains on its staff a significant proportion of 'ex-convicts'. In its experimental stages it was found that young reformed offenders often make very gifted teachers. Strong Quaker influence is still in evidence, though not in the curriculum.

School G is one of the European centres for training international voluntary workers.

School H is a college for young adults specializing in the visual arts, science and theology. It is organized as a commune-cum-monastery. It runs a small symphony orchestra, a farm and a publishing house. Some Friends think there is undue Catholic influence in it, but the corporate worship there is still largely in the Quaker manner.

School I did not survive.   (Hodgkin 1984, 298)

sity, they would clear the way for many urgent reforms in the existing secondary and tertiary systems. The value of occasional internal diagnostic tests and tests with an element of challenge and competition is *not* being questioned.

Independent secondary and preparatory schools really would begin to wither away, at least in their present form, once the selective examination system was abolished. In an open, partially subsidized secondary system of the kind described here there should be a big place for responsible innovation and for private enterprise.

Another casualty, alas (or not alas), would be the life-long profession of secondary schoolmaster and schoolmistress. There would be plenty of opportunities for mathematicians or crafts-men who can teach, for scientists or linguists whose special interest it is to understand the structure and pedagogy of their disciplines. But once you free secondary education from the thrall of compulsory schooling and from the black art of sorting out alleged goodies from the alleged 'academically less able' – once you do this you free teachers from their dreariest bonds. They could become interested once again mainly in students and in active knowledge rather than in testable facts. Many would renew their interest in those 'frontier' problems which fringe all disciplines with uncertainty and which never cease to allure the enquiring mind.[6] If we are to have professional organizations in the next millenium it would be refreshing if they could evolve more in the direction of learned societies which help to generate and protect the excellencies to which they are committed.

There are practical things, bearing on all this, which we could do now. We could generate a more critical attitude to all external exams as well as to the universities and employers who rely far too heavily on these false guides.[7] And less negatively we could welcome diversity of many kinds in our existing secondary schools. Everything that gets children out into the world of factory or workshop, river or mountain, which gets them out, not as passive spectators *but in some active role* – all this should be encouraged. So should every possible alternative route to excel-lence such as new types of college on the pattern of Ruskin College or the Bauhaus.[8] And at the primary level why should we not conduct one or two national experiments aiming at 13-year-old success for every child in all the core skills? Double and treble the teacher-child ratio, experiment with young volunteer hel-pers, give the best primary teachers their head in a wide explora-tory investigation in one of the less affluent corners of Britain! Why not?

I saw some children looking at the stocks in a museum recently and I wondered which of our present instruments of degradation would come to be eyed with a similar curious shudder by the year 3000. At least the stocks spoke of the past – 'he – or she – has done wrong'. Our instruments of selection in education, may not mean to, but they do, speak of the future and say: 'the good, the best, the mysterious, is not for you, you can't make it'. Yet the truth is that he or she – somewhere or somehow – *could*.

Notes

1 This passage was marked heavily in the margin of V. L. Griffiths' copy, which he took with him to the Sudan. There, starting in the depression of the 1930s, he and a group of Sudanese and British friends undertook the reform of the country's primary teaching and curriculum (Griffiths 1976).

2 The basis of this chapter was a BBC Radio 3 talk in May 1977. It was published, more or less in its present form, in *The New Era* 59 (February 1978).

3 The reference is to a request by the Prime Minister, James Callaghan, in a speech at Ruskin College (1976), that the country needed to embark on a radical discussion of educational priorities. The discussion which then ensued was carefully guided and produced little of note.

4 In the mid-1980s one is bound to reflect on the worsening employment situation in Britain and on the many experiments by the Manpower Services Commission and similar organizations in the creation of short-term jobs. The situation would certainly be worse without them, but many questions have to be asked. For example: where, in the perception of the young, do such schemes appear to lead – what vistas open? Is the educational content (openness, questioning and all that makes for competence) being squeezed out, in favour of skill training and narrow 'industrial' objectives? Are the schemes too centralized, standardized, risk-avoiding?

5 Some such extensive counselling and guidance network would obviously be important. Nevertheless, normal teachers in secondary and higher colleges should not be encouraged to give up their own counselling functions – a tendency which has gone a long way in the United States. In my opinion British teachers would be unwise to dilute their tradition of broad influence on students in favour of narrow specialist instruction.

6 See David Hargreaves' interesting case against the hardening of the teaching profession (1982, ch. 8).

7 The Oxford Certificate of Educational Achievement was a pioneering move in this direction, launched in the early 1980s.

8 Abbs and Carey (1977) give a favourable view of both of these.

Postscript: On human talents

Whatever patterns of education grow out of our present, patchily sclerotic Western systems, the need for adaptability, openness and bold experiment will continue. It is not just a question of arriving at some better state, or of surviving something worse; education must be constantly experimental to stay alive at all. Such experiment may sometimes produce hard statistics and data useful for Ph.D.s but that kind of knowledge is only a by-product. A shared, experimental attitude is essential at the very heart of education because the experience of thoughtful change is part of life itself; and the fruit of such change is not social science but good morale and new, shared achievements. And it always starts when people begin to recognize problems: 'We, all of us, have helped to identify this problem (vandalism, falling standards in French or whatever) and we are all involved in trying to do something about it, together'.

'All of us' means teachers and learners of many diverse gifts – the artists, the poets, the part-time clowns as well as the narrowly academic or athletic high-fliers. In the early 1980s there was a groundswell of renewed interest in the education of diverse talents. There had been bursts of protest, during the previous thirty years, against the narrowness of the secondary curriculum, especially in England, and of its testing and 'failing' procedures at every level. Then, almost imperceptibly, new theoretical considerations began to surface. There was Suzuki music teaching in Japan and the ideas behind it. There was Seymour Papert's work, referred to in chapter 7; and, scarcely rippling the educational pool, there had been twenty years of research on the significance of hemispheric differences. In 1983 Jerry Fodor produced a book whose title seemed to encapsulate the new trend – *The Modularity of Mind*. All of a sudden people started rediscovering that there had been sense in Gall's old faculty psychology, though not in the fashionable phrenology, which resulted from it.

Then, in 1984, there appeared a wide survey of this area, Howard Gardner's *Frames of Mind: The Theory of Multiple Intelligences*.[1] I found Gardner's book both exciting and frustrating. It was exciting because it offered yet another pointer to the new direction which education has to take. The frustration came from the realization that Gardner was missing certain ideas of crucial importance. The most serious of these shortcomings was that, like Bruner, he generally used a degraded and diffuse concept of symbolism and, correspondingly, failed to stress the importance of frontiers and exploration.

Gardner describes seven *'relatively autonomous* human intellectual competences' or 'intelligences' and these almost tally with my own scheme; I compress two of his pairs under single headings. Here are the two lists.

Intelligences or human intellectual competences (Gardner)	My terms, referring either to human competences or to the corresponding mode of cultural representation
(1) Linguistic intelligence	(1) Language-like (predominantly left hemisphere processing; includes notational systems of algebra, logic, music, etc.)
(2) Logical-mathematical intelligence	
(3) Musical intelligence	(2) Musical
(4) Spatial intelligence	(3) Iconic
(5) Bodily-kinaesthetic intelligence	(4) Enactive
(6) Intrapersonal	
(7) Interpersonal	(5) Interpersonal

Whichever terminology one uses, it is important to remember that any cultural or curricular 'subject' should draw on all or most of these competences in varying degrees.

Frames of Mind is wide-ranging, controversial and interesting. It brings together studies of brain injury, case histories of exceptionally gifted individuals and anthropological studies of traditional systems of education in which special talents have been developed. Thomas Gladwin's studies of the methods of navigation and training used by the islanders in the Pacific offers a notable example of how spatial intelligence and bodily kinaesthetic intelligence can combine to make enormously complex achievements possible – achievements which we in the West would expect to be impossible without abstract mathematics.

Gardner is, perhaps, too dismissive of testing. Obviously if intelligence is multiple then a test which aims at measuring predominantly linguistic facility is going to be of little use as a general predictor. Indeed it may be positively harmful if it is used for placing people in a rank order upon which future economic opportunities and cultural privileges may depend. However, if a verbally biased test is designed and used *diagnostically* to help both learner and teacher to find out what went wrong, that can be extremely valuable. Gardner would probably agree; but as we whet our knives for cutting back and eventually eliminating all norm-referenced selective tests in our educational systems, we ought also to be pressing for the development of more informative diagnostic tests across the whole spectrum of human talent.

The question about how many intelligences there are could, perhaps, become a red herring. Certainly there is scope for more research here.[2] However such research will be valuable in so far as it helps us to understand the interaction of these semi-autonomous systems rather than by enumerating them and understanding them in isolation. As when we count the senses – are there five or six or more? – questions of definition can confuse the issue.

In discussing the way in which intellectual competences work together I used the example of a small chamber orchestra. One might improve this by imagining a family of musicians – the Bachs, perhaps. A varied, semi-autonomous group has, in this instance, grown up within a shared musical tradition; yet different individuals specialize in different skills and use quite different instruments – harpsichord, violin, flute, etc. And they are trained to integrate their talents in an organic whole. As with our example of the two blocks of government offices, analogous to the two brain hemispheres, this model fails if we focus on the people in it, rather than on the interaction of their complementary information patterning systems. The model emphasizes: (i) the shared experience; (ii) the shared script (these, together, are analogous to the acquisition of common, but differently processed memories); (iii) the relative autonomy of the musicians – what Fodor calls 'the encapsulation' of the separate brain systems; (iv) the suggestion that exploration – any extension of the systems' joint capacity – depends, to a considerable extent, on *practice*, and this must involve continuous yet inconspicuous listening, watching and learning – each from each – *in action*; (v) finally, that it is possible for one member to take a definite lead or to relinquish it – the harpsichord, say, or the violin.

We have a great deal to learn about the ways in which these different competences make use of each other's strengths and exploit each others' characteristic storage systems. I gave details of one such exploration in chapter 9 when a colleague and I tried to unravel the different types of iconically assisted learning. Papert's analysis of juggling points to similar lines of enquiry in the iconic/enactive interaction.

There is one crucial perspective which is not made manifest by Gardner. It is to do with the centrality of personal commitment to exploration. It involves understanding the existential reality of play and frontier and, hence, of the toys and symbols with which we learn to explore. A symbol should never be thought of as 'mere'; it is, in its very essence, anti-reductionist, being always *for* some project, out there on the frontier. I doubt if we will make an adequate revolution in pedagogy unless we develop a philosophy appropriate to such issues.

If, from time to time in a learner's life, he or she does not grasp and use a tool or a machine or some powerful cluster of ideas with passionate intention of making or discovering something new, then his or her education will have been a poor business. Ambiguities and problems are where all exploration starts; they are education's chastening friends. We encountered the idea of resolving limited contradictions in the words 'two eyes for seeing in depth, and two (or more) brains for getting to know in depth'. Our multiple pattern-sensing and processing systems are designed to exploit moderate ambiguities. Symbols and lively myths and rituals in the strong 'non-mere' sense of these words, are cognitive devices for holding on to, and sometimes for resolving, hopeful tensions.

The varieties of our competences and the experiences which they mediate are all for a continuing purpose. They can cohere to form a personal belief system, which we use in order to get a deep view, a more comprehensive view, of the wood in which we find ourselves. 'Although the path chosen will be one of many, it must be inside the forest. It must give us the assurance *"that we are moving inside philosophy and not outside it"* ' (Steiner 1978, 26, quoting Heidegger). Then we may see, not only some distant interesting trees, but some vistas between them too. The wood is the universe – the natural world, ourselves and the whole universe of thought – Karl Popper's 'World 3' – whose recorded patterns, harmonies and discords, myths and theories fill our libraries, our electronic memories, our galleries and the languages and traditions through which we travel. Yet these worlds will only come to life if someone acts on them, plays with and explores them and shares the resulting surprises.

Notes

1 The book is the first of a series from The Harvard Graduate School of Education's Project on Human Potential.
2 Fodor claims, for example, that left/right hemisphere dichotomies are 'too gross' to be examples of modular systems of the kind he is trying to detect (1983, 104). While he instances face recognition as a possible candidate (see note 1 on p. 185) Gardner rejects this, partly on the surprising grounds that face recognition is 'insufficiently valued' by culture (1983, 61). This illustrates the fluid nature of the debate at present. For a useful overview see Gardner (1984, 280–5).

Bibliography

Where books not mentioned in the text have been included this is because they offer either interesting support for, or qualification of, the relevant subject matter. Journal references are only given when I do not know of an equivalent book reference.

Abbs, P. and Carey, G. (1977) *Proposal for a New College*. London: Heinemann.

Armstrong, M. (1980) *Closely Observed Children*. Richmond: Chameleon.

Atkins, P. W. (1982) *The Creation*. Oxford: W. H. Freeman.

Balchin, W. G. and Coleman, A. M. (1972) 'Graphicacy', *Geography* 57, 185–95.

Bannister, D. and Fransella, F. (1971) *Inquiring Man*. Harmondsworth: Penguin Books.

—— and Mair, J. M. M. (1968) *The Evaluation of Personal Constructs*. London: Academic Press.

Barfield, O. (1952) *Saving the Appearances: A Study in Idolatry*. London: Faber & Faber.

Barnes, D. (1975) *From Communication to Curriculum*. Harmondsworth: Penguin Books.

Bateson, G. (1958) *Naven: The Culture of the Iatmul People of New Guinea as revealed through a Study of Naven Ceremonial*. Stanford, Calif.: Stanford University Press.

—— (1973) *Steps to an Ecology of Mind*. St Albans: Granada.

Bennett, N. (1976) *Teaching Styles and Pupil Progress*. London: Open Books.

Benton, M. G. and Benton, P. (1969) *Touchstones: A Teaching Anthology*. London: English Universities Press.

Bereiter, C. (1972) 'Schools without education', *The Harvard Educational Review*, August, 390–411.

Berger, P. L. (1976) *Pyramids of Sacrifice: Political Ethics and Social Change*. London: Allen Lane.

—— (1980) *The Heretical Imperative: Contemporary Possibilities of Religious Affirmation*. London: Collins.

—— and Berger, B. (1972, 1976) *Sociology, A Biographical Approach*. Harmondsworth: Penguin Books.

—— and Luckman, T. (1967) *The Social Construction of Reality*. Harmondsworth: Penguin Books.

Berlin, I. (1976) *Vico and Herder: Two Studies in the History of Ideas*. London: Hogarth Press.

Bertalanffy, L. V. (1968) *General System Theory*. New York: Braziller.

Blakemore, C. (1977) *The Mechanics of the Mind*. Cambridge: Cambridge University Press.

Blakeslee, T. R. (1980) *The Right Brain*. London: Macmillan.

Boden, M. A. (1977) *Artificial Intelligence and Natural Man*. Brighton: Harvester Press.

—— (1979) *Piaget*. London: Fontana.

Bogen, J. E. R. (1975) 'Educational aspects of hemispheric specialization', *UCLA Educator* (Los Angeles), Spring 1975.

Bohm, D. (1980) *Wholeness and the Implicate Order*. London: Routledge & Kegan Paul.

Bohr, N. (1934) *Atomic Theory and the Description of Nature*. Cambridge: Cambridge University Press.

Boudon, R. (1971) *The Uses of Structuralism*. London: Heinemann.

Braham, M. (ed.) (1982) *Aspects of Education*. Chichester: John Wiley.

Brierley, J. (1976) *The Growing Brain: Childhood's Crucial Years*. Windsor: National Foundation for Educational Research.

Britton, J. (1970) *Language and Learning*. Harmondsworth: Penguin Books.

Bronowski, J. (1966) *The Identity of Man*. London: Heinemann.

Bruner, J. S. (1960) *The Process of Education*. New York: Vintage Books.

—— (1968) *Toward a Theory of Instruction*. Cambridge, Mass.: Harvard University Press.

—— (1971) *The Relevance of Education*. New York: W. W. Norton.

—— (1973) *Beyond the Information Given: Studies in the Psychology of Knowing*. New York: W. W. Norton.

—— (1983) *Child's Talk: Learning to Use Language*. Oxford: Oxford University Press.

Bruner, J. S., Jolly, A. and Sylva, K. (eds) (1976) *Play*. Harmondsworth: Penguin Books.

Bryant, P. (1974) *Perception and Understanding in Young Children*. London: Methuen.

Buber, M. (1937) *I and Thou*. Edinburgh: T. & T. Clark.

—— (1947) *Between Man and Man*. London: Fontana.

Buckley, W. (1967) *Sociology and Modern Systems Theory*. Englewood Cliffs, NJ: Prentice-Hall.

Buzan, A. (1974) *Use Your Head*. London: BBC.

Capra, F. (1975) *The Tao of Physics*. London: Fontana.

—— (1982) *The Turning Point*. London: Wildwood House.

Cassirer, E. (1944) *An Essay on Man*. New Haven, Conn.: Yale University Press.

—— (1953) *Language and Myth*. New York: Dover.

Child, D. (1973) *Psychology and the Teacher*. London: Holt, Rinehart & Winston.

Chomsky, N. (1968) *Language and Mind*. New York: Harcourt, Brace & World.

Clark, S. R. L. (1984) *From Athens to Jerusalem*. Oxford: Oxford University Press.

Coade, Thor (1966) *The Burning Bow*. London: Allen & Unwin.

Collingwood, R. G. (1938) *The Principles of Art*. Oxford: Oxford University Press.

—— (1946) *The Idea of History*. Oxford: Oxford University Press.

Coomaraswamy, A. K. (1956) *Christian and Oriental Philosophy of Art*. New York: Dover.

Coulson, J. (1981) *Religion and the Imagination*. Oxford: Oxford University Press.

Coulson, M. (1972) 'Role: a redundant concept in sociology?', in J. A. Jackson (ed.) *Role*. Cambridge: Cambridge University Press.

Croall, J. (1983) *Neill of Summerhill*. London: Routledge & Kegan Paul.

de Bono, E. (1970) *Lateral Thinking*. Harmondsworth: Penguin Books.

Devlin, D. D. (1975) *Jane Austen and Education*. London: Macmillan.

Dewey, J. (1956) *The Child and the Curriculum* and *School and Society*. Chicago: University of Chicago Press.

Donaldson, M. (1978) *Children's Minds*. London: Fontana.

Dore, R. (1976) *The Diploma Disease: Education, Qualification and Development*. London: Allen & Unwin.

Dunlop, F. (1984) *The Education of Feeling and Emotion*. London: Allen & Unwin.

Dunn, J. and Kendrick, C. (1982) *Siblings: Love, Envy and Understanding*. London: Grant McIntyre.

Dyson, F. (1979) *Disturbing the Universe*. New York: Harper & Row.

Edwards, E. (1981) *Drawing on the Right Side of the Brain*. London: Souvenir Press.

Egan, K. (1979) *Educational Development*. New York: Oxford University Press.

Eigen, M. and Winkler, R. (1982) *Laws of the Game: How the Principles of Nature Govern Chance*. London: Allen Lane.

Emery, E. F. (ed.) (1967) *Systems Thinking*. Harmondsworth: Penguin Books.

Erikson, E. (1950) *Childhood and Society*. Harmondsworth: Penguin Books.

Evans-Pritchard, E. E. (1937) *Witchcraft, Oracles and Magic among the Azande*. Oxford: Oxford University Press.

Fagen, R. (1981) *Animal Play Behaviour*. New York: Oxford University Press.

Fodor, Jerry A. (1983) *The Modularity of Mind*. Cambridge, Mass.: MIT Press.

Fores, M. and Glover, I. (eds) (1978) *Manufacturing and Management*. London: HMSO.

Foster, M. (1934) 'The Christian doctrine of creation and the rise of modern science', *Mind* 43, 446–68.

Freire, P. (1972) *Cultural Action for Freedom*. Harmondsworth: Penguin Books.

—— (1973) *Education for Critical Consciousness*. London: Sheed & Ward.

Gallwey, W. T. (1974) *The Inner Game of Tennis*. New York: Random House.

Gandhi, M. K. (1949) *An Autobiography: The Story of My Experiments with Truth*. London: Phoenix.

Gardner, H. (1984) *Frames of Mind: the Theory of Multiple Intelligences*. London: Heinemann.

Gazzaniga, M. S. and LeDoux, J. E. (1978) *The Integrated Mind*. New York: Plenum Press.

Gelwick, R. (1977) *The Way of Discovery: An Introduction to the Thought of Michael Polanyi*. New York: Oxford University Press.

Geschwind, N. (1983) 'The organisation of the living brain', in J. Miller (ed.) *States of Mind*. London: BBC.

Gibson, J. J. (1966) *The Senses Considered as Perceptual Systems*. London: Allen & Unwin.

Goffmann, E. (1969) *The Presentation of Self in Everyday Life*. London: Allen Lane.

Gombrich, E. H. (1950) *The Story of Art*. Oxford: Phaidon Press.

—— (1960) *Art and Illusion*. Oxford: Phaidon Press.

—— (1979) *The Sense of Order*. Oxford: Phaidon Press.

Gooch, S. (1980) *The Double Helix of the Mind*. London: Wildwood House.

Goodman, N. (1969) *The Languages of Art*. New York: Oxford University Press.

Goody, J. R. (1977) *The Domestication of the Savage Mind*. Cambridge: Cambridge University Press.

Gould, S. J. (1980) *Ever Since Darwin*. Harmondsworth: Penguin Books.

Gregory, M. S. *et al.* (eds) (1978) *Sociobiology and Human Nature*. San Francisco: Jossey-Bass.

Gregory, R. L. (1970) *The Intelligent Eye*. London: Weidenfeld & Nicolson.

—— (1972) *Eye and Brain: The Psychology of Seeing.* London: Weidenfeld & Nicolson.

—— (1981) *Mind in Science.* London: Weidenfeld & Nicolson.

—— and Gombrich, E. H. (eds) (1973) *Illusion in Nature and Art.* London: Duckworth.

Grene, M. (1963) *A Portrait of Aristotle.* London: Faber & Faber.

—— (1966) *The Knower and the Known.* London: Faber & Faber.

—— (1974) *The Understanding of Nature: Essays in the Philosophy of Biology.* Dordrecht and Boston: D. Reidl.

Griffiths, V. L. (1976) *Teacher Centred.* London: Longman.

Hamlyn, D. W. (1978) *Experience and the Growth of Understanding.* London: Routledge & Kegan Paul.

—— (1983) *Perception, Learning and the Self.* London: Routledge & Kegan Paul.

Hargreaves, D. H. (1982) *The Challenge for the Comprehensive School.* London: Routledge & Kegan Paul.

Harré, R. (1970) *Principles of Scientific Thinking.* London: Macmillan.

—— (1979) *Social Being.* Oxford: Blackwell.

—— (1983) *Personal Being: A Theory for Individual Psychology.* Oxford: Blackwell.

—— and Secord, P. F. (1972) *The Explanation of Social Behaviour.* Oxford: Blackwell.

Hawes, H. (1979) *Curriculum and Reality in African Primary Schools.* London: Longman.

Heron, R. E. and Sutton-Smith, B. (1971) *Child's Play.* New York: John Wiley.

Hinde, R. A. (ed.) (1972) *Non-verbal Communications.* Cambridge: Cambridge University Press.

—— (1979) *Towards Understanding Relationships.* London: Academic Press.

—— and Stevenson-Hinde, J. (eds) (1979) *Constraints on Learning: Limitations and Predispositions.* London: Academic Press.

Hodgkin, R. A. (1956) *Education and Change.* Oxford: Oxford University Press.

—— (1970) *Reconnaissance on an Educational Frontier.* Oxford: Oxford University Press.

—— (1976) *Born Curious.* London: John Wiley.

—— (1980) 'Mountains and education', *The Alpine Journal* 86 (330), 201–11.

—— (1981) 'Where law and order start: the genesis of boundaries and norms', *Journal of Moral Education* 11 (2).

—— (1984) 'Estranged faces', *The Friends Quarterly* 23 (6).

Hofstadter, D. R. (1979) *Gödel, Escher, Bach.* New York: Basic Books; Brighton: Harvester.

Holbrook, D. (1979) *English for Meaning*. Windsor: National Foundation for Educational Research.

Horton, P. C. (1981) *Solace: The Missing Dimension in Psychiatry*. Chicago: University of Chicago Press.

Horton, R. and Finnigan, R. (1973) *Modes of Thought*. London: Faber & Faber.

Hudson, L. (1966) *Contrary Imaginations*. London: Methuen.

Huizinga, J. (1949) *Homo Ludens*. London: Routledge & Kegan Paul.

Illich, I. (1976) *After Deschooling What?* London: Writers and Readers Co-operative.

Israel, J. and Tajfel, I. (1972) *The Context of Social Science*. London: Academic Press.

Jackson, J. A. (ed.) (1972) *Role*. Cambridge: Cambridge University Press.

James, W. (1899) *Talks to Teachers on Psychology and to Students on some of Life's Ideals*. New York and London: Longmans.

—— (1917) *Selected Papers on Philosophy*. London: J. M. Dent.

Jaynes, J. (1982) *The Origin of Consciousness in the Breakdown of Bicameral Mind*. Harmondsworth: Penguin Books.

Jones, R. M. (1972) *Fantasy and Feeling in Education*. Harmondsworth: Penguin Books.

Jung, C. G. (1946) *Psychological Types*. London: Kegan Paul, Trench & Trubner.

Kaiser, C. B. 'Niels Bohr and Michael Polanyi: some interesting parallels'. Unpublished D.Phil. thesis, Edinburgh University.

Kelly, G. A. (1955) *The Psychology of Personal Constructs*, 2 vols. New York: W. W. Norton.

—— (1962) 'Europe's matrix of decision', in M. R. Jones (ed.) *Nebraska Symposium on Motivation*. Lincoln: University of Nebraska Press.

Kennedy, J. M. (1974) *A Psychology of Picture Perception*. San Francisco: Jossey-Bass.

Kenny, A. (1980) *Aquinas*. Oxford: Oxford University Press.

Kingsbourne, M. (1978) *The Asymmetrical Function of the Brain*. Cambridge: Cambridge University Press.

Knowlton, J. Q. 'On the definition of "pictures"'. *Audio-Visual Communication Review* 14(2).

Koestler, A. (1959) *The Sleepwalkers*. London: Hutchinson.

—— and Smythies, J. R. (eds) (1969) *Beyond Reductionism*. London: Hutchinson.

Konner, M. (1982) *The Tangled Wing: Biological Constraints on the Human Spirit*. London: Heinemann.

Kuhn, T. S. (1962) *The Structure of Scientific Revolution*. Chicago: University of Chicago Press.

—— (1974) *The Essential Tension*. Chicago: University of Chicago Press.

Langer, S. K. (1957) *Philosophy in a New Key: Studies in the Symbolism of Reason, Rite and Art.* Cambridge, Mass.: Harvard University Press.
—— (1967) *Mind, an Essay on Human Feeling,* vol. 1. Baltimore: Johns Hopkins University Press.
Laszlo, E. (1972) *The Systems View of the World.* New York: Braziller.
Leach, E. (1970) *Lévi-Strauss.* London: Fontana.
Leakey, R. and Lewin, R. (1977) *Origins.* London: Macdonald & Janes.
Leavis, F. R. (1975) *The Living Principle: 'English' as a Discipline of Thought.* London: Chatto & Windus.
Lishman, W. A. (1976) *The Two Hemispheres.* Totnes: Dartington Hall.
Lorenz, J. (1953) *On Aggression.* London: Methuen.
—— (1977) *Behind the Mirror: A Search for the Natural History of Human Knowledge.* London: Methuen.
Lovelock, J. E. (1979) *Gaia.* Oxford: Oxford University Press.
Lucas, J. (1980) *On Justice.* Oxford: Oxford University Press.
Luria, A. K. (1977) *Cognitive Development.* Cambridge, Mass.: Harvard University Press.
Macintyre, A. (1981) *After Virtue.* London: Duckworth.
MacKay, D. M. (1982) *Nature* 295, 690.
McLuhan, M. (1962) *The Gutenberg Galaxy.* London: Routledge & Kegan Paul.
MacMurray, J. (1938) *Reason and Emotion.* London: Faber & Faber.
—— (1957) *The Self as Agent.* London: Faber & Faber.
—— (1961) *Persons in Relation.* London: Faber & Faber.
Magee, B. (1978) *Men of Ideas.* London: BBC.
Mander, J. (1978) *Four Arguments for the Elimination of Television.* New York: William Morrow.
Marland, M. (1978) *Head of Department.* London: Methuen.
Marshack, A. (1972) *The Roots of Civilization.* London: Weidenfeld & Nicolson.
Martin, B. (1982) *A Sociology of Contemporary Cultural Change.* Oxford: Blackwell.
Mead, G. H. (1934) *Mind, Self and Society.* Chicago: University of Chicago Press.
Medway, P. (1980) *Finding a Language: Autonomy and Learning in School.* London: Writers and Readers Co-operative.
Merleau-Ponty, M. (1962) *Phenomenology of Perception.* London: Routledge & Kegan Paul.
Midgley, M. (1979) *Beast and Man: The Roots of Human Nature.* Brighton: Harvester; London: Methuen.
—— (1984) *Wickedness, A Philosophical Essay.* London: Routledge & Kegan Paul.
Miller, J. (ed.) (1983) *States of Mind.* London: BBC.
Monod, J. (1972) *Chance and Necessity.* London: Collins.

Morris, B. (1972) *Objectives and Perspectives in Education*. London: Routledge & Kegan Paul.

Mumford, L. (1946) *Technics and Civilization*. London: Routledge & Kegan Paul.

Musgrove, F. (1964) *Youth and the Social Order*. London: Routledge & Kegan Paul.

Nash, R. (1973) *Classrooms Observed*. London: Routledge & Kegan Paul.

Needham, J. (1970) *Clerks and Craftsmen in China and the West*. Cambridge: Cambridge University Press.

Needleman, J. (1983) *The Heart of Philosophy*. London: Routledge & Kegan Paul.

Neisser, U. (1976) *Cognition and Reality*. San Francisco: W. H. Freeman.

Newsom, J. and Newsom, E. (1979) *Toys and Playthings*. Harmondsworth: Penguin Books.

Nuttgens, P. (1977) *Learning to Some Purpose*. London: Society of Artists and Designers.

Oatley, K. (1978) *Perceptions and Representations*. London: Methuen.

Olson, D. R. (ed.) (1974) *Media and Symbols: The Forms of Expression, Communication and Education*. Chicago: University of Chicago Press.

Ong, W. (1982) *Orality and Literacy*. London: Methuen.

Ornstein, R. E. (1975) *The Psychology of Consciousness*. Harmondsworth: Penguin Books.

Pallis, M. (1939) *Peaks and Lamas*. London: Cassell.

Papert, S. (1980) *Mindstorms: Children, Computers and Powerful Ideas*. Brighton: Harvester.

Peacocke, A. R. (1979) *Creation and the World of Science*. Oxford: Oxford University Press.

—— (ed.) (1985) *Reductionism in Academic Disciplines*. Guildford: SRHE and NFER-Nelson.

Piaget, J. (1971a) *Structuralism*. London: Routledge & Kegan Paul.

—— (1971b) *Science of Education and the Psychology of the Child*. London: Longman.

—— (1979) *Behaviour and Evolution*. London: Routledge & Kegan Paul.

Pivčevič, E. (1970) *Husserl and Phenomenology*. London: Hutchinson.

Polanyi, M. (1951) *The Logic of Liberty*. Chicago: University of Chicago Press.

—— (1958) *Personal Knowledge*. London: Routledge & Kegan Paul.

—— (1966) *The Tacit Dimension*. New York: Doubleday.

—— (1969) *Knowing and Being*. London: Routledge & Kegan Paul.

—— and Prosch, M. (1975) *Meaning*. Chicago: University of Chicago Press.

Pope, M. and Keen, T. R. (1981) *Personal Construct Theory and Education*. London: Academic Press.

Popper, K. (1972) *Objective Knowledge: An Evolutionary Approach*. Oxford: Oxford University Press.

Rahner, H. (1965) *Man at Play*. London: Burns & Oates.

Raine, K. (ed.) (1957) *Coleridge: A Selection of his Poems and Prose*. Harmondsworth: Penguin Books.

Read, H. (1945) *Education Through Art*. London: Faber & Faber.

Richards, M. P. M. (ed.) (1974) *The Integration of a Child into a Social World*. Cambridge: Cambridge University Press.

Richardson, E. (1973) *The Teacher, the School and the Task of Management*. London: Heinemann.

Richardson, R. and Chapman, J. (1973) *Images of Life: Problems of Religion, Belief and Human Relations in Schools*. London: SCM Press.

Ritterbush, P. C. (1972) 'Aesthetics and objectivity in the study of form in the life sciences', in Rousseau, G. S. (ed.) *Organic Form*. London: Routledge & Kegan Paul.

Robertson, S. M. (1982) *Rosegarden and Labyrinth*. Lewes: Gryphon Press.

Rorty, R. (1980) *Philosophy and the Mirror of Nature*. Oxford: Blackwell.

Rose, S. (1976) *The Conscious Brain*. Harmondsworth: Penguin Books.

Ross, M. (ed.) (1978) *The Creative Arts*. London: Heinemann.

Ryle, G. (1949) *The Concept of Mind*. London: Hutchinson.

Schumacher, E. F. (1977) *A Guide to the Perplexed*. London: Cape.

Schutz, A. (1964) *Collected Papers*, vol. I. The Hague: Martinns Nijhoff.

Scott, D. (1985) *Everyman Revived: The Common Sense of Michael Polanyi*. Lewes: The Book Guild.

Searle, J. (1984) *Mind, Brains and Science* (The Reith Lectures). London: BBC.

Selfe, L. (1977) *Nadia: A Case of Extraordinary Drawing Ability by an Autistic Child*. London: Academic Press.

Sen, A. K. (1981) *Poverty and Hunger*. Oxford: Oxford University Press.

Shah, I. (1966) *The Exploits of the Incomparable Mulla Nasrudin*. London: Cape.

Shallis, M. (1984) *The Silicon Idol*. Oxford: Oxford University Press.

Sheldrake, R. (1983) *A New Science of Life*. London: Granada.

Shostak, M. (1982) *Nisa: The Life and Words of a !Kung Woman*. London: Allen Lane.

Shotter, J. (1984) *Social Accountability and Selfhood*. Oxford: Blackwell.

—— and Gauld, A. (1977) *Human Action and its Psychological Investigation*. London: Routledge & Kegan Paul.

Sless, D. (1981) *Learning and Visual Communication*. London: Croom Helm.

Smith, P. (ed.) (1984) *Play in Animals and Humans*. Oxford: Blackwell.

Sperry, R. W. (1983) *Science and Moral Priority*. Oxford: Blackwell.

Spitz, R. (1965) *The First Year of Life*. New York: International Universities Press.

Springer, S. P. and Deutsch, G. (1981) *Left Brain, Right Brain*. San Francisco: W. H. Freeman.

Stanley, M. (1978) *The Technological Conscience: Survival and Dignity in an Age of Expertise*. New York: The Free Press.

Steiner, G. (1969) *Language and Silence*. Harmondsworth: Penguin Books.

—— (1978) *Heidegger*. London: Fontana.

Stenhouse, L. (1971) 'Some limitations on the use of objectives in curriculum research and planning', *Paedogogica Europaea*. Brunswick: Georg Westermann.

—— (1980) *Curriculum Research and Development in Action*. London: Heinemann.

Stubbs, M. and Delamont, S. (1976) *Explorations in Classroom Behaviour*. London: John Wiley.

Swietecka, M. J. (1980) *The Idea of the Symbol: Some Nineteenth Century Comparisons with Coleridge*. Cambridge: Cambridge University Press.

Taylor, C. (1975) *Hegel*. Cambridge: Cambridge University Press.

—— (1979) *Hegel and Modern Society*. Cambridge: Cambridge University Press.

Thompson, D. A. W. (1961) *On Growth and Form* (abridged). Cambridge: Cambridge University Press.

Thorpe, W. H. (1956) *Learning and Instinct in Animals*. London: Methuen.

Tinbergen, N. (1958) *Social Behaviour in Animals*. London: Methuen.

—— (1960) 'The evolution of behaviour in Gulls', *Scientific American* (December).

Torrance, T. F. (ed.) (1980) *Belief in Science and Christian Life*. Edinburgh: Handsel Press.

—— (1981) *Divine and Contingent Order*. Oxford: Oxford University Press.

—— (1984) *Transformation and Convergence in the Frame of Knowledge*. Grand Rapids: Eerdmans.

Turner, J. (1984) *Cognitive Development and Education*. London: Methuen.

Turner, V. (1974) *Dramas, Fields and Metaphors*. Ithaca, NY: Cornell University Press.

—— (1982) *From Ritual to Theatre: The Human Seriousness of Play*. New York: Performing Arts Journal.

Ullmann-Margalit, E. (1978) *The Emergence of Norms*. Oxford: Oxford University Press.

Vygotsky, L. (1962) *Thought and Language*. Cambridge, Mass.: MIT Press.

Waddington, C. H. (1957) *The Strategy of the Genes*. London: Allen & Unwin.

—— (ed.) (1968, 1969) *Towards a Theoretical Biology*, 2 vols. Edinburgh: Edinburgh University Press.

Wall, W. D. (1977) *Constructive Education for Adolescents*. London: UNESCO & Harrap.

Wallas, G. (1945) *The Art of Thought*. London: Watts.

Ward, C. (1979) *The Child in the City.* Harmondsworth: Penguin Books.

Warnock, M. (1976) *The Imagination.* London: Faber & Faber.

Warr, D. (1982) 'The influence of visual aids on teaching and learning in schools'. Unpublished D.Phil. thesis, University of Oxford.

Watts, A. (1962) *The Way of Zen.* Harmondsworth: Penguin Books.

Weiss, P. A. (1975) *Knowledge in Search of Understanding.* New York: Futura.

Weizenbaum, J. (1976) *Computer Power and Human Reason.* San Francisco: W. H. Freeman.

White, L. L. (1965) *Internal Factors in Evolution.* London: Tavistock.

White, R. H. (1959) 'Motivation reconsidered: the concept of competence', *Psychological Review* 66, 5, 297–333.

White, T. H. (1938) *The Sword in the Stone.* London: Collins.

Wickes, L. (1982) *The Genius of Simplicity* ('About Suzuki' series). Princeton, NJ: Summy Birch and Music.

Wiener, N. (1958) *The Human Use of Human Beings.* New York: Sphere Books.

Wigner, E. P. and Hodgkin, R. A. (1977) 'Michael Polanyi', in *Biographical Memoirs of Fellows of The Royal Society 1977.* London: The Royal Society.

Wilson, B. (ed.) (1970) *Rationality.* Oxford: Blackwell.

Winnicott, D. W. (1971) *Playing and Reality.* London: Tavistock.

Wittgenstein, L. (1968) *Philosophical Investigations.* Oxford: Blackwell.

—— (1980) *Culture and Value.* Oxford: Blackwell.

Yates, F. (1966) *The Art of Memory.* London: Routledge & Kegan Paul.

Young, M. F. D. (1971) *Knowledge and Control. New Direction for the Sociology of Education.* London: Collier Macmillan.

Ziman, J. (1980) *Teaching and Learning about Science and Society.* Cambridge: Cambridge University Press.

Note

In the United Kingdom Janet Adler's film, *Looking for Me* may be hired from Concord Films, Ipswich.

Index